D1548067

IN
THE
SHADOW
OF
OLYMPUS

SUNY Series in Feminist Criticism and Theory
Michelle A. Massé, Editor

IN THE SHADOW OF OLYMPUS

German Women Writers Around 1800

Edited by

Katherine R. Goodman
and
Edith Waldstein

STATE UNIVERSITY OF NEW YORK PRESS

Published by
State University of New York Press, Albany

© 1992 State University of New York

All rights reserved

Printed in the United States of America

For information, address State University of New York
Press, State University Plaza, Albany, N.Y., 12246

Production by Diane Ganeles
Marketing by Theresa A. Swierzowski

Library of Congress Cataloging-in-Publication Data

In the Shadow of Olympus : German women writers around 1800 / edited by
    Katherine R. Goodman and Edith Waldstein.
        p.   cm. — (SUNY series in feminist criticism and theory)
    Includes bibliographical references and index.
    ISBN 0–7914–0743–8 (CH : acid-free). — ISBN 0–7914–0744–6 (PB :
acid-free)
    1. German literature—18th century—History and criticism.
    2. German literature—19th century—History and criticism.
    3. German literature—Women authors—History and criticism.
    4. Feminism and literature—Germany. I. Goodman, Katherine, 1945–
        II. Waldstein, Edith Josefine.   III. Series.
PT289.S48   1992
830.9'9287'09033—dc20   90–46558
                                                                     CIP

10   9   8   7   6   5   4   3   2   1

Contents

Foreword

Marianne Hirsch, Ruth Perry, and Virginia Swain

In 1981, Elaine Showalter defined the task of feminist criticism as gynocriticism, "a sustained investigation of literature by women, . . . the study of women as *writers*, . . . the history, styles, themes, genres, and structures of writing by women, the psychodynamics of female literary creativity, the trajectory of the individual or collective female career, and the evolution and laws of a female literary tradition."[1] In the late 1980s the notion of *women's* writing has become more problematic. Some have shifted attention from *women's writing* to *gendered writing*, defining gender as the operative category of literary analysis. Others have been speaking instead of *feminist writing*, in Nancy Miller's terms, writing which, among other things, articulates a "self-consciousness about woman's identity," and which "contests the available plots of women's development or *Bildung* and embodies dissent from the dominant tradition. . . ."[2] Others still have called the very category *women* in question, arguing its "volatility" and radical "historicity".[3] *In The Shadow of Olympus* reaffirms the category of "women's writing" and demonstrates that the process of gynocriticism continues to be a vital and instructive one.

This anthology represents the first sustained feminist examination in English of eighteenth and early nineteenth-century German women writers. The women whose literary accomplishments are displayed and examined in the following pages wrote novels, poems, letters—published and unpublished—and plays. All were inspired by classicism and romanticism, by the male standard bearers of their day; hence the ambivalent title of this collection.

These women authors all revolve like lesser lights around a luminary, Goethe. There is no comparable figure in French or English culture who so dominated the literary scene in general or the literary lives of women writers in particular. Samuel Johnson—with much less sexual interest in his protegés than Goethe exhibited—encouraged a number of individual women writers in England but he was not, as a literary sensibility, particularly inspirational to women.[4] Indeed, Goethe's wider influence on literary women throughout Europe must be acknowledged, along with Rousseau: both writers fed the controversy over sentiment and individualism that dominated *belles lettres* at the end of the eighteenth century.[5] In England, for example, *The Sorrows of Young Werther* enjoyed a tremendous vogue among women readers and writers alike.[6] It is hardly surprising, then, that women writers in Germany were under Goethe's sway—whether directly inspired by personal contact or imitating and admiring him from a distance.

None of the German women writers examined here had a particularly distinguished career, for reasons that begin to emerge with comparison to the literary situation of women writers in France and England. For one thing, the German enlightenment was more scholastic than in England and France, with more deference to earlier scholarship, more dependence on classical languages, and a more contemptuous attitude toward vernacular speech as the proper vehicle of rational discourse—attitudes which served to disempower women, who were not, for the most part, classically educated. Whereas Chaucer, Shakespeare, and Milton were recognized as uncontested classics in England, constituting a local vernacular tradition (almost) equally available to men and to women, Germany had no such strong vernacular tradition for women to draw on. It makes sense, then, that the point of reference for German women would have been this contemporary male author, the most proximate locus of the new vernacular tradition in German letters.

The example of English culture was important to German women writers insofar as it derived from another non-Catholic society that prized learning both in the arts and the fledgling sciences, and in which intellectual women were visible as writers, critics or bluestocking salonieres—and constituted a sizeable market for literary production. By the late eighteenth century in England, women had been writing and publishing as women for a hundred years, beginning with such poets as Katherine Philips or Anne Finch and the playwright and novelist Aphra Behn in the seventeenth-century, and continuing in an unbroken line to best-selling writers such as Charlotte Smith, Elizabeth Inchbald, Maria Edgeworth at the end of the eighteenth century. Both in and out of books, Englishwomen provided for German women writers imitable models of self-conscious, female subjectivity—both in fictive representations of sensible womanhood and in the "real world" as readers and writers in the literary marketplace.

Earlier capitalist expansion may account for women's greater participation in the literary affairs of England. Voltaire argues in his *Lettres philosophiques* (1734)—sometimes translated as *Letters on the English Nation*—that the energizing force of thriving commerce and representative government combined to produce in England a culture in which literature was more honored than in France. "In London," he wrote, "there are some eight hundred people with the right to speak in public and uphold the interests of the nation; about five or six thousand aspire to the same honour in their turn, all the rest set themselves up in judgement on these, and anybody can print what he thinks about public affairs. So the whole nation is obliged to study."[7]

On the other hand, France, without all this mercantile activity, produced a lively tradition of women's writing long before the eighteenth century. Indeed, women's literary salons and literary productions flourished in France a century before they could be found in England. By the end of the eighteenth century, however, this tradition was being undermined in France for reasons that we still do not entirely understand.

It is ironic that German women writers found their voices at the turn of the nineteenth century, just when their French counterparts were being effectively silenced. After at least two centuries in which women were able to make their opinions known in salons and in print, the French Revolution marked a giant step backward for French women's self-expression. During the twenty years covered by the essays in this volume (1790–1810), women writing in French were mostly living outside France's borders.[8] With the exception of a few, such as Olympe de Gouges and the anonymous authors of the *Cahiers de doléances des femmes*, who were writing within the Revolution in the vain hope of winning rights for women, only a handful of women authors continued to write—in exile—and their works show the impact of the upheaval in France. Because of these very great differences in the effects of the Revolution in the two countries, we must go back in time in order to find any basis for comparing German women authors and women writers in France.[9]

Women writing in France in the earlier eighteenth century had to face many of the same problems which would later beleaguer

German women: the lack of an adequate education; attacks against "public" women throughout the century, which caused many women to write anonymously or under male pseudonyms and forced them to arrange for the publication or presentation of their works through male intermediaries;[10] the extreme difficulty of earning a living through writing, frequently coupled with the necessity of doing so; the burden of censorship, which more often than not deprived women of the royal "permission" to publish; and well-known but unwritten restrictions which considered the most prestigious genres, like verse tragedy and other types of poetry, off-limits for women.[11]

However, French women did have several advantages over German women of the Revolutionary period. The first of these is probably the one we think about the least: French women were writing within a culture secure in itself and in its hegemony. Women struggling to find their voices in eighteenth-century France did not have to contend with a wave of emerging national-ism that thrust them forward even as it threatened to drown them out. More specifically, they had the benefit of a well-established salon culture dating from the early seventeenth century, a culture which allowed women from the aristocracy and the upper bour-geoisie the free expression of their ideas. There were literally hun-dreds of salons in Paris and in the provinces, spanning the century. In Germany these do not begin to become firmly estab-lished until well into the eighteenth century.

Once they were actually in print, French women also had the advantage of a larger, though still very limited, public which they could reach through lending libraries and reading rooms in the capital and in the provinces. The book trade was not restricted to the degree that made circulation nearly impossible for so long in Germany.

And finally, French women of the eighteenth century, like their English counterparts, did not labor in the shadow of any one male "Olympian" figure. With the possible exception of Rousseau, whose influence on French literature and educational theory ex-tends from the early 1760s until well beyond the Revolution, no single man commands the attention of an entire generation the way Goethe does in the German states. Rousseau did receive "fan letters" from many women in response to his novel *Julie, ou la Nouvelle Héloïse*;[12] other women, interested in education, took a stand for or against the theories he put forward in *Emile*. While Rousseau's intellectual pull was great, in these later years of his career, his paranoia was such that he repeatedly complained about authors' efforts to capitalize on his fame, seeing in their potentially flattering advances further evidence of plots against him.[13] Women in France had to contend with many other obstacles put in the way of their development as authors, but they did not have to resist the fatal attraction of an intellectual "deity."[14]

By contrast, the gendered "minefield" of the German cultural scene and the, again gendered, strategies of response to the literary hegemony of one gigantic, male figure are well documented in the following essays, which reveal what life was like for women "in the shadow of Olympus." These sustained readings of eighteenth-century women/feminist writers can teach feminist literary critics and theorists a great deal about writing in dialogue with a mainstream, about revision, appropriation, redefinition, subversion, compliance and contestation.

But there is more. There is much to learn here about the relation of gender and genre, about the *Familienroman,* the utopia, the letter. There is much to learn about the salon as a literary and cultural force, and about the unique role women played in the culture of the salon. There is much to learn, as well, about the social and cultural forces that make writing possible and about the social and cultural forces that inhibit it. As we read these essays we discover a body of writing which takes shape, sometimes too comfortably, sometimes angrily, sometimes disturbingly, against the background of the, again gendered, Enlightenment notion of reason and humanity and of the lofty claims Romanticism makes for literature. We discover a body of writing that takes shape originally in the context of shockingly low literacy rates for women, and that helps to construct a greater and more educated female readership. And we are led to think about the relation between the individual text and its social, economic, political, spiritual and gendered scene of production and reception.

Most importantly, perhaps, we learn about women's lives in eighteenth-century German society, about friendship and love, marriage and divorce, heroism and failure. We look at how women wrote about their lives, how they imagined and reimagined them, and at how feminist critics can interpret their representations today.

As we study this vital tradition of eighteenth-century German women's writing, we know that our reading of other traditions will shift in subtle but important ways. For as Virginia Woolf reminds us, "books continue each other, in spite of our habit of looking at them separately."

1

Introduction

Katherine R. Goodman and Edith Waldstein

Introite, nam et hic Dei sunt![1]

German women writers became a force to be reckoned with in
the 1790s. To be sure, no Jane Austens emerged, but if literary
moguls had previously celebrated the talent of an occasional writing woman, they now had to worry occasionally about molding
the explosion of that talent in their own image. Intellectuals of
the Enlightenment had marveled at the potential of the human
race in the achievements of an Anna Luise Karsch (1722–1791)
or a Luise Adelgunde Gottsched (1713–1762), but intellectuals
around 1800 doggedly sought "feminine" virtues in the writing of
Caroline von Wolzogen (1763–1847), Therese Huber (1764–1829),
Sophie Mereau (1770–1806), Dorothea Schlegel (1763–1839), Caroline Auguste Fischer (1764–1842), Benedikte Naubert (1756–
1819), Friederike Unger (1751–1813), and others.

The emergence in the German states of women writing in
such large numbers paralleled what had happened in England and
France. It was tied to the expansion of a new bourgeois class and
its culture, which led to changes in the public sphere, like the
growth of the publishing industry; in social forms, like the development of the bourgeois salon; and in literary forms, like the
merger of the letter and the novel. Thus, in broad terms, many of
the issues addressed by these German women writers are similar
to those of their English and French sisters: the role of women in a
middle-class society and in the family. But because it occurred in a
language that belonged to no nation-state and because it occurred
somewhat later, the phenomenon itself acquired a somewhat different shape. The contingencies of time and place, of history, had
definite consequences for the production and reception of German
women's writing.

The two single most important historical facts that shaped the specific form the emergence of German women's writing took, were the fragmentation of the German states and the course of the French Revolution. The implications of this situation are infinitely complex—and remain to be discussed in some detail. But if speculation is permitted at this point, then it shall be proposed that, without these, German women's writing would have developed earlier and would not have been forced to contend with the aesthetic turn which literature in Germany took in the wake of the French Revolution. As it happened, however, what might be labeled the first generation of women writers in Germany began to publish at precisely the moment when the literary scene focused itself most particularly on the figure of Goethe. This had a definite effect both on women writers of the time and on the reception of their works since that time. The image of Goethe reigning over a spiritual and German "Olympus" has been entrenched in the minds of many Germans for almost two hundred years. Those who have stormed this "Olympus" have not fared well; and it is therefore with a sense of irony that we title this book *In the Shadow of Olympus*. But all of this requires some further explanation.

The Fragmentation of the German States and the Emergence of a Public Sphere

In part, at least, the emergence of women writers in the German states was tied to the emergence of middle-class male writers. As an independent profession, writing only came into existence with this class. This "larger" phenomenon was impeded considerably by the fragmentation of the German states. There was no single German-speaking nation, rather there were separate principalities, each governed by its own autocratic ruler. Not until 1871, after a series of wars, when Bismarck united several major German states, can one speak of "Germany."

The consequences of this political fragmentation for cultural life were multi-faceted. For most of the eighteenth century the lack of a national identity meant that German courts were virtual cultural colonies of France, and the cultural differences between the classes were therefore enormous. The emerging bourgeois intelligentsia was confronted with the fact that the language and culture of the courts was French. Frederick the Great of Prussia, who reigned from 1740 to 1786, spoke French on all occasions. He con-

ducted personal and court business in French, read French literature, and wrote his political treatises in French. When he invited
intellectuals to court, they were often French. When he wrote his
verdict about the lack of a German literature, "De la littérature
allemande," he wrote it in French. And, when the poet Anna Luise
Karsch wanted to draw the King's attention to her poetic adula-
tions (with hopes of income), she had to have them translated into
French. For the most part, aristocrats in other courts were no different. It is impossible to imagine the emergence of a professional
writing class when so many of a country's rulers and so many of
its subjects did not read the same language. This situation began
to change after the French Revolution.

For the literary life of the middle-classes, and the expansion
of the public sphere, this fragmentation into hundreds of small
states posed other obstacles as well. On the simplest level, for instance, there was no capital city in which intellectuals could con-
gregate to exchange ideas. They were isolated throughout the
landscape in provincial settings. Even more important, however,
was the fact that this political situation meant that the emergence
of a broad-based, modern, industrial, middle-class was impossible.
Laws, including copyright laws, varied from state to state, making
profits from published works difficult to collect. Medieval guilds
were still strong. Trade with other principalities was difficult because of the tariffs imposed in transit across borders, and because
currencies varied.

This chaotic situation influenced the development not only of
the middle-class and modern industry in general, but of book
trade and literary production in particular. While a literary marketplace was already established in England and France by the
middle of the eighteenth century, the situation in the German
states was quite different. For instance, in the 1750s, book dealers
still conducted their business with one another on the basis of
commodity exchange. This meant that large amounts of potential
capital were held in inventory and were unavailable either for
printing new books or for advance payments to authors. Most titles were strictly scholarly. And here, naturally, women were at a
disadvantage. Only in the mid-1770s, with a changing reading
public, did large Leipzig book dealers, like the Weidmannsche
Buchhandlung, begin to convert to currency transactions.

Governmental and guild restrictions also inhibited the growth
of a literary industry. For instance, in order to receive the right to
publish books in Austria after 1772, a person had to have studied

the trade for six years, served as apprentice for four, have evidence from an imperial university of knowledge of the best authors, and possess 10,000 Gulden (Schmidt, 79). Guild requirements could be equally restrictive. For instance, type makers were not allowed to work as typesetters, typesetters were not allowed to work as printers, printers were not allowed to work as bookbinders, bookbinders were not allowed to work as book dealers. Production rights and markets were therefore distributed between individual guilds. Once again, not until the late eighteenth century did Breitkopf in Leipzig manage to bring under one roof guild members from enough guilds to produce books in one place. Then he employed 130 people, no mean financial feat.

Only once the book industry had been organized along more "modern" lines was it financially possible for professional authors to emerge. Until then those who wrote books were either at court, employed by a court, or had other occupations such as professor, lawyer or pastor. It goes without saying that under these circumstances few women wrote literature. Naturally there were exceptions: some aristocratic women, a few court poets, an occasional professor's wife or daughter. But just as it is difficult to speak of a German literature before the last half, even last third, of the eighteenth century, so, too, is it difficult to speak of a women's literature in Germany until the last decade of the century.

When male literati emerged as a class at the end of the century, they identified themselves with the enlightened progress of history and viewed their role in public terms. They saw themselves as part of a broad, essentially middle-class movement and desired to contribute to the formation of a new and better society. The vehicles for this emerging common sensibility were similar to those in England and France: print media (journals, books, newspapers); reading societies; lending libraries; clubs; salons. However, none of the literature on reading societies, lending libraries, or clubs mentions the participation of women. Therefore, in the absence of affirmative statements, we assume they were not members. We shall return to the moral weeklies and salons.

The slow growth of the institutions of the public sphere not only affected reading habits and literacy rates, it was affected *by* them. Only at the end of the century did these begin to change in any radical way. Then, partially fueling the expansion of the book trade, partially fueled by it, reading habits underwent radical transformations. Individuals no longer read one or two books intensively (usually the Bible), but began to read extensively. The number of titles published increased dramatically: in 1740 there were 755; in 1770 there were 1144; and in 1800 there were 2569. Moreover, while the percentage of titles on theology, law, and philosophy decreased between 1740 and 1770, titles in the *belles lettres* increased by 327 percent, in political science by 220 percent, practical handbooks by 650 percent, in education by 400 percent, and popular periodicals by 1650 percent! Increases in the next thirty-year period were not as dramatic, but confirmed the trend towards the production of books that were more popular in nature. To increase their market, publishers needed to broaden the appeal of their books. They needed to reach those who could read, but had not yet done so extensively. It is at this point in history that women became important consumers of literary titles. In fact it might be asserted that an appeal to female readership was essential for the new literary marketplace to develop at all.

Again, the means by which this was accomplished were not unlike those used in England and France. However, in the German states the low literacy rate among women certainly dampened the pace of the rise of literature. Around 1789 there were approximately 23 million people living in the German states. By one estimate (Schumann, 140), about 20 percent of these could read at all, perhaps 4.5 million people, but by another (Schenda, in Lutz, 37) there were only 2 million actual readers. Around 1800 the novelist Jean Paul (1763–1825) estimated that his audience was only about 300,000 readers (Martino/Stützel-Prüsener, 55). But if one assumes that barely half as many women as men were literate, then less than 10 percent of the women could read, perhaps as many as 1 million women. Or, in Jean Paul's terms, only 100,000 women read "high" literature.

Without literacy any proposal—derived from the enlightened philosophy of the incipient bourgeoisie—for the education of women was meaningless. But as the public sphere began to take shape and the word "Bildung" (education) became more and more important for men, it did so for women as well. Their education was sometimes part of the explicit goal of the German Enlightenment, for until roughly the 1790s women were considered to be rational creatures, just like men. They were generally thought, however, to possess less capacity in this direction, and were almost never intended to acquire *equal* education.[2] To be sure, in 1742 Dorothea Christiane Leporin pleaded for gifted women to be allowed to study with men and even to enter professions, if they remained unmarried. After her direct appeal to the newly crowned, "enlightened" Frederick the Great, the University of Halle admitted her as its first female candidate for a degree in medicine. Her study was interrupted by marriage and childbirth, but she was awarded her degree in 1754, and her case became a cause célèbre. So, too, in the case of Dorothea Schlözer, whose professor-father encouraged her studies. In 1787, at the age of 17, attired in bridelike white and with flowers in her hair, she was examined by Göttingen professors and awarded a Doctor of Philosophy, the first German woman to be so honored.

Far more common than these unique cases are those described, for instance, in the first women's novel in Germany, *The History of Sophie von Sternheim* (1771) by Sophie von La Roche (1731–1807).[3] Its exemplary young heroine from the lower nobility had studied philosophy, history, languages, music, and dancing. (La Roche, 51) This was an exceptional education for a young woman in a well-to-do family. Advanced study or the study of Latin or Greek, considered necessary for educated young men, were naturally out of the question for young women.

The merchant's daughter and novelist Johanna Schopenhauer (1766–1838) wrote in her memoirs about her childhood education in Danzig. She noted that it was exceptional and included French, English, geography, history, and mythology. She read the *Spectator*, the letters of Lady Montague, Homer, Young, Milton, and Shakespeare. Of this education she recalls being somewhat ashamed—she even rejected one tutor's offer to teach her Greek—for it was more than was considered appropriate for most young women. Indeed, she looks back most fondly on her attendance at Madame Ackermann's "Société des jeunes dames" where she learned how to make graceful entrances, write with a beautiful hand, pour tea correctly, and embroider while being read to aloud. She equates this education with the "university days" of young men.

If the passive participation of women in the public sphere increased slowly, so too did their active participation. Curiously, perhaps, it was in some ways their lack of formal education that gave German women their entrance into the literary profession. In the course of the century, as the bourgeoisie was defining itself more consciously in opposition to the aristocracy, it began to esteem women's lack of training in the contorted phraseology of the court or the stilted style of academic writing. In 1751, for instance, Christian Fürchtegott Gellert (1715–1769) wrote the most influential eighteenth-century manual on how to write letters. Women's letter writing was held to be the model of a more natural German style.

He acknowledged that their spelling was erratic, their grammar was faulty, their style was clumsy. These he turned into virtues since women wrote without hypocrisy and without ulterior motivations but, from the heart. Moreover the familial and social functions of women, so often carried out by letter, began to draw new respect as a model for the kind of bourgeois interaction that demonstrated the moral superiority of their class and hence their legitimacy. Women were therefore encouraged to write letters when they were not encouraged to write anything else.

But if there were indigenous reasons for the middle-classes to praise women's writing, as for so much else in the German states at this time, the influence from abroad was critical in shaping this development. The emphasis placed on natural expression and style owed much to the writings of Rousseau. More important, however, for the gradual entrance of women into the literary profession in Germany, was the influence of the British moral weeklies and of Samuel Richardson's novels. As in England, moral weeklies were an important source of reading matter for women. In the course of the eighteenth century roughly eighty-five appeared which specifically addressed what they perceived as women's interests (Schumann, 142). Prior to the French Revolution these often attempted to popularize certain academic subject matters, so that women might have some appreciation of the issues discussed by men. Later, for a variety of reasons, these journals began to focus more concertedly on issues related to *belles lettres* or the "destiny" of women: motherhood and domestic affairs (Schieth, 107ff.). The first important weekly for women, *Die Vernünftigen Tadlerinnen,* was edited by Johann Christoph Gottsched (1700–1766) in the mid-1720s. Gottsched encouraged the collaboration of women, especially in the role of correspondents. While he actually wrote most of the articles himself under feminine pseudonyms, his notoriously learned wife, Luise Adelgunde Gottsched (1713–1762), also wrote for it.[4] Indeed, in mid-century Luise Gottsched translated *The Spectator* into German. In the 1770s *Iris,* the most well-known periodical for women, edited by the rationalists Johann Georg Jacobi and Wilhelm Heinze, was recognized as actually encouraging significant contributions by women. The best-known woman poet in the eighteenth century (a woman born and raised in poverty), Anna Luise Karsch (1722–1791), published there. But it was Sophie von La Roche who was the first woman to edit a journal for women, *Pomona,* in the mid 1780s. Throughout the century women's contributions to the moral weeklies had increased,

especially in the role of letters to the editor, but also in other re-
spects. Thus, what had begun as reading matter for women became gradually a medium for women to exercise their own literary
skills.

The novels of Samuel Richardson were to form another bridge
to women's participation in the creation of fiction. *Pamela* (1740/
41) was not translated until 1772, but the translation of *Clarissa*
(1747/48) was begun within the same year of the English publication: 1748/51. Its success was immediate and profound. Of course
the subject matter was of interest to women readers, who now
found their own personal concerns treated in fiction. Richardson
soon found his German imitators: Johann Fürchtegott Gellert in
his *Das Leben der schwedischen Gräfin von G.* 1747/48, and Johann Timotheus Hermes in his more popular *Sophiens Reise von
Memel nach Sachsen* in 6 volumes (1769–73). These were the titles
Johanna Schopenhauer named as the first German novels appropriate for women readers. Because they placed a heroine at the
heart of the novel, these *Familienromane,* or family novels, were
particularly popular among German women.[5]

Almost from the moment women's own lives became the subject of literature, they become emboldened enough to write it—
especially when the form is one that they have been encouraged to
use: the epistolary form. Sophie von La Roche would write the
first epistolary novel by a woman, *The History of Sophie von Sternheim* (1771). The influence of Rousseau is strongly felt in this
woman's *Bildungsroman,* as is that of Richardson. But in its own
right La Roche's novel is credited with having influenced other authors, including the young Johann Wolfgang Goethe whose first attempt at fiction, the epistolary novel *The Sorrows of Young
Werther* (1774), would soon sweep Europe.[6] And Lydia Schieth has
demonstrated that it was a model for the German *Frauenroman*
up to modern times. In the last two decades of the century, but
especially in the 1790s, other women novelists continued the tradition of the family novel when "high" literature no longer considered such themes important. (In fact, as a relative late-comer to a
literary scene dominated by classical aesthetics, the novel in general had difficulties establishing itself as a legitimate genre in the
German states.)

Thus, while women had not been educated in traditional
"high" forms of literature, when forms and themes emerged in
which they felt competent they were not shy to set pen to paper.
They generally did not have trouble finding publishers, but fre-

quently did hide behind pseudonyms or "anonymous." To be sure, their public reception was not always as positive as that of Sophie von La Roche. But then they did not all have her aspirations, talent, or luxury of time. One writer of popular novels of fallen women was Isabella von Wallenrodt (1740–1819). After unsuccessfully begging the King for a pension for years, and trying her hand at manufacturing, she actually managed to earn most, if not all, of her living from writing. As her critics assaulted not only her subject matter, but her style as well, she complained in her autobiography that she was paid by the page and so could not afford to write as refined a prose as her critics would like to read.

In sum, one can conclude that the noteworthy and rapid expansion of the literary market around 1770 was tied, at least in part, to an increased appeal to female readership. The evolution of writing as a profession for women follows immediately upon this historical event, beginning in the 1780s, but particularly during the 1790s. Relative to the emergence of women writers in England and France, the same phenomenon occurs somewhat later in the German states. In terms of the emergence of a significant number of professional male writers in Germany, however, it occurs at about the same time. This by no means suggests that it was as easy for women as for men; there was still a social stigma attached to a woman earning money, they were not as well prepared, and although there are currently no figures for this, they probably did not earn as much as men. Since they most commonly wrote in popular rather than esoteric forms, they frequently received poorer reviews. But it was a profession that was marginally possible for women and just as marginally respectable.

The French Revolution and the Turn towards Aestheticism

The German reaction to the course of the French Revolution was a major force in shaping the role played by women writers in German literary history. In this context the *nature* of the emerging public sphere in the German states is significant. In eighteenth-century England there were public debates on politics or public policy matters as well as on aesthetic and moral issues. In the German states, due to their fragmentation and the plethora of autocrats, this was not true. We know, for instance, that a majority of the holdings in reading societies were related to what might be called professional matters, not political affairs. *Belles lettres* were more likely to dominate private libraries or clubs sponsored by publishers. Public discussion centered around narrow professional matters or remained mainly moralistic, as opposed to social or political. Not only did large scale discussions of natural rights (whether for bourgeois men or for women) tend not to occur, but literature and philosophy tended to claim a proportionally larger role of the public attention in the German states than in England.

It is difficult to reconstruct the impact the French Revolution must have had on the essentially apolitical imaginations of the neighboring German intelligentsia. In its initial phase the Revolution opened the scope of vision for many. Surely German women had heard of Olympe de Gouges, for instance. But what they may have thought remains a mystery. No sooner might they have had the occasion to hear of her declaration of the rights of women in 1791 than the reign of terror, which began in 1792, caused many to rethink totally the goals of the Enlightenment, goals they had identified with the progress of the Revolution. In addition, the invasion by French Revolutionary troops, their conquest of Mainz in October 1792 for instance, caused severe differences of opinion among the middle-classes. National pride, what there was of it, was now also assaulted. If after 1789 many *Bürger* felt that all winds that blew from France were benevolent, then after 1792 they likely scrambled to opine that, after all, the German states would find a better, third alternative. France was no longer to be imitated, rather it provided a negative moral to be learned—for aristocrats as well.

As fragmented and chaotic as middle-class opinions were, they had one common effect: to fuel the desire for public debate and literary endeavors. If the literary public sphere in the German states was just beginning to establish itself prior to the Revolution, the Revolution itself was a catalyst for an even faster paced increase in reading. In the 1790s around two hundred new reading societies were founded in the German states—roughly a 46 percent increase. In the Hanseatic city of Bremen alone, ten new lending libraries were established. And the women, through whose hands more books passed now than ever before, began more and more frequently, in-between reading books, to pick up the pen.

From the moment the French Revolution occurred German supporters could be found. These German Jacobins remained in the minority (especially after 1792), but there were also women who sympathized with their position. Their visions tended to correspond to those of the French Jacobins. In this volume Ute

Brandes and Jeannine Blackwell discuss the utopian visions of women authors who could be said to have allied themselves with the Jacobins, and who continued to write after 1792: Henriette Frölich and, to some extent, Therese Huber.

In the main, however, male writers began reconstructing ideologies to ensure that the French terror would not be repeated. This put not only women, but also women writers, at a disadvantage. Protagonists in novels were no longer named Clarissa, the Countess of G. or Sophie, but rather Wilhelm Meister or Faust, and male stories began to predominate. Naturally it is too easy to blame the French Revolution for all the consequent ills, since in part at least the intellectual basis for classical and romantic aesthetics had already been laid. Still, while for a brief time there had been some chance that history might take a different course, now even the most enlightened tendencies of the Revolution seemed questionable. In short, there was an intellectual purge of many of the ideals of the Enlightenment, or at least a reworking of them.

The Revolution had thrown intellectuals back to the theoretical drawing board. For answers, many looked to the preeminent German author of the time, Johann Wolfgang von Goethe (1749–1832). In his youth Goethe had acted out the role of *enfant terrible,* rebelling against the rigidity of the class system and the antiquity of the legal system. Many hopeful eyes turned to him for some kind of national guidance in those turbulent revolutionary times. But Goethe had since become a court minister in the small duchy of Sachsen-Weimar (106,000 inhabitants, 36 square miles), and declined to play the role of the intellectual leader of revolutionary thought.

Nevertheless, the town of Weimar would now become the focus of much cultural activity, and many German hopes lay with its intellectual leaders. When Goethe had first arrived in the town of Weimar (6,000 inhabitants) in 1775, he had found another reknowned poet there, Christoph Martin Wieland (1733–1813), the literary mentor of Sophie von La Roche. In 1776 he arranged for his own mentor, the theologian Johann Gottfried Herder (1744–1803), to come there. Eventually, in 1788, the poet Friedrich Schiller (1759–1805) became professor of history in the not too distant university town of Jena in the same duchy. In 1799 Schiller, too, moved to Weimar. Weimar (and Jena) became the seat of classical German literature and aesthetics.

This concentration of intellect lent Sachsen-Weimar the aura of a spiritual mecca, an *Olympus.* Many traveled there just to meet the most inspired minds of the age and to hear their pronouncements.

Something of the flavor of this sentiment is captured by Schelling, the philosopher-husband of Caroline Schlegel-Schelling, in his statement following Goethe's death in 1832:

> There are times in which men of great experience, of imperturbably healthy spirit, and of a sublime purity of conviction which is beyond question, sustain and strengthen others merely by their very existence. In a time like this not only German literature, Germany itself suffers the most painful loss it could endure. A man is taken from it who during all internal and external disorders stood like a mighty pillar on which many supported themselves, like Pharus lighting all the paths of the mind, by his very nature an enemy of all anarchy and lawlessness, and who claimed to owe the sovereignty he exercised over minds only to truth and to the moderation he found in himself. In his mind, I might say in his heart, Germany was sure to find for everything which moved it in art and science, in poetry or in life a judgment of paternal wisdom. Germany was not orphaned nor impoverished; in all its weakness and internal strife it was great, rich and powerful in spirit as long as—Goethe lived.

> Es gibt Zeiten, in welchen Männer von großartiger Erfahrung, unerschütterlicher gesunder Vernunft, in einer über allen Zweifel erhabenen Reinheit der Gesinnung, schon durch ihr bloßes Dasein erhaltend und bekräftigend wirken. In einer solchen Zeit erleidet—nicht etwa die deutsche Literatur bloß, Deutschland selbst den schmerzlichsten Verlust, den es erleiden konnte. Der Mann entzieht sich ihm, der in allen inneren und äußeren Verwirrungen wie eine mächtige Säule stand, an der viele sich aufrichteten, wie ein Pharus, der alle Wege des Geistes beleuchtete, der, aller Anarchie und Gesetzlosigkeit durch seine Natur Feind, die Herrschaft, welche er über die Geister ausübte, stets nur der Wahrheit und dem in sich selbst gefundenen Maß verdanken wollte; in dessen Geist, und wie ich hinzusetzen darf, in dessen Herzen Deutschland für alles, wovon es in Kunst und Wissenschaft, in der Poesie oder im Leben, bewegt wurde, das Urteil väterlicher Weisheit, eine letzte versöhnende Entscheidung zu finden sicher war. Deutschland war nicht verwaist, nicht verarmt, es war in aller Schwäche und inneren Zerrüttung groß, reich und mächtig von Geist solange—Goethe lebte. (cited in Oeser, 22)

In this spirit, the intellectual achievements of Weimar became more than a compensation for the lack of a revolution on German soil, they became the real alternative (Ueding, 74). The Germans would create a "Republic of the Spirit." The classical literature produced there became the "the glimmer of the political perfection of German history as a unified and free nation-state" (Ueding, 67). For some it remains "even today our most important historical credential" (Ueding, 75).

The close intellectual friendship between Goethe and Schiller, which began in 1794 and lasted until Schiller's death in 1805, provided the core for this ideology. In some sense the friendship itself became a model of how two great individuals could productively collaborate; but without the classical aesthetics of both men, that friendship would not have carried its ideological weight. While this ideology was attractive to many women, it also both intimidated and objectified them in ways not conducive to their own artistic creation.

Schiller's extended treatise *On the Aesthetic Education of the Human Race* (*Über die ästhetische Erziehung des Menschen*, 1794) was clearly written after considerable reflection on recent events in France. He castigated capricious autocrats who bled their subjects to death, *and* he denounced the unruly, brutish mobs that had overthrown them in France. The solution, he claimed was education to the beautiful "because it is through the beautiful that one reaches liberty" (Ueding, 86). The French crisis had occured because autocrats violated fundamental needs of their subjects and because the lower and more numerous classes had grown savage. A more just state would require for its foundation a better human race. Art and artists could reestablish a lost human totality by providing it themselves in an ideal incarnation. The artist (and author) should become the ideal of human education, to purify human endeavors. Not only the work of art, but also its creator, represent the anticipatory creation of human ideals. The writer, in Schiller's mind, has a grave national (indeed, human) responsibility to become a prophet of the divine ideal.

Though it has the highest public function, this role is not political. It is above all politics, indeed all dailiness. In 1795 Schiller began editing the journal *Die Horen* (*The Horae*) which was to carry out the ideals expressed in his treatise. In the prospectus for his journal, he makes a reference to the Revolution and to the role he intended the journal to play in healing the wounds of the times.

> To be sure the times do not bode well for a journal which will impose on itself silence regarding the favorite topic of the day and which seeks its fame precisely by appealing to something

other than what currently appeals. But the more the limited interests of the present pressure the spirit, cramp and suppress it, the more urgent becomes the need to free it through a general and lofty interest in what is *purely human* and beyond all influence of the times, to unify again the politically divided world under the flag of truth and beauty.

In der Tat scheinen die Zeitumstände einer Schrift wenig Glück zu versprechen, die sich über das Lieblingsthema des Tages ein strenges Stillschweigen auferlegen und ihren Ruhm darin suchen wird, durch etwas anders zu gefallen, als wodurch jetzt alles gefällt. Aber je mehr das beschränkte Interesse der Gegenwart die Gemüter in Spannung setzt, einengt und unterjocht, desto dringender wird das Bedürfnis, durch ein allgemeines und höheres Interesse an dem, was *rein menschlich* und über allen Einfluß der Zeiten erhaben ist, sie wieder in Freiheit zu setzen und die politisch geteilte Welt unter der Fahne der Wahrheit und Schönheit wieder zu vereinigen.

Thus literature and intellectual life were explicitly to address elevated and broad issues, not daily and particular (read overtly political) ones. It was to harmonize the social body and to calm human discord. When he explained the title, *Die Horen,* Schiller told the story of the Horae who received the newborn Venus in Cyprus and clothed her in divine garments. Then they led her, clothed by their hands, into the circle of the immortals:

> ... a charming story, in which it is implied that, even when newly born, beauty must submit to rules, and only through abiding the law can it appear worthy of obtaining a place in Olympus, immortality and moral values.

> ... eine reizende Dichtung, durch welche angedeutet wird, daß das Schöne schon in seiner Geburt sich unter Regeln fügen muß und nur durch Gesetzmäßigkeit würdig werden kann, einen Platz im Olymp, Unsterblichkeit und einen moralischen Wert zu erhalten. (Schiller, II, 668)

These sublime claims about literature by the intellectual giants of the day would have their effect on women authors. At the most basic level of course women were ill-equipped to write literature which met these lofty requirements. They were not trained in the classical literatures or languages, often not even in German style. Indeed until this time their literary style (in letters, for instance) had been praised as a model precisely *because* it was lacking in training, and therefore seemed more "natural." Now "natural" had become identified with mob rule and the reign of terror. Moreover the weighty claims of these aesthetics distanced the content and style of literature from the realm in which most women felt comfortable by training: daily and personal life.

In addition, the products of these aesthetic views provided idealized images of women which were inappropriate to their own enlightened exodus from any self-incurred powerlessness (Kant). The essay "On Grace and Nobility" (1793) contains "nearly the entire body of thought of Schiller's classical aesthetics, ethics, and anthropology" (Herbert G. Göpfert in Schiller, II, 834). According to Schiller, women were particularly likely to manifest the quality of grace:

> The more delicate feminine form absorbs every impression faster and lets it disappear again faster. Solid constitutions are only moved by a storm, and when strong muscles are acquired they cannot show the ease demanded of grace. What is still beautiful sensitivity in a feminine face would express suffering in a masculine one. The delicate fibre of woman bends like a thin reed with the gentlest breath of emotion. In gentle and charming waves the soul glides over the expressive countenance, which quickly smoothes itself again into a serene mirror.

> Der zärtere weibliche Bau empfängt jeden Eindruck schneller und läßt ihn schneller wieder verschwinden. Feste Konstitutionen kommen nur durch einen Sturm in Bewegung, und wenn starke Muskeln angezogen werden, so können sie die Leichtigkeit nicht zeigen, die zur Grazie erfordert wird. Was in einem weiblichen Gesicht noch schöne Emfindsamkeit ist, würde in einem männlichen schon Leiden ausdrücken. Die zarte Fiber des Weibes neigt sich wie dünnes Schilfrohr unter dem leisesten Hauch des Affekts. In leichten und lieblichen Wellen gleitet die Seele über das sprechende Angesicht, das sich bald wieder zu einem ruhigen Spiegel ebnet. (Schiller, II, 409)

As much as Schiller honors grace as the freely chosen expression of genuine sentiment, and therefore the union of freedom and necessity, women will seldom be able to attain the highest form of humanity.

> Seldom will feminine character raise itself to the highest idea of moral purity and seldom will it be capable of more than *affected* actions. It will often resist sensuality with heroic strength, but

only *through* sensuality. . . . Grace will therefore be the expression of feminine virtue and may frequently be missing from masculine virtue.

Selten wird sich der weibliche Charakter zu der höchsten Idee sittlicher Reinheit erheben und es selten weiter als zu *affektionierten* Handlungen bringen. Er wird der Sinnlichkeit oft mit heroischer Stärke, aber nur *durch* die Sinnlichkeit widerstehen. . . . Anmut wird also der Ausdruck der weiblichen Tugend sein, der sehr oft der männlichen fehlen dürfte. (Schiller, II, 409)

Male virtue is more likely to be manifested in "nobility" ("*Würde*"). The implicit relative value of female and male virtue is then expressed in the sentence: "The highest level of grace is that which *enchants;* the highest level of nobility is *majesty.*" ("Der höchste Grad der Anmut ist das *Bezaubernde;* der höchste Grad der Würde die *Majestät.*" Schiller II, 422)

The aesthetics, ethics and anthropology of German classicism provided models of character and behavior for women that made it difficult for admirers of Goethe and Schiller to be active or rebellious, strong-willed or independent. The idealized claims were both impossible and attractive for women. The complex literary reactions of women like the salonnière Rahel Varnhagen, the lady-in-waiting Charlotte von Stein, and the authors Friederike Unger and Bettine von Arnim to the literature of this "golden age" are explored in this volume in essays by Liliane Weissberg, Katherine Goodman, Susanne Zantop, and Edith Waldstein.

The *real* situation of women was certainly quite different from any described in classical literature—and, of course, classical German literature was never intended to be realistic. Lydia Schieth has recently narrated the history of Schiller's *Horen* and its relationship to women. Of the twenty-five first listed contributors, none was a woman. The tone began as elevated as Schiller had announced; but he sought desperately for a novel to serialize in order to increase readership. None was immediately available. By the third year he had picked up seven women contributors and in October of 1796 began publication of the anonymous novel *Agnes von Lilien.* The novel was a success, and some even guessed that it was Goethe's sequel to *Wilhelm Meisters Lehrjahre.* In reality it was the product of Caroline von Wolzogen. But the appearance of the novel and of female contributors coincided with the complaints of more than one critic that they missed the journal's "striving for the eternal" (Streben nach dem Unendlichen, Körner, in Schieth,

85). The efforts of dilettantes, with which women's works were identified, mistook the end result of art, the effect on the reader, for its essence and ignored matters of objective causes and motivations, noted Goethe in "Über den Dilettantismus" (1799) (in Schieth, 93). All writing that did not contribute to this idealist project was judged to be dilettantish. Goethe and Schiller undertook to battle this kind of dilettantism, or, as Goethe phrased it in his *Farbenlehre* (1810), to oppose the "feminization and infantilization" of serious fields (in Schieth, 94).

It is not hard to imagine that the creator of female characters like "Lotte," "Gretchen," or even "Iphigenie" would have had a somewhat limited view of the kind of literature that women might write or the role of female characters. Although Goethe appeared to support the concerns of women and the efforts of women writers, he did so by restricting their sphere of activity. Thus in a favorable review of one novel written by a woman, he noted:

> But shouldn't intelligent and talented women be able to acquire intelligent and talented male friends to whom they could show their manuscripts, so that all unfeminine traits would be expunged and nothing would remain in such a work which would depart from natural feeling . . . like a burdensome counterweight.

> Sollten denn aber geistreiche und talentvolle Frauen nicht auch geist- und talentvolle Freunde erwerben können, denen sie ihre Manuscripte vorlegten, damit alle Unweiblichkeiten ausgelöscht würden und nichts in einem solchen Werke zurückbleibe, was dem natürlichen Gefühl . . . sich als ein lästiges Gegengewicht anhängen dürfte. (in Schieth, 146)

Interestingly, what a woman produced might be unnaturally unfeminine, and a male friend would be able to render the text suitably, "naturally," feminine. In another favorable review of a woman's novel Goethe wrote:

> Epic and semi-epic writing demands a main character which will be introduced by a man in the case of the dominance of action, by a women in the case of the dominance of suffering.

> Epische, halbepische Dichtung verlangt eine Hauptfigur, die bei vorwaltender Tätigkeit durch den Mann, bei überwiegendem Leiden durch die Frau vorgestellt wird. (in Schieth, 155)

So the gender of a novel's hero is determined by whether or not the author envisions action or suffering as its main theme. Goethe was universally admired for his creation of female characters as well as for his talent in general. What must it have been like to be a woman author, who could appreciate Goethe's talent, but who tried to portray in fiction the lives of women? The attraction of the elevated philosophy of Goethe and Schiller, their verbal virtuosity and their idealization of limited female roles made negotiations about the literary field particularly difficult for these writers. The case of Sophie Albrecht probably represents but one example of the plight of women authors whose writings failed to accrue the praises of the male literary establishment. Ruth Dawson explores her reliance on an alternative network of female friends in this volume.

While Goethe and Schiller expressed positive attitudes towards women in their idealized philosophy, their writings clearly revealed a double standard in which explicitly male virtues were held to be the superior ones. By contrast, values explicitly associated with women were in some ways more important to the aesthetic theories of a younger generation of intellectuals who formed the Romantic Movement.

Romantics included women as a category in several ways that made them seem more central. For instance, they encouraged women's expression in art and society because they understood it to fill a void that had been furthered by Enlightenment philosophy. Women, according to the male romantics, were the embodiment of nature, the necessary counterpart to reason and science. The subjective, the emotional, the "natural" had to be synthesized with the rational in order to transcend the political and social failure of the present.

In aesthetic terms, the romantics were also generally interested in the transcendence of that which is known through a synthesis of all aspects of human experience. Their philosophy and art sought to synthesize elements of both mysticism and tangible reality. The authentic and complete expression of men's and women's personal and social experience was believed to make possible the transcendence of that reality, which would then be articulated as an improved state of existence. Ideally, this process would repeat itself infinitely and provide art, life and society with the benefit of constant reevaluation. The expression of these improved states of existence manifested themselves in a variety of ways, whether in personal letters, epistolary or "objective" novels, ranging from explicit and concrete suggestions for social change, as exemplified in Bettine von Arnim's *Königsbuch* (1843; 1852),[7] to the more utopian sketch of the future hinted at in Sophie Mereau's *Das Blüthenalter der Empfindung* (1794). But in general women might have felt that their concrete experience was attended to. Furthermore, a constant in the works of most, if not all, romantic writers, was their interest in the mediation between the individual and the community, for they viewed the individual as one component of the organic whole of the universe. The quality of social ties was a vital concern. Women, of course, were traditionally adept at sociability (*Geselligkeit*) and therefore formed the nucleus of their social groups.

The romantic philosophy of synthesis demanded the *real* articulation of these theories in the concept of *Lebenskunst*, the art of life. And microcosms of the romantic vision manifested themselves in the Jena "commune," in collective work on the journal *Athenäum*, and in the salons. For a time the university town of Jena, near Weimar, hosted a romantic "commune." 1799 saw the romantic theoreticians A.W. and Friedrich Schlegel settled there in one house centered around A.W. Schlegel's wife Caroline and F. Schlegel's lover Dorothea Veit, who had divorced just one year earlier the banker Simon Veit). The poet Ludwig Tieck arrived in October, the philosophers Fichte and Schelling soon thereafter, the poet Novalis often came over from nearby Weißenfels, and the poet Clemens Brentano, brother of Bettine von Arnim, was studying there. Some of them lived in the same house, many of them assembled regularly. Schlegel might read a poem, Novalis or Brentano an essay, while philosopher Fichte listened. They wandered through the moonlight, kept company till dawn, and wrote. They became personally embroiled in national debates about free love and atheism. For the period it was an altogether scandalous arrangement.

Although the group dispersed in 1801, by that time the women had become heavily involved in the literary work of the men. Caroline Schlegel worked with A.W. Schlegel on a translation of Shakespeare and on various reviews. She provided material for Friedrich Schlegel's periodical *Athenäum* and proofread his novel *Lucinde* (1799). Dorothea Veit wrote her novel *Florentin* (1801) and contributed articles to *Athenäum* and *Europa*. Later she published various translations under Friedrich Schlegel's name and for a time supported him in this manner.

The center of salon life in the German states was Berlin. Interestingly enough many of the salonnières were Jewish women and of these Rahel Varnhagen was (and is) the most famous. Her salon enjoyed the greatest popularity and influence around 1796 but came more or less to a standstill in 1806 when French troops occupied Berlin. Together with her husband, Karl August Varnhagen von Ense, she opened her second salon in 1819, and it lasted until 1832. The names of a few of the guests in attendance at both salons will suffice to show the diversity and prominence of her social gatherings: the philosopher and student of Hegel, Eduard Gans; the classical philologist, Friedrich August Wolf; the historian, Leopold Ranke; the Prussian general, Wilhelm von Willisen; Prince Louis Ferdinand of Prussia and his lover, Pauline Wiesel; the writers, Heinrich Heine, Achim and Bettine von Arnim, Clemens Brentano, Jean Paul, Ludwig Tieck, Adelbert von Chamisso, Friedrich von Fouqué; the explorer and scientist, Alexander von Humboldt; the theologian, Friedrich Schleiermacher; the philosophers, Johann Gottlieb Fichte and Friedrich Schlegel; the government official, Friedrich Gentz; and noblemen, such as Gustav von Brinkmann and Wilhelm von Burgsdorff. Precisely this social mixture lent the salon an aura of titillation. For aristocrats to socialize with the middle class, with Jews, with actresses, was slightly scandalous, and no doubt a little exciting. For middle class intellectuals who sought public advancement, it could be a place for valuable connections.[8] While the Varnhagen salon was known for its concern with *belles lettres,* especially its adoration of Goethe, its guests also discussed music and politics, and Varnhagen was known for her talent in mediating these sophisticated debates. Moreover, her forcefully idiosyncratic letters have attracted the interest of German women for nearly two centuries.[9]

Around the time of Rahel Varnhagen's death in 1833, Bettine von Arnim opened her salon in Berlin. During the tumultuous times preceding the Revolution of 1848, the Arnim salon was at the height of its popularity and influence, while becoming far more political than the Varnhagen salon. Bettine von Arnim, the granddaughter of Sophie von La Roche and raised by her after her mother's death in 1793, was exposed very early in life to both the French Revolution and the institution of the salon. Artists, academics, German and French Jacobins, and French emigrants met at her grandmother's house in Offenbach to discuss the issues of the day, in particular the French Revolution. Here the young Bettine first encountered critical discussions of Goethe and the beginnings of the Romantic Movement as well as radical political thought. As a result, she read and admired not only the prominent German writers of her time, but also the French revolutionist Mirabeau (1749–1791). And thus the mold had been cast for the "democratic" salon Bettine von Arnim hosted later in her life.[10] The guests attending it were much the same ones who had frequented the Varnhagen house. Von Arnim attracted liberal thinkers, such as the Varnhagens, the literary historian Adolf Stahr, and the political activist and Young-Hegelian Bruno Bauer. She deliberately used her salon as a cultural *and* political forum, where to the end of her life she discussed democratic ideals that had had their origin in the French Revolution and had taken many shapes over the course of the first half of the nineteenth century. Bettine von Arnim's salon was one of the last of its kind in Berlin, coming to an end in the late fifties, shortly before her death in 1859.

While some of these romantic women published novels, what is particularly striking is the fact that several consciously devoted themselves to letters as a literary form. Previously, women's epistolary style had been proposed as a model of natural style. Now, the letter could integrate itself into romantic aesthetic theory as a whole. It was an ideal medium in which to synthesize the real and the ideal. It could fulfill the romantic criterion for fragmentary form, both internally (moving rapidly from topic to topic, with no formal requirements) and externally (a piece of reality lifted from its context). And it was the aesthetic expression of utopian sociability. Caroline Schlegel-Schelling, Rahel Varnhagen, and Bettine von Arnim rightly prided themselves on their epistolary styles. Therefore, while the letter is not a genre that has remained significant for the literary canon, its theoretical importance for the romantics clearly gave women the freedom to explore their expression in it. Sara Friedrichsmeyer, Liliane Weissberg, and Edith Waldstein evaluate various aspects of the contributions of these authors to epistolary forms.

The romantic predilection for blending reality and fantasy to the point where they become indistinguishable resulted in another form that intrinsically encouraged women's literary production: the fairy tale (*Märchen*). These derived in part from an oral tradition in which women felt comfortable. In addition to writing literary fairy tales, the romantics, in the persons of the Grimm brothers, had begun to collect (and modify) folk fairly tales told to them by women. Bettine von Arnim and her daughter Gisela, who later married a son of one of the Grimm brothers, both tried their hands at this form. In the current volume Shawn Jarvis explores the alternative spaces created by women in the fairy tales of

Benedikte Naubert. Perhaps the communities of women she portrayed are the fantastic transformations of the female networks upon which Sophie Albrecht had relied.

Nevertheless, even in the relatively woman-friendly cultural environment of the early romantics, women's lives were still narrowly circumscribed by male society and male romantics. It was still a fact of life, after all, that women were not as well educated as their male counterparts and it was still the case that women were not equal to men before the law. Women's participation in "high" culture, therefore, remained necessarily limited. But in addition to these concrete restrictions, romantic philosophy participated in Schiller's and Goethe's turn to aesthetic idealism, despite theoretical positions favoring *real* life. As in the case of these two classical authors, the romantic position paralleled a somewhat negative reaction to the French Revolution. Friedrich Schlegel was perhaps at his most radical in his "Essay on the Concept of Republicanism" ("Versuch über den Begriff des Republikanismus", 1796). And yet even he placed himself somewhere between Schiller and the Jacobins in his claim that moral education and political freedom had to be mediated through a dialectic between governmental institutions and the individual intellect, the *Geist*. Like that of a few other romantics, his radical position consisted of supporting a constitutional monarchy, not the rule of the people which had taken such a bloody turn in France.

The aesthetic parallel situated art with the divine elites. Goethe, for instance, may not have been an unflawed idol to them, but they still imagined an "Olympus" and located him on it. Poets, in general, were priests in a privileged position to divine truth. The aesthetic idealism of the Romantic Movement placed women in a paradoxical situation. While virtues associated with women were deemed central to any notions of change, women themselves were seemingly barred from the possibility of experiencing transcendent wholeness. As Friedrich Schlegel wrote:

> It is not the destiny of women which is domestic, it is their *nature* and *situation*. And I consider it more a useful than a happy truth, that even the best marriage, motherliness itself and the family can entangle them and degrade them so easily with the needs of economy and the earth, that they no longer remain mindful of their divine origin and image . . .

> Nicht die Bestimmung der Frauen sondern ihre *Natur* und *Lage* ist häuslich. Und ich halte es für eine mehr nützliche als erfreuliche Wahrheit, daß auch die beste Ehe, die Mütterlichkeit selbst

und die Familie sie gar leicht so sehr mit dem Bedürfnisse, der Oekonomie und der Erde verstricken und herabziehen kann, daß sie ihres göttlichen Ursprunges und Ebenbildes nicht mehr eingedenk bleiben.... (F. Schlegel "Über die Philosophie" in *Athenäum*, 2 (1799), 1, in Schieth, 117)

In the romantic scheme of things, women were the embodiment of nature in its totality, and the male romantic philosophers and writers, such as Novalis and Friedrich Schlegel, longed for union (in the sense of an androgynous synthesis) with a woman in their search for wholeness. It then follows that it would not be possible for women to attain a comparable transcendence, since they were bound by virtue of their gender to the fixed "totality" of nature. And, according to romantic thinking, it was precisely such a transcendence that allowed the writer to be a visionary, to establish a connection not only with the future, but also with the infinite— with the divine. The privilege of the male voice is evident in such thinking, in that women, although praised and idealized, functioned as a means to an end. And although one could reverse the synthetic argument, it was not done. Men were still the bearers of "high" culture. It is not surprising, then, that many romantic women writers, like many of their precursors, published anonymously or under their husbands' names when their writings did in fact appear in print.

English and French literature possessed their geniuses, but only in the German states was the ideological and aesthetic distance between "high" and "low" literature formulated so dramatically. German women continued to write in the same genres that they had used before the Revolution, fairy tales, epistolary fiction, and the family novel, for instance. And because these forms (and the topics they implied) comprised the vast portion of popular literature in the eighteenth and nineteenth centuries, they did not receive the critical acclaim that drama, poetry, or other variations of the novel, such as the *Bildungsroman,* enjoyed.

The romantic women discussed in this volume responded in different ways to the troubled political position of the German states at the turn of the century. Their answers incorporated their very specific position as women in German society in a way that was neglected by their male counterparts. Ute Brandes discusses the divergent responses of Sophie von La Roche and Sophie Mereau, grandmother and wife respectively of the romantic poet Clemens Brentano, to German women's social and cultural situation around 1800. While the political position of each is quite different, La Roche and Mereau share a concern with issues relating to their gender. And it is not expressed in terms of a treatise on androgyny à la Friedrich Schlegel, like in his novel *Lucinde* (1799), but rather speaks to the very concrete problems women faced both domestically and in the public sphere from the perspective of gender-specific personal experience.

On the heels of the Enlightenment and the French Revolution, both of which inspired German versions of the French originals, followed Germany's attempts to find a "third way," a more perfect social union, in the aesthetic idealism of the classicism of Goethe and Schiller and the Romantic Movement of the younger generation. In their desire to include polyphonous expressions of all human experience, the early romantics at least partially legitimized women's participation in the cultural sphere. But the emphasis on gender difference and the divine status accorded to literature still conspired to denigrate the possibilities for a full participation of women writers in the undertaking of this project for a more just and generous society. Even today the canon refuses to recognize the most talented of them.

In the Shadow of Olympus

We have assembled chapters about only a few of the women who wrote "in the shadow of Olympus." But considering our intention to draw attention to their works, some explanation of our title is necessary. That we perpetuate the concept of an "Olympus" in whose "shadow" women writers toiled does not reflect our ideal understanding of the time. It does reflect the very real difficulty of coming to terms with this period, even in the late twentieth century. Not only contemporaries of Goethe have tended to connect all literary activity of the period to one writer. Even before Hermann August Korff's influential multi-volume study of German literature covering the period from the 1770s to 1830, *Geist der Goethezeit* (1923–40), that period had been identified with the works of this one major author.[11] The designation "Goethezeit" (Age of Goethe) subsumes all writing in Germany for sixty years and organizes it around that one beacon.

Clearly this was a period in which much more was happening than can be expressed by this label. In terms of literary movements alone the period encompasses at least the late Enlightenment, "Storm and Stress," classicism, romanticism (early, middle, and late), and the "Biedermeier" era. Historically, Germans reacted to the French Revolution, Napoleon's conquest of Germany as well as his expulsion, and the institution of new monarchies after 1815. It was a period of great social shifts from the cultural dominance of the courts to the cultural dominance of the bourgeois intelligentsia. The basis for trade began to shift from commodity exchange to cash, medieval guilds began to lose their importance, and the German states moved toward a market economy.

But despite all these developments, many German literary critics (perhaps the majority) still view the intellectual atmosphere of this period as reflecting the spirit of one man, and still view the aestheticism of the period around 1800 in utopian terms. It would take at least one additional volume to explain the popularity of the term "The Age of Goethe" or the image of an "Olympus."

To be sure, there have been critics of this nomenclature. Outside Germany, literary scholars like to refer to all of these authors as romantics. But this is a designation strongly resisted by an indigenous insistence on referring to the writings of Goethe and Schiller as classical. Moreover it tends to blur some of the valid distinctions highlighted by the other labels applied to various literary styles in this period.

Inside Germany the term "Age of Goethe" has been criticized for neglecting male authors of other classes and literary and political persuasions, not to mention women authors of any persuasion. This is precisely why we criticize this term, as well as the term *Kunstperiode* (aestheticism), which some scholars have recently advanced.[12] The term is taken from the poet Heinrich Heine's designation of the literary period prior to 1830. To be sure, it highlights some of the characteristics of the period that seem relevant for our discussion of women writers; namely, the elevated status accorded the arts and the importance of technical virtuosity. But as a label, it does nothing to help us with our desire to find a term which allows us to include what most women actually wrote.

In short, we cannot yet find an adequate label for the period we describe. We have only begun to illuminate the "shadows" surrounding "Olympus." To date nothing demonstrates as clearly as the expression "The Age of Goethe," or the image of an "Olympus," our dilemma in confronting both the relative dominance given to Goethe's voice and to aesthetic idealism during this period, *and* the privileged position they have been given in the literary canon. As we hope to show in this introduction and the chapters which follow, to begin to appreciate what women wrote in this period, it is vital to bear in mind both *their* chronological relationship to the phenomenon "Goethe" and *our* chronological relationship to the image of an "Olympus." Therefore we place the title in provisional quotation marks.

All the chapters in this volume are sensitive to the attraction of this image. Indeed, pioneering monographs about the relationship of women and literature in this period have, for the most part, emphasized the ways in which "real" women and their literary voices have been absorbed, or "dissolved" by this dominant literary culture. Sylvia Bovenschen, Barbara Becker-Cantarino, Helga Meise, and Lydia Schieth have all tended to stress the virtually total oppression of women's voices and the orchestration of a massive ideological network that brook no deviation.

While recognizing the gravitational attraction of this dominant culture, the scholars writing for this volume have usually sought to find individual moments of orbital pull against "Goethe" and the dominant culture. It is not that the chapters assembled here propose a tradition of the eternal or essential feminine, against which some German feminists justifiably argue. Nor do they propose a history of concerted and determined struggle against oppression. Rather, in various ways, these chapters tend to examine the tension embodied in these texts. We might be tempted to claim an investigation of what Nancy Miller has termed "feminist writing" were it not for the fact that in some cases the self-consciousness of the text is in question. Therefore it is probably more appropriate to claim the tradition of Elaine Showalter's "gynocriticism."

These selections are, therefore, attempts at locating individual moments of slippage, moments in the history of women's writing when women did not conform perfectly to the ideology that dominated the "Age of Goethe." To be sure, in one or two instances, the critique was quite explicit and conscious, and in one, at least, it does not seem to exist at all (Weissberg on Varnhagen), but for the most part one suspects that any slippage or "oppositional" tendency was a product of attempts simply to elaborate the specific situation of women. After all, women's perspectives on the problems they face quite simply differ from men's perspectives on women's issues. Nowhere in this period is there any systematic opposition; there are no declarations of independence. There are merely repeated registrations of differences of perspective and indications of discontent. These women were neither blind to their situation nor simply entangled in an ideological network. And while in the end they may have accommodated themselves to society, it is the negotiation for that space which is the primary focus of the chapters collected here.

On his deathbed Goethe is reputed to have demanded, "More light!" It is indeed time for more light, time to bathe this whole period in a wash of light and bring these authors out of the shadows for good.

2

The Beautiful Soul Writes Herself: Friederike Helene Unger and the "Große Göthe"

Susanne Zantop

In May 1796, the forty-seven-year-old Goethe received a letter that read:

> Ever since I started to think and to feel, ever since the first spark of your genius fell into my ever so receptive heart, I wanted to have an opportunity to express to you, most respected Sir, my warm and heartfelt admiration. The deceased Moritz used to promise me, whenever our conversations of and about you rekindled my desire, to mention me once to you; for it was my pride to know that you were not unaware of my existence. But alas! the poor man died, and with him my hope to see you, and venerate you, in Weimar. Now my husband is at the Leipzig fair—I am the wife of your publisher Unger—and my friend Zelter provides me through his songs with this natural opportunity. But will I be able to use it? My heart was overflowing, but now that I feel close to you, I remain speechless. I desired at last to vent the feelings that your greatness inspired in me. But how will you believe that I have the mind to appreciate this greatness if I lack the words to tell you something as simple and as natural as that? For what is more natural than to love the most charming poet and philosopher—never have I uttered your name without a quickening of my pulse and secret longings—like when one reencounters the love of one's youth!

> Seit ich zu den denkenden und fühlenden Wesen gehöre, seit der erste Funke Ihres herrlichen Geistes in mein so empfängliches Herz fiel, wünsche ich mir Veranlassung, Ihnen, Hochverehrter Mann, meine so warme und innige Verehrung zu erkennen zu

geben. Schon der seelige [Karl Philipp] Moritz versprach es mir, wenn er durch seine Gespräche von, und über Sie, diesen Wunsch aufs neue anregte, mich wenigstens einst, gegen Sie zu nennen; *denn es war schon mein Stolz, zu wissen, daß Ihnen meine Existenz nicht unbekand sei.* Aber Leider! der Gute starb, und mit ihm meine Hoffnung, Sie in Weymar zu sehen, und zu verehren. Jetzt ist mein Mann zur Leipziger Messe—Ich bin die Frau Ihres Verlegers Unger—und mein Freund Zelter, gibt mir durch seine Lieder, eine unverkünstelte Veranlassung. Aber möchte ich sie nun benutzen können? ich hatte viel auf dem Herzen, *bin aber stumm, da ich mich in Ihrer Nähe fühle.* Mir lag daran, endlich einmal, dem Gefühl Luft zu machen von welchem ich für Ihre Größe durchdrungen bin. Wie werden Sie es mir aber glauben, daß ich Sinn habe, sie zu fühlen, wenn es mir an Worte gebricht, Ihnen so ganz etwas einfaches und natürliches zu sagen. Denn was ist natürlicher, als daß man den liebenswürdigsten Dichter u. Philosophen liebt, nie nannte ich Ihren Nahmen ohne Herzklopfen, und geheime Ahndung, wie wenn man den Geliebten, der früheren Jugend begegnet! (Biedermann, 67f.)[1]

The author of this erotic fan letter was the fifty-five-year old Friederike Helene Unger, wife of Johann Friedrich Unger, the publisher of Goethe's *Wilhelm Meisters Lehrjahre* (1796)[2]. When her husband returned from the Leipzig book fair, Friederike "confessed" her improper advances to the great master; the embarrassed Johann Friedrich felt compelled to apologize for his wife who, as he said, had been seduced by the "snake"—Zelter's songs— to make overtures to the "great Goethe". The poet responded condescendingly; he graciously acknowledged Madame Unger's effort to make available to him Zelter's "masterful compositions" and thanked her for her devotion: "I certainly appreciate the interest taken by kindred cultured souls in me and in my works, which help me to relate a part of my existence even to unknown minds far away." (Glauben Sie, daß ich den Anteil zu schätzen weiß, den gute und gebildete Seelen an mir und an den Arbeiten nehmen, durch die ich einen Teil meiner Existenz auch entferntern mir unbekannten Gemütern nahe bringen kann.) No reference to her own aesthetic interests and her own quite remarkable literary production.[3]

I have quoted this incident at length, because Unger's letter clearly illustrates a profound psychological dilemma faced by most German women writers—and some male writers as well—at the end of the eighteenth century: Torn between their erotic and aesthetic fascination with Goethe and their desire for self-expression, they feel overwhelmed, speechless. Yet they recuperate their own language precisely in their need to overcome their spell-bound state, their anxiety of *not* being heard. We can observe this phenomenon in Bettina von Arnim, whose book *Goethes Briefwechsel mit einem Kinde (Goethe's Correspondence with a Child)* fictionalizes this interaction. We can see it in Rahel Varnhagen, whose admiration for Goethe both silenced her (as a writer) and made her eloquent (as a salonnière). We find it in Johanna Schopenhauer and Friederike Helene Unger.[4] It is not just the man Goethe to whom everybody is attracted—Unger for example never met him personally—it is what he embodies. He is undoubtedly the king of German poetry, the tastemaker, the "genius" par excellence. The seduction the young and not-so-young authors feel is not only due to the power of Goethe's erotics but to an erotics of power. Paradoxically, by associating with the Olympian Goethe, the women writers both partake of this power *and* are annihilated. Thus one of the most detailed accounts of Unger's life to date, Ludwig Geiger's 1895 entry in *Allgemeine Deutsche Biographie,* sums up her literary significance with the following words:

> Although Madam Unger was certainly not a pre-eminent writer, she deserves our respect for having been an immensely hard worker. Her special merit consists in having directed the attention of Goethe—with whom she apparently shared no other relation—to Zelter and for having thus helped to promote an association that must be counted among the most beautiful in our classical literary period. (ADB 39:295)

While Unger's literary production is brushed aside, her place in literary history as facilitator of male friendship and male creativity is thus guaranteed.

Both the positive and pernicious effects of the association with Goethe become even more obvious when we move from the biographical to the intertextual interaction. Goethe was, of course, not only the embodiment of the dominant discourse and thus of market power, but above all a powerful literary model: a writer who, perhaps more than any German author before him, had expanded the notions of the "eternal feminine" to include an ever wider and ever more seductive range of female characters—without, however, advocating that women transcend their "true calling," the triple role of wife, mother, and housekeeper. Indeed, with the exception perhaps of Philine, the self-assured, sensuous, bohemian actress in *Wilhelm Meister,* Goethe provided no examples of successful, independent women artists, let alone of women writers.[5] Women trying to become authors and invent their own heroines thus had to break the spell cast by such heroines as Iphigenia, Aurelie, Nathalie, or Eugenie and redirect the course of female development given in Goethe's paradigmatic female *Bildungsroman, Bekenntnisse einer schönen Seele (Confessions of a Beautiful Soul).*[6]

Again, Friederike Helene Unger's writings typify this tension between conformism with and resistance to the male models, a tension we can discover in most women's novels of the period and which, as Gilbert and Gubar have shown, produces such duplicitous, disjointed texts. In fact, although Unger had, in every sense, privileged access to the means of literary production and distribution,[7] almost all her novels, from *Julchen Grünthal* onward, constitute an *Auseinandersetzung*—literally both an engagement and a disengagement—with Goethe's works, which she imitates and rejects, retells from a woman's perspective and discusses critically. Her "tease" with the "Great Goethe" is particularly visible in her novels *Gräfinn Pauline* (1800), *Melanie das Findelkind (Melanie, the Foundling,* 1804), and *Albert und Albertine* (1804) written at the peak of her literary productivity and at the peak of Goethe's fame. By creating heroines who slip into female "roles" distilled from Goethe's characters, yet who act out rather than fulfill these roles, Unger manages to establish a distance to her model and create a space to insert her own experiences and projections as woman writer, to add what Nancy K. Miller has called a special "emphasis" (343), a difference in "intonation".[7] While this "literary parasitism," as one might call it, apparently cemented the dependency of the woman writer on the man even in the realm of the imagination, paradoxically it also facilitated the emergence of the female author. In the following, I shall try to show how these mechanisms of dependence operated in some exemplary texts.[8]

Gräfinn Pauline, or: the Sorrows of Young Iphigenia

Does man alone have the right to unprecedented action?

Hat denn zur unerhörten Tat der Mann allein das Recht?
(Goethe, *Iphigenie auf Tauris*)

In Unger's first work of fiction, *Julchen Grünthal. Eine Pensionsgeschichte* (1784), Goethe's novel *Die Leiden des jungen Werthers (The Sorrows of Young Werther)* and his play *Stella* appear at a critical juncture in the plot: Julchen, removed from the harmful influences of the French boarding school to the home of her married cousin Karoline, is introduced to German sentimentalist literature—"the entire Werther paroxism, and the sentimental period following it" (den ganzen Wertherparoxismus und die darauf folgende empfindsame Periode, 180)—by Karoline's sentimental and not so virtuous husband Karl. Soon Julchen and Karl not only read together, but are engaged in adulterous activity, as Karoline observes through the key-hole:

> Karl recited to her Goethe's Stella, with the most ardent expression. I don't know, dear uncle, whether you know that play, in which the basest standards are clad in the most attractive, seductive language. They took turns reading. Julchen read in a similarly passionate tone the role of Stella. They sat on a sofa opposite to the door; I clearly saw that they were locked in an embrace. O God, I almost fainted!

> Karl deklamirte ihr mit dem feurigsten Ausdruck Göthens Stella vor. Ich weiß nicht, lieber Onkel, ob Ihnen dies Schauspiel bekannt ist, das mit den elendesten Grundsätzen in der reizvollsten verführerischsten Sprache ganz durchwebt ist. Sie lasen wechselweise. Julchen las eben so im leidenschaftlichsten Tone die Rolle der Stella. Sie saßen auf einem Ottomann (sic) der Stubenthüre gegenüber; ich sah deutlich, daß sie einander mit ihren Armen fest umschlungen hatten. O Gott, wie wankte ich zurück! (223–24)

Not surprisingly, Goethe's seductive text corrupts Julchen, the personification of the naive reader, and completes her downfall, a fall that was triggered by Rousseau's *Nouvelle Héloïse*[9]. Unger's distinction between Goethe's greatness as an artist, which she appreciates, and the "immorality" of his works, which she laments, also characterizes her future approach to the poet. After her overtures to the "Great Goethe" in 1796 (and possibly because of a commercial interest in remaining on a good footing with him),[10] the split assessment is displaced onto the audience: While Unger apparently recognizes that a critical engagement with Goethe's works could release creative energies in his (female) readers, she repeatedly warns of the dangers of false, i.e., sentimental, identificatory reading.

Unger's first original novel after *Julchen Grünthal, Gräfinn Pauline* (1800), confronts these two types of reading. The tightly constructed melodrama combines, in the form of a thematic collage, elements of Goethe's *Die Leiden des jungen Werthers* (1774), *Iphigenie* (1787), and *Wilhelm Meisters Lehrjahre* (1796).[11] On the one hand, it appropriates the images of ideal femininity so masterfully propagated by Goethe: the virtuous, disembodied "beautiful soul," and the self-effacing, selfless "Entsagende," which associate female heroism with suffering, self-denial and renunciation.[12] On the other hand, it creates a heroine whose lofty image of herself, formed through identification with heroic literary models, causes both her empowerment *and* her demise. Rather than extolling *Entsagung* (renunciation) as the way for women to achieve a reconciliation between reality and ideal, a "higher humanity," as Goethe does (and as she occasionally seems to do herself), Unger exposes the pitfalls of living a "fiction".

The plot of *Gräfinn Pauline* is structured around three tests in which the heroine exhibits her willingness to sacrifice personal happiness to the dictates of state and morality. Passionately attached to Prince Aemil since early childhood, Countess Pauline renounces her love when dynastic concerns, moral conventions, and political convenience demand such a sacrifice. The novel focuses entirely on Pauline's intense inner struggle to overcome her desire for Aemil, to control her physical and emotional needs, to abide by her strict moral code and thus transform her love into "eternal love" and herself into the personificaiton of female virtue. In the conflict between *Neigung* (desire) and *Pflicht* (duty), *Sinnlichkeit* (sensuality) and *Sittlichkeit* (morality), she chooses the latter, emerging as a true "beautiful soul."[13]

Yet while Pauline elevates herself to superhuman heights, becoming "the true ideal of womanhood" (das reine Ideal des Weibes, 49), the story subtly undermines the heroic plot by insisting on the destructiveness of abstract virtue to the individuals involved: Prince Aemil's officially arranged marriage facilitated by Pauline's sacrifice almost ruins the state, driving its ruler to distraction; a shot directed at Aemil cripples and disfigures the "divine" Pauline; away from home, in self-imposed exile, she wastes away and eventually dies a miserable death, sweetened only by Aemil's last-minute arrival on the scene.

The moral rigor of the protagonist is revealed to be a trap set by patriarchy, i.e., the rigorous moral dualism Pauline has internalized. Pestered by the advances of a libertine count, she ex-

claims: "Count, I will never, never marry anybody! Never! This is
my word to you and all the others. It is my last word, count." (Herr
Graf, ich werde nie, nie eines Mannes Weib! Nie! Dieß für Sie und
für Alle. Dieß ist mein letztes Wort, Herr Graf, 70). Although she
immediately realizes that with this vow, "she has gone too far,
driven by the force of circumstances," she cannot take it back. As
Pauline becomes aware—a knowledge she desperately tries to re-
press throughout her brief ordeal—she is caught in a system of
morality that conceives of only two kinds of women, virtuous and
vicious ones. Once on the path of virtuous renunciation, Pauline
must continue till the end or lose her identity. Ironically, her
death by a violent hemorrhage replicates the death of her antagonist, the sensuous, devilish Florentine, suggesting that, at least in
death, *les extrêmes se touchent*.

The novel thus seems to be engaged in multiple, even contradictory projects, which may indicate Unger's unease with existing
models of female perfection and her (or her society's) inability to
conceive of viable alternatives. On the one hand, the novel extols
women's empowerment through the uncompromising pursuit of
"virtue," which it defines broadly to encompass not just chastity
but civic virtues ("honor," service to the state, etc.) as well. On the
other, it questions the extreme subjectivity, the self-absorption and
self-destructiveness of this quest.

The heroine's empowerment is manifest when we compare the
beginning of the novel with its end. The text starts out with the
emphatic lines: "Nobody will miss me. Nobody . . . If nobody has no-
ticed my presence, how will they notice my absence?" (Niemand
wird mich vermissen. Niemand! [. . .] Hat doch keiner meine Gegenwart bemerkt: wie sollten sie meine Abwesenheit gewahr werden?) By means of a long process of physical withdrawal and
spiritual merging, Pauline manages to inscribe herself in the conscience of all around her, who share the guilt of having caused her
suffering. In the end, the dying Pauline has achieved transcendence; she has transformed her absence into eternal presence
through her spiritual legacy, her letter on children's education
presented to Aemil on her deathbed. The novel thus partakes of
the popular topos introduced by Richardson and brought to perfection by Wilhelmine Karoline Wobeser, whereby women manipulate
men through suffering and guilt, emerging at least morally, if not
socially, superior. By sticking to her principles of abstract morality,
yet refusing the domesticity plot, Pauline can become a heroine
of her own making, as she emphatically asserts: "I don't belong to

anyone; no one belongs to me; for a long time, I have been the property of my own love. Not even to Aemil can I sacrifice the quiet consciousness of myself." (Ich gehöre Niemandem, Niemand gehört mir an; längst sah ich mich als das Eigenthum meiner Liebe an.... Denn auch einem Aemil kann ich das ruhige Bewußtseyn meiner selbst nicht hingeben, 167). This emphatic self-creation has clear narcissistic overtones: Like Werther, Pauline seems to be more involved with her own feelings, the construction of her self as the "eternal beloved," than with the needs and feelings of her lover. Like the Beautiful Soul, Pauline's spirituality takes a turn toward extreme subjectivity or self-absorption. Yet by focusing on the psychological and physical cost of such a heroic effort, Unger makes unmistakably clear that the goal of female perfection thus conceived is, literally, a dead-end street, and not necessarily an attractive model to be emulated by her women readers. In fact, Pauline's heroic path sets a dangerous precedent, as the narrator hastens to explain:

> Wenn Pauline nach dem gemeinen Maaßstabe weiblicher Begriffe, die sich in gewöhnlicher häuslicher Beschränkung bildeten, gerichtet wird, kann sie, wo nicht geradehin fehlerhaft, doch in seltsamer Eigenthümlichkeit erscheinen. Allein man sehe auf ihre Erziehung, ihre natürliche Sphäre, den Hof, ihre frühe Liebe, ihre Abgeschiedenheit nachher, die hohe Ausbildung ihres Geistes, das ernste Studium der Geschichte, aus der sie eine große Ansicht der Dinge und eine Kraft, sich über die gewöhnlichen kleinlichen Rücksichten der Gesellschaft zu erheben, hernahm, die es ihr leicht machte, das drückende Gewicht gemeiner Hausmoral abzuwerfen; welches für Gemüther, die nicht so wie unsere Freundinn, fest und unverrückt, allein der Tugend, und ihren Begriffen von dem, was recht ist, huldigen, gefahrvoll werden könnte.

> If Pauline is judged by common standards of femininity, she may appear strange, if not outright faulty. But one should consider her education, her natural environment, the court, her early love, her seclusion afterwards, the high elevation of her spirit, the serious study of history, which instilled in her an elevated view of things and a strength to lift herself above the common petty considerations of society, and made it easy for her to throw off the heavy burden of common morality; something that can be rather dangerous for those minds who, unlike our friend, do not exclusively extoll virtue and all that is right. (168–69)

Despite her transcendence, Pauline is presented less as a heroine than as a victim of society, whose image of ideal femininity dictates her behavior and actions and destroys her in the end. Not only is Pauline's emotional fulfillment sacrificed to state interest and conventional ideals of female virtue, but the sacrifice itself proves utterly futile, an empty gesture, precisely because of her limited options.

Whereas Unger seems to question the masochistic, destructive implications of this type of *Entsagungsmodell* (type of renunciation), she suggests that sublimation could be a creative force for women as well. Unlike Werther, whose creative faculties are paralyzed by his absorbing passion—although, ironically, passion makes him eloquent in his letters to Wilhelm (6:53)—Pauline discovers that unfulfilled love and distance from the beloved serve as powerful stimuli for artistic production: "She wrote poetry, she composed, she painted, and everything was infused with the spirit of tender love, *her love*. She had always painted the beloved darling of her soul truthfully, in all its aspects, so warmly did his beautiful image live in her active imagination." (Sie dichtete, sie komponirte, sie malte, und in Allem wehete der Athem inniger Liebe, *ihrer Liebe*. Sie hatte den theuren Liebling ihrer Seele, in allen Beziehungen, immer treffend ähnlich gemalt, so warm lebte sein schönes Bild in ihrer regen Phantasie, 150). And not only is her creativity awakened, but she becomes active as a founder of country schools and as social reformer. The ideas that unfulfilled love can be sublimated into artistic and social practice, that work and art provide a "means to transcend the dislocation" (Hirsch, 46), are elaborated again when Pauline returns to court, where she must maintain a proper distance so as not to be mistaken for the Prince's mistress. As the Prince's friend, confidante, and collaborator, Pauline participates in the planning and governing process of the state and makes her benevolent presence felt. In these moments of artistic and political fulfillment, Unger ties the rational *Entsagungsmodell* of Sophie von La Roche's practical protagonists—who even in greatest distress find ways to educate others—to the artistically active, passionate heroines of Caroline Auguste Fischer, suggesting alternatives to sentimental *Tugendschwärmerei*, the exaggerated, self-destructive enthusiasm for virtue.[14] Caroline Schlegel's vicious aside to Rahel Varnhagen, "I found it particularly interesting how the beautiful Pauline with all her virtue and nobility finally turns into Mme. Unger" (Ich habe es besonders interessant gefunden, wie die schöne Pauline endlich aus lauter Tugend und Edelmut zur Mme. Unger wird),[15] hits the mark: Curiously, more productive alternatives to the sacrificial heroine emerge whenever Unger's own experiences as a woman writer and literary collaborator interfere with Pauline's melodramatic quest. Unger's identification with what she called her "best educated daughter"[16] provides at least a glimpse of an escape from a socially imposed female dilemma.

Insight into the female psyche, questions as to the value of self-effacement, and suggestions of a less heroic but more practical redefinition of *Entsagung* thus create "moments of resistance" in a novel which, at first sight, seems to follow conventional patterns. Unger's novel leaves the (feminist?) reader with more questions than answers, for it stretches heroic femininity to its limits, where self-effacement borders on the grotesque, the sublime on the ridiculous. The text carries Goethe's dictum that female protagonists in novels must be represented through their suffering, male through action, to its logical extreme, thereby revealing its function as part of a repressive gender ideology.[17]

Melanie das Findelkind or: Melanie's Theatrical Mission

> It seems we are playing a comedy here!
>
> Wir spielen hier, wie es scheint, Komödie!
> (Unger, *Melanie das Findelkind*)

The novel *Melanie das Findelkind* attests further to Unger's struggle with the self-sacrificial, purely spiritual model of female perfection and her search for a way to achieve "rational happiness" without self-denial. Magdalene Heuser has suggested that most of Unger's novels (and, for that matter, most of her non-fiction as well) are attempts to conceive of a female *Bildungsroman,* inspired by, or modelled after, Goethe's *Wilhelm Meister.* As I want to argue, *Melanie das Findelkind*—which Heuser does not mention in this context—can indeed be considered Unger's female equivalent to that famous male novel of formation. Not only do the names (Wilhelm, the male protagonist; Mariane) or characters (Mariane = Philine) suggest such an elective affinity—the whole idea of theater as a station in the protagonist's education and of role-playing as an initiation into society is directly derived from Goethe' narrative. Unger's rewriting exposes the dilemma faced by a female protagonist in search of *Bildung* (education). Barred from Wilhelm's freedom of movement *in* society and unwilling to follow the Beautiful Soul's example of complete withdrawal *from* society, she is compelled to accept as a "third way" the constricted female role of wife offered *by* society. If Pauline fell into the trap of a model which, paradoxically, granted women heroic status as victims, Melanie is trapped by the lure of conventionality. Her harmonious integration into domesticity is, however, undercut by the novel's ostentatious theatricality, which suggests Unger's subconscious, if not conscious, discomfort with the option she proposes.

As the title indicates, Melanie the foundling's origin and status are undefined at the onset of her story. Her search for an identity and a proper place in society organizes the plot into a series of encounters with representatives of almost all social strata, which provide her with the experience necessary to be accepted into her "paternal home" (13).

Melanie's *Bildung* is initiated by a violent rupture: Expelled by the jealous Princess from the court where she was raised and educated, Melanie must re-establish herself through her own inner resources. She is abducted by a libertine nobleman to his love nest in the forest, where she struggles successfully to remain virtuous; she joins a troupe of actors; gains fame as an actress, wins the love of count Wilhelm despite her precarious social situation as "public woman"; renounces him when his family puts pressure on her to do so, yet wins him back after years of trials and tribulations as lady companion and servant to noble and bourgeois mistresses. In a final test of loyalty, Melanie, led to believe that Wilhelm was crippled in the war against the Turks, consents to marry him despite his injury. Melanie's reward is all the greater: Her sacrifice, which turns out to have no basis in reality—the amputation was a ploy—entitles her to assume the elevated social status she has morally held all along. She is recognized by her legitimate father, the Prince, marries count Wilhelm—and wins a large sum of money in the British lottery . . .

As the retelling of this Cinderella plot indicates, Melanie's trajectory differs substantially from Wilhelm Meister's more or less linear development: although downward and upward, it is basically circular. After her experiences with both higher and lower ranks of society, with professional life as an actress and woman companion, and with a public existence, she returns home in a double sense: to her origins, her "legitimate place" among the nobility, and to domestic bliss. Nor does her *Bildungsweg* consist, like

Wilhelm's, of a "gradual organic unfolding of inner capacities, culminating in active social involvement and civic responsibility"
(Hirsch, 29), i.e., a continuous widening of the horizon, a becoming. Instead, it is marked by a series of abrupt dislocations, most
of them imposed on her by circumstances, which test her endurance and emotional resourcefulness and which end in a constricted
space, in every sense. The beautiful soul Melanie, a woman in
whom *Anmut* and *Würde,* grace and dignity, are in perfect harmony (62) from the onset, almost instinctively finds her way
through the romantic trappings of the current literary and social
scene to avoid the ignominy of Meister's Mariane,[18] the *Raserei*
and *Liebestod* of Aurelie, or the *Tugendschwärmerei* (93) of the
"beautiful souls" who model themselves after Goethe's saint:

> However, Mesdames, if that were the case? If it were my book's
> intention to show you, for a change, a young woman who, healthy
> in body and mind, without that hysterical sensitivity which is the
> essence of romantic-beautiful souls, feels enough strength in her-
> self to conquer her first love, to submit to duty and necessity,
> and thus become worthy of the best man by demonstrating the
> strength and courage to renounce him; would that be of no inter-
> est to the beautiful souls of my beautiful readers? I certainly
> hope not!

> Allein, Mesdames, wenn dem nun so wäre? Wenn es nun in der
> Tendenz meines Buches läge, Ihnen zur Veränderung ein Mäd-
> chen zu zeigen, das gesund an Leib und Seele, ohne jene hy-
> sterische Reizbarkeit, die das Wesen romantisch-schöner Seelen
> ist, Kraft genug in sich fühlte, eine erste Liebe zu verschmerzen,
> der Pflicht und der Nothwendigkeit nachzugeben, und sich so des
> ersten Mannes würdig machte, indem es Kraft und Muth äußerte,
> ihn aufzugeben; würde das für die schönen Seelen der schönen
> Leserinnen gar kein Interesse haben? Ich will nicht hoffen! (185)

Self-styled "beautiful souls" appear as Melanie's true antagonists.
"Coelestine," as she is appropriately called, could indeed have become an excellent person, had she not tried to be a beautiful soul.
In these, as a respectable writer says, everything is hysterical:
their love, their worship, their laughter, their anger, their enjoy-
ment, their sorrow. And is it their fault if they have an organ
which seems to be a material soul that meddles with everything?"
(Coelestine hätte in der Tat vortrefflich werden können, wäre sie
nicht zu sehr darauf aus gewesen, eine schöne Seele zu seyn. Bei

diesen ist, wie ein achtungswerther Schriftsteller sagt, ihre Liebe, ihre Andacht, ihr Lachen, ihr Zorn, ihre Freude, ihre Betrübniß, alles ist hysterisch. Und was können sie dafür, daß sie ein Organ haben, das eine materielle Seele zu seyn scheint, die sich in alles mischt? 196)

In her *Wanderjahre* through society, Melanie supposedly learns to distinguish between true and false sentiment, true and false virtue, between genuine nobility, practical virtue, and "hysterical" women posing as "beautiful souls." Her "inborn" moral superiority, reinforced by her reading of morally uplifting enlightenment authors such as Gellert (whom Unger implicitly opposes to "immoral" contemporaries such as Goethe and the Romantics) withstands public scrutiny, before it is finally rewarded with marriage, with its typical later eighteenth-century division of labor (252–53).

Rather than presenting an analogous *Bildungsweg* for women which would not only bring to fruition specific innate talents but allow for continued growth and openness to new experience,[19] the novel thus reproduces Melanie's initiation into the only role bourgeois society has to offer to women. If the male *Bildungsroman,* according to Martin Swales, "is written for the sake of the journey, and not for the sake of the happy ending toward which that journey points" (34), Unger's female *Bildungsroman* appears to do the very opposite—unless we take into consideration the novel's theatricality, its self-conscious sense of producing a "stage-managed reality," which subverts the happy ending as it reaffirms it (Swales, 60).

The idea that all protagonists are playing culturally prescribed roles rather than discovering "selves," pervades the whole narrative. Melanie's innate talent for acting makes her perceive her life in theatrical terms, on-stage and off. Each "stage" in her development implies a different social scenery and different social roles: "Fräulein Melanie" at court; a "Tugendheldin nach Richardsonschem Zuschnitte" (a virtuous heroine à la Richardson, 115), a mix between Lessing's "Emilia Galotti" and Goethe's "Gretchen" on stage; "woman companion" or "servant" on the great and small "stages of vanity" (156) of the noble or bourgeois salons; and "wife" her final role, which she plays with special dedication and skill. Each act of "renunciation" precedes dramatic "exits," yet the moments of high drama are undercut by buffoonery, by the narrator's "stage directions" and the "audience's" direct interference, all of which combine to create a sense of playfulness and distance from the tragic events befalling Melanie:

She saw few men, and among them nobody who could have satisfied her much-demanding heart or who could even have equalled the dark sides of her first beloved, when, one day—
"Oh, excuse me for interrupting," says one of my pretty readers, who shares with many others the custom of interrupting by claiming she does not want to interrupt. Well, "excuse me for interrupting; if I'm not wrong, this is going to be a novel without love. How can you, Sir or Madam, expect us to enjoy such a boring piece? A novel without love is like a face without a nose, which has no physiognomy left." I would be very happy, beautiful reader, if I managed to write a novel without love; for love—is love. It contains the ingredients for the highest human virtue and the most hellish vices. But what do you think? Hasn't enough, too much, been written about this torturer of humankind? If Melanie is not completely wrapped up in it, if she does not constantly cry out her eyes and waste away with love's grief like the former Miss Byron; if the motivation in Melanie's life is not just love, but if pride and vanity play their role as well—this is quite germane to young girls and quite alright; we praise her for it.

Sie sah wenige Männer, und unter den wenigen keinen, der diesem viel fordernden Herzen genügt, oder auch nur die Schattenseite des ersten Geliebten hätte repräsentieren können; als eines Tages—
"O daß ich Sie nicht unterbreche" sagt eine meiner schönen Leserinnen, die mit vielen anderen die Gewohnheit hat, zu versichern, sie wolle nicht unterbrechen, indem sie eben unterbrach. Also: 'Daß ich Sie nicht unterbreche; das wird, wie es scheint, ein Roman ohne Liebe. Wie können Sie uns zumuthen, mein Herr oder Madame, ein so fades Machwerk zu goutiren? Ein Roman ohne Liebe ist wie ein Gesicht ohne Nase, dem alle Physiognomie abgeht.' Es wäre mir recht lieb, meine schöne Leserin, wenn mir ein Roman ohne Liebe gelänge; denn die Liebe—ist die Liebe. In ihr liegt die Ingredienz zur höchsten menschlichen Tugend, wie zu höllischen Lastern. Aber, wo denken Sie denn hin? Ist nicht schon mehr, als zuviel, von der Menschenquälerin die Rede gewesen? Wenn gleich Melanie nicht ganz allein in ihr lebt und webt, und sich unaufhörlich die Augen roth weint und wie Fräulein Byron weiland, vor Liebesharm in die Abzehrung fällt; wenn die Triebfeder in Melaniens Leben nicht allein die Liebe ist; wenn Stolz und einige Eitelkeit mitwirken, so ist das ganz mädchenhaft und in der Ordnung; wir loben sie deswegen. (184)

The heroic plot of *Gräfinn Pauline* has thus given way to the mock heroic domesticity plot in *Melanie;* tragedy turns to comedy, the high-mimetic to the low-mimetic—with role playing as the major female activity. This emphatic theatricality not only undermines Melanie's sense of high drama, but also the book's overt message.

The text's incongruity stems from the incompatibility between two genres that appear superimposed in the novel—the female *Bildungsroman* and the *Künstlerroman* (artist novel) and between two female roles—the housewife and the artist. Endowed with a remarkable talent for acting, Melanie seems to be predestined for the career of actress. Her education at court, acting in amateur plays, and public representation prepare her for the public stage and make her decision to join an acting company and "dedicate herself wholly to art" plausible (57). The social ostracism and dubious reputation actresses enjoyed in the eighteenth century compels the narrator, however, to excuse Melanie's decision to join the troupe (38).[20] Catering to the perception that "public women" are "immoral," the narrator insists that Melanie, used to the "highest decency of decorum" (61), does not succumb to the free ways of the actresses, but chooses instead those roles in which she can play "herself". This trick allows Unger to represent Melanie's acting as "natural," "artless," and thus render her stage experience acceptable to her bourgeois readers. The identification of the roles she plays on stage with those she plays in life makes her switch back to "life" unproblematic and belies the implicit assumption that Melanie has learned anything from her stage experiences. Melanie abandons the public for the domestic stage gladly, and without remorse. The incipient *Künstlerroman* is aborted when the *Bildungsroman* and love plot claim center stage, so to speak. Rather than constituting a serious goal or occupation, art serves but to bridge—or finance—the transition from Melanie's public role as lady-in-waiting to her private role as homemaker, from her exclusion from home to her re-insertion into her "rightful place."

Mariane, Melanie's frivolous actress friend, is even more candid about the "intimate" and purely commercial relationship between her life on stage and the stage in her life: her acting serves no other purpose than to win her admirers and, eventually, a rich husband dumb enough to overlook her previous amorous adventures. Art practiced by women is thus portrayed in purely practical, commercial terms, not as a possible calling. While an incipient artist's novel was repressed by the powerful *Entsagungsmodell* in *Gräfinn Pauline*, the *Künstlerroman* in *Melanie*—although conceived of as a viable alternative for at least a short period—is suffocated by the exigencies of a female *Bildungsroman* in which *Bildung* is equated with successful adaptation. Whereas Pauline was "barred from the redemption of art" (Hirsch) because of her fixation on heroic self-sacrifice, Melanie is prevented from becoming an artist because of her heroic (and realistic?) compliance with social expectations.

If Melanie's and Mariane's "theatrical missions" are aborted, or rather withdrawn and displaced onto the private stage, the scene of domestic dramas, the woman writer fares even worse. An elderly, sickly bourgeois (140), "Madame Leerheim" is described in the most vicious terms, both physically and spiritually. "The lady laid much claim to genius; just as any bizarre deformation is nowadays labelled geniality." (Die Dame machte viel Anspruch auf Genialität; wie denn überhaupt jede Bizarrerie der Verbildung jetzt unter die Rubrik der Genialität geschoben wird, 145). Her literary salon, a "cabinet of caricatures," a "club of the ugly" (148), is peopled by social parasites who live off her money; Leerheim's literary fame in turn rests on her plagiarizing her deceased husband's works, as Melanie soon discovers. The fact that Unger directs her satire at a woman writer, whom she depicts as derivative, presumptuous, and vain, may indicate an attempt to gain recognition by the male literary establishment by savaging her own kind. It may also be read as a polemic against unprofessional dilettantes who copy ideas instead of writing their own texts, or as one of Unger's many attacks on romantic salons. In any case, neither the artistically endowed heroine Melanie, nor the fake salonnière Leerheim (who, ironically, bears some resemblance to Unger herself) are allowed to sustain or display their talent. In a society which values as the only female profession the wife/housewife/mother triad, serious professional involvement with the arts is inconceivable. A female *Bildungsroman,* i.e., a woman's socialization into "normal" eighteenth-century adulthood, cannot coexist with a female *Künstlerroman.* They are contradictions in terms.

Albert und Albertine: The Emergence of the Artist as a Woman

Even the spirit of your Elise produces and substitutes for bodily progeny. Dear niece, I, I daydream a novel, as my rich phantasy conjures it up.

Auch Eurer Elise Geist producirt und ersetzt die leibliche Descendenz. Nichtchen, ich, ich schwärme einen Roman, wie meine reiche Phantasie ihn mir hinzaubert.
(Unger, *Albert und Albertine*)

In the two novels discussed so far, Goethe's literary models loomed large. They served as subtexts and counter-texts to create space for inter- and intratextual dialogues. In *Albert und Albertine,* Goethe's writings and Goethe the writer move outside to become the measure by which the protagonists are identified and judged. Not only does Unger distinguish good female readers from bad ones by their response to the male Olympian, but she suggests that interaction with and separation from the male model may allow for the imagining of an, albeit rudimentary, female-centered "counter-culture."

In the two former novels, Unger had concentrated on young women who either fail or succeed in their effort to secure for themselves the ideal husband and whose failure or success depended on the literary model they chose to emulate. In her novel *Albert und Albertine,* Unger explores the complications faced by a newlywed, Albertine, whose husband Louis had left for the battlefield where he is reported to have died. The different status of the heroine allows Unger to abandon the rigorously moral, almost prudish stance exhibited formerly in favor of a relatively greater tolerance for women's erotic needs. Before Albertine can find true happiness with Albert, her friend and soul-mate, she has to endure a series of trials. She is seduced and almost raped by an attractive impostor; she almost loses all her money and jewelry through gambling; her problematic marriage to the headstrong soldier Louis, who returns alive but crippled from the battlefield, is not dissolved until he (conveniently) dies in a hunting accident; she almost expires in a violent fever; and her blindness incurred during a smallpox disease is not cured until Albert has proven his love for her by his willingness to marry and "save" the disfigured woman. All of these near-castrophes not only prove Albertine's steadfastness, but— and this is very different from the former novels centered on female protagonists only—they test the endurance, loyalty, and humanity of her male alter ego, Albert. In fact, Albert has to renounce and suffer even more than Albertine in order to win the object of his desire; he is the one who must step back when Louis returns, who selflessly stands by her in all her difficulties, believes in her, forgives all her trespasses, and remains a loyal friend, even when her beauty is gone. As its title implies, the novel seeks to establish a balance between male and female *Bildung,* male and female characteristics, to achieve *Herzensbildung,* an education of the heart, for both and thus allow for an ideal union based on friendship, loyalty, and common interests.

But *Albert und Albertine* transcends the former novels in other, significant ways as well. For the first time, it presents a female character, Henriette Euler, who not only is a serious artist, but who lives independently, earning her living through art. After having lost an unfaithful husband who had gambled away her savings, she works as a painter of portraits and still-life paintings; she consciously chooses those genres which will sell, but abandons commercial art for "autonomous" art as soon as she has the financial security to do so.

Similarly, Albertine begins to dedicate herself to painting under Henriette's guidance, against the opposition of her husband. This provides Unger with an opportunity to express her anger at the double standard used against women artists, who are scolded if they neglect their duties as wife, and ridiculed because they cannot dedicate themselves fully and uncompromisingly to their professed interests:

> He [Louis] did not realize that this is only natural, and that it would be unfair to demand of the woman that which only the exceptional man can do: to meet all expectations. Wouldn't female talent develop more freely in competition with male talent, if the woman did not, at the same time, have to dedicate herself to a hundred fragmenting activities? And honestly, you women artists and writers, when you put down the brush, when you are just about to utter a verse or invent a lively image—do you then go to the kitchen or the linen closet with the same lively interest as you would sit at your writing desk or the easel? I say no, and the man who demands from you that your intellectual entertainment be subjected, is unjust. Who would want to drink sour country wine if he could have nectar! But that woman who, conscious of her duty and dignity, does the one without abandoning the other, is the best.

> Er [Louis] bedachte nicht, daß es in der Natur der Dinge liegt, und daß es unbillig ist, vom Weibe zu fordern, was der seltne Mann nur vermag: allem zu genügen. Würde sich weibliches Talent im Wettstreite mit dem männlichen nicht ungehemmter entwickeln, müßte sich das Weib nicht zugleich hundert zeitversplitternden Arbeiten hingeben? Und die Hand aufs Herz, ihr Künstlerinnen, und schriftstellerischen Weiber, wenn ihr den Pinsel aus der Hand legt, wenn euch eben ein Reim oder lebhaftes Bild auf der Zunge schwebt, gehet ihr dann mit eben so lebhaftem Interesse in die Küche oder an den Wäschschrank, als

ihr euch an euren Schreibetisch oder an die Staffelei setzet? Ich
sage nein! und der Mann, der es von euch fordert, daß die Geistes-
unterhaltung untergeordnet bleiben soll, ist ein unbilliger. Wer
wird, wenn er Nectar haben kann, noch gern sauren Landwein
trinken! Aber das Weib, das im Gefühl ihrer Pflicht und Würde,
eines thut und das andere nicht läßt, ist das beste. (283)

Although Unger carefully tries not to challenge the division of labor at the heart of the gender dichotomy, her dual-role model in
fact expands existing concepts of femininity. Like her sisters Pauline and Melanie, Albertine practices her artistic talent to fill a
void in her life and give expression to her longing (294): during her
unhappy marriage she paints, and during her brief blindness, she
composes and plays the piano. Artistic activity is sustained, however, not abandoned during marriage. In the community of equals,
the small bucolic idyll formed by congenial male and female beautiful souls, art and life are one.

This lofty utopian vision is also accompanied by its travesty.
The three serious Goethe connoisseurs Albert, Albertine, and Henriette are contrasted with a trio of grotesque Goethe enthusiasts:
Aunt Elise, writer of lyrical poetry; Laurette, the cynical, bad-
mouthed "philosopher," and Madam Rosamund, an aging prosti-
tute. In a caricature of a romantic salon, these three gather
around the poet and philosopher Wassermann—a take-off on
Friedrich Schlegel—and indulge in Goethe worship, poetic readings, and vicious literary critiques. Aunt Elise keeps the handker-
chief into which she cried upon reading *Werther,* unwashed; she is
also the proud owner of a toothpick Goethe once used and left behind in an inn. Rosamund plays "muse;" and Wassermann considers himself the world's expert on Goethe's aesthetics. The group's
mindless hero-worship and Wassermann's pontifications on Goethe's "harmonious forms" anticipate much of nineteenth-century
Goethe reception:

"Ah! Ah! Goethe!" [. . .] "Please, please dear von Ulmenhorst,
tell us something, tell us a lot about Papa Goethe!" the dear old
child Elise, Dämmrig's sister, twirped. [. . .] Albert was about to
open his lips in kind compliance when Wassermann intercepted
furiously. The uninitiated, he said, should never speak about
Goethe, whom he alone understood and grasped. Indeed he was a
philosopher who knew everything, explored everything, and never

made use of those abominable crutches of an invalid humanity, experience, which he abhorred. Only in that large hospital for mental cripples did one need such a sad support . . . He did admit that he had never seen Goethe in his whole life, but in imperfect reproductions; however, the image of the adored poet emerged from his writings and stood so lively before his soul that he was able to portray him trait by trait. And thus good Wassermann began his oeuvre: he spoke about eternal features, the corners of the mouth, the opening of the lips, the glimpse of the eye, the nose. You must know, my ladies, the truly formed human being, the purely humane, has to be surrounded by beautiful form. But the crude masses don't know about form, all they want is matter, and again matter. You understand me, my beautiful ladies!

"Oh! Oh! Göthe!" [. . .] "Bitte, bitte, lieber Herr von Ulmenhorst, sagen Sie uns doch recht viel, aber recht recht sehr viel, von Papa Göthe," zwitscherte das liebe alte Kind Elisa, Dämmrigs Schwester. [. . .] Schon öffnete Albert freundlich die Lippen, den Frauen zu willfahren, als Wassermann sich wüthig dazwischen stürzte. Ein Ungeweihter sollte nie über Göthe sprechen, sagte er; den er ganz allein nur verstand und begriff. Überdem war er ein Philosoph, der alle Dinge wußte, alles ergründete und sich nie der erbärmlichen Krücke der invaliden Menschheit, der Er- fahrung, bediente, die ihm ein Greuel war. Nur in dem großen Lazarethe geistiger Krüppel brauchte man diesen traurigen Nothbehelf. . . . So gestand er zwar jetzt, daß er Göthe in seinem ganzen Leben nie anders, als in sehr unvollkommenen Abbildun- gen gesehen habe; indeß stehe ihm das Bild des Verehrten so lebendig aus seinen Werken vor der Seele, daß er ihn Zug für Zug abzucontrefayen im Stande sei. Und so begann der gute Wasser- mann das Werk; er sprach vom ewigen Schnitte des Gesichts, von Mundwinkeln, von Lippenöffnung, vom Augenauffschlagen, von Nasenflügeln. Sie begreifen es, meine Damen, das ächt gebildete Wesen, das rein menschliche, muß stets von schöner Form umgeben seyn. Aber der rohe Haufen hat keine Ahnung von dem Formellen, will nur immer Stoff und wieder Stoff. Sie verstehen mich, meine Schönen!— (12–13)

Unger's satire takes on the Goethe enthusiasts, while it spares the author, whose works, although read, no longer figure as models. But while Unger, in her known fashion, ridicules would-be writers and would-be beautiful souls, we can detect incipient sympathies for her "kin". The eternal adolescent Elise, for example, "the good old miseducated woman with the young heart" (die gute Verbil- dete, mit dem jungen Gemüthe, 41), bears affinity with the Unger of 1796: "Good old Elise always pronounced Goethe's name with a divine shudder, like that of a first love." (Die gute Elise sprach den Namen Göthe stets mit heiligem Schauer, wie den einer ersten Liebe, aus.) She constitutes perhaps a superseded stage in Unger's development, which has now approximated Albertine's, as the next sentence suggests: "This was almost the only connection between her and her niece, who knew the great poet intimately and who venerated him, although her view of him differed considerably." (Dies war beinahe der einzige Berührungspunct zwischen ihr und ihrer Nichte, die den großen Dichter innig kannte und verehrte, obschon sie eine sehr verschiedene Ansicht damit verband, 41). Elise's move to Goethe's Weimar to enjoy "free love" and breathe the same air as her divine model (172) brings not only disillusionment—Wassermann runs off with her money—but a rich spiritual harvest. Inspired by the great poet, Elise produces sentimental novels—all of which appear in print, as she proudly announces to her incredulous family (301). "And your superhuman novel in which nothing happens naturally, and where a chest of drawers is the prima donna?"—"Will be published!" and she adds: "Go ahead and make fun of me! It makes much more sense to introduce a speaking closet or a chunk of wood than old knights, whom you so cherish. In the wide realm of the imagination, in its creations everything is alive. The divine poetic fire makes stones alive and moves mountains, just like faith." (Und dein übermenschlicher Roman, worin nichts natürlich zugeht, wo eine Komode die prima Donna ist?—Erscheint!—Spotte nur, spotte! Einen Schrank, einen Klotz kann man immer noch vernünftiger, als einen alten Ritter, worein ihr so verliebt seid, redend einführen. Im weiten Reiche der Phantasie, in ihren Schöpfungen ist alles Leben. Das heilige Dichterfeuer belebt Steine und versetzt, wie der Glaube, Berge, 302).

Unger's mocking tone barely hides the affinities between Elise's and her own situation. In both cases, enthusiasm for the "Great Goethe" has not only released creative energies, but, once introduced to the "wide realm of the imagination," has permitted them to develop their own themes and literary forms—which are, as nobody would deny, a far cry from Goethe's. Elise, although a superseded stage, remains a close relation; and so is Henriette Euler, who joins the "family of artists" by marrying Albertine's brother.

Conclusion

If we look at the three novels in succession, multiple projects and conflicting, even contradictory tendencies in Unger's writing become apparent, creating a situation which eludes critical summary and appraisal. Steeped in the tradition of rationalist enlightenment literature and convinced of the educational mission of the female author, Unger feels compelled to reject the sensual, "immoral" qualities of Goethe's writing, while at the same time acknowledging their seductive power.[21] Her own works reflect this double pull or double bind: purporting to attack naive readings of Goethe, Unger's novels in fact reproduce them. Rather than developing her own stories based on her own experience or perception of "reality," as she claims literature should do, she remains fixated on classical formulae, caught in the dialectics of appropriation and rejection. However, her interaction with Goethe, her rubbing shoulders with the great, also produces creative friction. As I said in my introductory remarks, Unger's characters are made to play Goethean roles they cannot fulfill; like Goethe's female readers, they dress up in costumes of Iphigenie, Eugenie, or Nathalie that do not fit, costumes that are both too loose (unattainable perfection) and too tight (the restricted role of wife). The characters' discomfort, which is also the author's discomfort, translates into satirical impulses: both the heroics of renunciation and the heroics of domesticity are undercut by theatricality or ironic authorial intervention. While in her redefinition of "Entsagung," "schöner Seelen," and of bourgeois matrimony Unger manages to expand or slightly revise Goethe's archetypes to infuse them with a down-to-earth "normalcy" (which borders on the banal) or utopian longings (which have lost none of their attraction), it is above all in the satirical depiction of her minor characters that Unger's genuine concerns and talents come to the fore. Increasingly, her would-be poets, failed salonnières, sentimental actresses and self-stylized aesthetes gain ground and prestige, until, in *Albert und Albertine's* utopic vision, the "true artists" are integrated into the community of equals, while the fakes discredit themselves and disappear. The gradual (and certainly limited) emancipation of the woman artist, which we can discern in the three novels, parallels Unger's own emancipation from Goethe, which finds verbal expression in her subsequent novel *Confessions of a Beautiful Soul. Written by Herself* (1806).[22] After 1806, there is not visible trace of Goethe's works in Unger's. One reason for this sudden abstinence, I want to suggest, is that Unger may have realized the paradox of defining her own literary project in terms of a paradigm that actively discourages artistic creativity in women.[23] Her last two novels, *Die Franzosen in Berlin* (1809) and *Der junge Franzose und das deutsche Mädchen* (1810), in which direct personal experience—the French occupation of Berlin and its impact on the city's female population—intertwines with fictions of political-sexual alliances, are indeed entirely "written by herself," the detached, critical, and sometimes satirical female observer of contemporary life.

3

Turns of Emancipation:
On Rahel Varnhagen's Letters*

Liliane Weissberg

I

Emancipation, the "deliverance from bondage or controlling influence,"[1] is a term that has its origin with the Roman family and describes the setting free of children as well as slaves from the paternal power. It developed into a political term associated with contracts, laws, and the declaration of civil rights, whose use itself is highly charged ideologically. The eleventh edition of the *Encyclopedia Britannica,* for example, does not list the term; the American Webster dictionary, on the other hand, refers to its country's history by listing Lincoln's proclamation. The German *Brockhaus* deflects from German history and cites the end of American slavery as well as the French Revolution, and points to a general history that seems to defy all national boundaries: to the emancipation of women and of Jews.[2]

Writing about a woman and a Jew in the context of emancipation, I am not referring to laws or paternal proclamations. Obviously, one cannot state the equality of women in the late eighteenth and early nineteenth century Berlin, or discuss the emancipation of Jews during a time when different Prussian laws took and gave various rights without establishing an equal status for the Jewish population. The influence of the French Revolution had

* A version of this paper appeared first in *Cultural Critique* 15 (1989). I would like to thank the editors for permission to include it in this anthology. The essay is part of a longer work on Rahel Varnhagen and Dorothea Schlegel that will appear in German in a special volume of the *Deutsche Vierteljahrsschrift, Perspektivenwechsel.*

its limits, even in French-occupied Berlin. If I would like to write about a Jewish woman writing in Berlin during this period, I will have to turn the discussion of emancipation from a statement of paternal will into the question of daughterly wishes, private acts and reflections, perhaps not of a less political kind. How could one be equal? Rahel Varnhagen seems to ask, and to whom should one be equal? Under which conditions, moreover, is this equality desirable?

In his study about Jewish female authors in Berlin in the late eighteenth century, Gert Mattenklott notes a relationship between the conditions of their literary production and the possibility of their own aesthetics.[3] The double "marginality" of being a woman and a Jew, designs for them a second-hand way of living, he writes. For these Jewish women, there could not have been any life beyond the participation in another's—and there could not have been any "free" life at all. Art, it seems, however, is only possible after emancipation. The impossibility of leading a free life makes the development of one's own aesthetics impossible:

> Surely art could not flourish here. Art presupposes freedom. A Jewish, a female aesthetics, this is a contradiction in itself, and the women of this circle were much too clever not to discover this. Art by Jewish women would presuppose a sovereignty over their sex and birth, nature and history, and this, as it were, had to be illusory.

> Erst recht konnte Kunst hier nicht gedeihen. Sie setzt Freiheit voraus. Eine jüdische, eine weibliche Ästhetik, das ist ein Widerspruch in sich selbst, und die Frauen dieser Kreise waren zu klug, als daß er ihnen hätte verborgen bleiben können. Kunst von jüdischen Frauen hätte Souveränität über Geschlecht und Herkunft, Natur und Geschichte vorausgesetzt, die nach der Lage der Dinge illusorisch sein mußte.

The writings of these Jewish women were structured by their lack of sovereignty; they had to choose, as Mattenklott insists, a medium that lacked sovereignty as well. In this relationship between gender and genre, he focuses on the essay and the letter: "These are forms that flourish when something can be disposed with, independent of any direction, or in which the hindrance, the inability or the resistance to conform to the representational forms of the old culture would find its expression." (Es sind Formen, die gedeihen, wo etwas zur Disposition steht, unentschieden in der einen oder anderen Richtung, oder in denen sich die Verhinderung, das Unvermögen oder die Weigerung bekundet, in den Repräsentationsformen der alten Kultur Ausdruck zu suchen.) Texts by Jewish women appear here not only as a replacement of their actions, but also as the replacement of proper literature,[4] despite the fact that the letter and the essay are, paradoxically, precisely genres that mark, like no other, the official literary discourse in the eighteenth century.[5]

Mattenklott repeats the statements of many other literary critics and sketches further consequences of this thesis. The growth of these semi-public literary forms, made possible through resistance and inability, indicates itself the deficits of the female and Jewish demi-monde. There is only one answer to this limitation. Because a "free life" is impossible for Jewish women, the letter and essay have to sketch alternative lives and utopian autobiographies. But any critic who censures these literary genres as a failure has to censure the sketch of an imaginary life as well.[6] The hopeful alternative is doomed to appear deficient. Here, as before, life meets art again.

Perhaps, however, the issue may not be whether these Jewish women discover their sovereignty *over* their gender, but whether they find the sovereignty *of* their gender; perhaps we are dealing here with the paradox that a sovereignty has to establish itself in the very moment of their writing—even if they are writing as women and as Jews. The object/subject distinction of author and text, which has to be established in any kind of judgment, will have to be called into question. The sovereignty that can be discovered in these women's writing, and the sovereignty of their writing, have to be different from that other, masterful discourse of literature.

In her letters, and by writing several letters a day, Rahel Varnhagen tries to establish herself, to describe herself as an individual. Rahel, the hostess of a well-known Berlin salon, receives numerous guests, many of whom become her correspondents. The concept of friendship and *Geselligkeit* as established by the culture of the salons, and that of oral conversation influence the style of her letters and often their content. Paradoxically, Rahel writes about herself while also reporting about others, and by sending her letters as part of a dialogue to her addressees.

Moreover, her production of tens of thousands of letters elucidates a strange fact. While denied any official inclusion in established literary history, Rahel's letters do not conform to the rules of epistolary guides, style manuals, or dictionaries, either. One is not always sure which qualifications of the "letter" they fulfill.

Which description and order can capture the abundance of her writings? and what "life" can we deduct as a result of Rahel's text?

To be able to read Rahel's letters and to find a descriptive term for them, the critic must compare them with other texts and find similarities. For Rahel, similarities are at stake as well. First, the similarities that Rahel recognizes between herself and the men of her circle of acquaintances: Christians, German bourgeois or bourgeois aristocrats, the authors of philosophical lectures or *Bildungsromane*. But as the gesture of establishing similarities implies that something is comparable, and can be established in comparison (in contrast to what appears to be different, or oneself as that which appears to be different), this gesture also produces the possibility to articulate a difference. The reader today, who would like to trace this gesture in her statement about Rahel's writing and in Rahel's writing itself, compares literary products. Are we able to understand these letters as a special, different literature; do we have indications of the possibility of another evaluation, another aesthetics? And how can this possible gesture made by the female, Jewish author be compared to the gesture made by the reader herself today, and the possibility of another kind of writing be compared with that of another kind of reading, without blurring the distinction between the conditions of writing and those of reading in this comparison itself?

II

In May 1809, Karl August Varnhagen introduced his friend Alexander von der Marwitz to Rahel Levin. The time of her first salon had passed, Berlin was occupied by the French, and Rahel herself was living alone and had financial difficulties. Marwitz was the descendent of an old and established aristocratic family. He administered his family estate and was soon to join the Austrian army. Rahel, at this time thirty-eight years old, was very taken by Marwitz, sixteen years her junior, but their relationship relied primarily on an exchange of letters. Five years after their first meeting, Marwitz was killed in a battle in France. At the time of his death, Rahel had already begun her relationship with Varnhagen; she converted and married him in 1814. The good-looking soldier Marwitz was, however, remembered by Rahel in many of her letters, and especially in her correspondence with Varnhagen. She wrote about him with fondness and with praise, and described Marwitz, who did not paint, who did not play any music, and who did not write any poetry, as an "artist."[7]

Rahel's correspondence with Marwitz tells the story of their relationship. Her letters are filled with questions, reports, and descriptions of her own life and adventures. Marwitz in turn reads her letters many times; he finds them agitating in a way that prevents an immediate answer.[8] Rahel calls Marwitz' description of his reading, and of her letters, a flattery, and his letter a *Schmeichelbrief*. In rejecting his flattery, however, Rahel also comments on her own letters. A few years earlier, in a letter to her Jewish friend David Veit, Rahel described them as the *Confessions de J. J. Rahel.*[9] Here, in her letter to Marwitz, she speaks again of her confessions:

> You should know that this letter of flattery has flattered me indefinitely; do you know, that it is quite true, that I need to be calmed down about my quite terrible letters; that I could not suspect that you would deal with them [*verführen*] in this way? Do you also know, that I wish quite different ones for you, to deal with them like that; but, on the other hand, that I do not think my own unworthy? And you should hear, first of all, what I have decided for myself: I will continue to write to you such letters; these are true *confessions*, I have thought about it and decided; and you should see, my soul, as only I can capture it.
>
> Wissen Sie, daß dieser Schmeichelbrief mich unendlich geschmeichelt hat; wissen Sie, daß es ganz wahr ist, daß ich Beruhigung über meine ganz entsetzlichen Briefe brauchte; daß ich nicht ahnden konnte, daß Sie so mit ihnen verführen? Wissen Sie aber auch, daß ich Ihnen ganz andere wünsche, um daß Sie so mit ihnen verfahren; meine aber doch nicht für unwürdig halte? Und hören Sie für's erste, was ich bei mir beschlossen habe: ich will ihnen ferner solche schreiben; es sind wahre *confessions*, hab' ich mir überlegt; und Sie sollen sehen, meine Seele, wie ich sie nur selbst erhaschen kann.[10]

Rahel, the author and heroine of a text in Rousseau's tradition, offers her letters as a confession, as a form of purifying autobiography. The gesture is ambiguous. Only after some thought, her confessions can show themselves as those of a soul that may not be beautiful, but that wants to be true. The truth of the confessions themselves will make Rahel's soul visible, and this becomes the justification for her letters.

An offering and a retraction are thematized here and acted out with the exchange of these letters. Only true confessions and

multiple avowals can prevent the replacement of Rahel's letters
with those other, nameless ones, that are not present here, but
that would be more deserving of a flattering reading and response.
A foreign word, the French *confessions,* enters her letter seduc-
tively. It indicates a polite tone as well as a literary tradition,
which is, despite all truth, important here as well. After all, the
reader's eye should not just capture the letters, but Rahel's soul;
her soul that is in view only fleetingly, as if the reader would have
to trace it in the process of reading, and find a meaning that is in
danger of escaping. The letter serves as a mirror and it casts a
double reflection. The reader captures the view of Rahel's soul,
just as the author herself can view it only while passing by. Rahel's picture appears in this reflection, in the moment when her
soul is offering itself, in its truth, in Rahel's writing.

In Rahel's letters, this moment is at stake; a moment that she
has to provoke by constant writing, so as to be able to hope for its
elusive appearance. If the text functions as a mirror, it cannot reflect an image from a smooth surface. Hannah Arendt describes
Rahel's writing as a putting together of the disconnected, and
compares it with the technique of the joke.[11] Connecting the disconnected, Rahel searches for her moment as one outside any linguistic order. If truth can show itself in Rahel's dialogue with her
reader, Rahel has, at the same time, to put into question what
seems to be the fundament of every introspective narrative, and
every autobiography: a constant, defined Self.

Autobiographical reflection presupposes a paradox; a stable
"I" who narrates, and its transformation in time. In this process
the other—the reader, the addressee—is necessary. Jean Starobinski writes:

> [Autobiography] only requires that certain possible conditions be
> realized, conditions which are mainly ideological (or cultural): that
> the personal experience be important, that it offer an opportunity
> for a sincere relation with someone else. These presuppositions
> establish the legitimacy of "I" and authorize the subject of the
> discourse to take his past existence as theme. Moreover, the "I" is
> confirmed in the function of permanent subject by the presence of
> its correlative "you", giving clear motivation to the discourse. I
> am thinking here of the *Confessions* of St. Augustine: the author
> speaks to God but with the intention of edifying his readers.[12]

Rahel sees the "truth" of her *confessions* already as sufficient reason for their formulation. Her confessions are beyond any judgment,

and beyond aesthetic judgment as well: "If a truth is coarse or not, nobody can question it as such; it corresponds to its being, if it is true; and where it settles on, this is the place that transforms it into coarseness of courtesy." (Ob eine Wahrheit grob ist oder nicht, darüber kann man ihr als solcher nichts anhaben; sie entspricht ihrem Wesen, wenn sie wahr ist; und wo sie hin trifft, das ist der Ort, der sie zur Grobheit oder Höflichkeit macht.[13]) Rahel's truth cannot be criticized, only the place in which it produces itself. "Truth" itself does not comply to this condition of its appearance. Therein seems to lie hope.

While truth does not orient itself according to the concretely placed subject, the legitimacy of that "I" and its authority are put into question by the structure of the representation itself. The separation between addressee, reader, and writer undermines in Rahel's letter the integrity of the Self, and the stability of the "place" itself. Her soul cannot exist otherwise than while quickly passing by. In her dialogue with the reader, truth does not become anything constructive or edifying, although it is the aim and object of her discourse. It becomes the third, fleeting, and never quite articulated side of a triangle that links writer and reader; that separates them, as any message would, but also reflects this separation in itself. Rahel needs Marwitz not only to be a reader of her missive, but to be a reader who makes the writing of truth possible, and the truth of her lines appear.

"That you would deal with them in this way?" Rahel asks. The subjunctive *verführen* derives from *verfahren,* to deal with, and hints at a procedure; but it is the infinitive of the verb *verführen,* to seduce, as well. Procedure and seduction, here ambiguously stated, are a necessary part of Rahel's writing. The letter that is her *confessions,* message and narrative of what can never be fully or permanently present, will finally also have to remove itself from that presence that insists on contemporary time. To be able to make herself understood by Marwitz in the future, at the time of his reception of her letter, Rahel does not write what is, but about that which has made her what she is. She describes what makes her view of the world possible. Rahel comments on it elsewhere, in a letter to Friedrich de la Motte Fouqué:

> I am, therefore, observing the world. Life, nature, are here for me. Calculate the *lutte* of my life, therefore; the big, the small and bitter moments. With the sharpest knowledge [consciousness] about myself. With the opinion, that I should be a queen (no

reigning one, however), or a mother: I discover that there is just n o t h i n g that I am. No daughter, no sister, no lover, no spouse, not even a burgheress.

Ich sehe also der Welt zu. Das Leben, die Natur, ist für mich da. Berechnen Sie also die lutte in meinem Leben; die großen, die kleinen bittern Momente. Mit dem schärfsten Bewußtsein über mich selbst. Mit der Meinung, daß ich eine Königin (keine regierende) oder eine Mutter sein müßte: erlebe ich, daß ich grade n i c h t s bin. Keine Tochter, keine Schwester, keine Geliebte, keine Frau, keine Bürgerin Einmal.[14]

Rahel observes the world. The happy moments that she sees in others seem only to indicate the negative in her; she lacks the properties, positions, definitions that she should have had. The subjunctive, however, "should be," constructs an alternative that does not resemble the sketch of a dream world, but leads her to record her dreams. To record them, and to make the analysis of her writing possible, Rahel needs the other: "Please calculate." The "sharpest consciousness" takes shape without a stable subject between the author and the reader.

III

Rahel's first salon lasted until the early nineteenth century. The French occupation, the following war provided a political context in which Berlin's social life changed. Just after 1809, when Rahel was not able to keep even her position as hostess, she often writes down her dreams in her letters to Marwitz. The narrative of her dreams is presented as a gift, functioning as a sign of greatest intimacy and at the same time provoking distance. As evidence of their friendship, Marwitz asks Rahel to show the narrative of her dreams to his friend, Henriette Schleiermacher. With this presentation, he wants to seal his new friendship with his old one, and he encouraged, moreover, the friendship between the women themselves and their exchange of dreams.[15] Following this request, Rahel's letters to Marwitz become more cautious; she is not sure if she would really like to be part of this triangle and pass on her dreams. Later, however, she records the dreams for a second time, this time for Varnhagen, who will marry her: *Verfahren* and *Verführung*, procedure and seduction, are here at play as well. Varnhagen prepares Rahel's letters for publication, and with her help.[16] He heads his copy of Rahel's dream narrative only with a date, "July 1812." He selects dreams from those Rahel had copied into a notebook, and introduces these excerpts into his printed edition of Rahel's correspondence with Marwitz. The dream that had been narrated as a letter, is returned as a narrative to the epistolary exchange.

The editorial procedure points at the special status of the dream that aspires to be a letter. The position of the reader—Marwitz or, later, Varnhagen—designates this other world that Rahel would like to encounter, even if she could only encounter it voyeuristically. Strangely, though, the relationship between the reading of her text and her view of the other generates a double blindness: "Do you know," she writes to Marwitz, "that your presence has become to me like the eye of the world? I see it, even if you are not there, but I cannot look into her [the world's] eyes: I also don't know if she [the world] is seeing me." (Wissen Sie dabei, daß Ihre Gegenwart mir wie das Auge der Welt geworden ist? Ich sehe sie, auch wenn Sie nicht da sind; aber in die Augen sehe ich ihr nicht: Ich weiß auch nicht, ob sie mich sieht.[17]) This blindness is marked by strangeness as well as gender. It is a blind sight, which love demands, and likened to that writing which directs itself blindly, and within some distance to the person who makes her search for truth possible. Without Marwitz, the world outside cannot perceive her.

Several critics have pointed out that Rahel's writing calls for a psychoanalytic reading, and that the writing itself bears the structure of psychoanalytical discourse.[18] Fritz Ernst published an article that ends with a quotation from one of Rahel's dreams in which he tries to use them to trace her "wishes" and "longings."[19] Hannah Arendt places a chapter "Night and Day" in the center of her monograph on Rahel Varnhagen, in which she interprets two of her dreams. Arendt uses the dream as an object to interpret her subject; she does not care about the process of analytical reading itself, but about a reading that attempts to stabilize the individual in the process of analysis. Arendt can therefore proceed to make a thematic selection. Rahel's dreams become for her biographical keys to her relationship with Karl von Finckenstein or Raphael d'Urquijo, and become "silent and consuming complaint of the night," "shadow images," which repeat themselves, to "assault, as memories, the waking person."[20] The night, however, which is calling for these ghosts, also repeats another dream that is neither quoted by Arendt, nor copied by Varnhagen for reproduction, and that is therefore censored from the chain of repetitions; much in the same way of censorship and repression in which dreams operate. The censored dream tries to confront art and life. It is not without obvious biographical references. It resembles, indeed, in many ways another dream that Varnhagen and Arendt record, and which places Rahel in a castle, observing a gathering of people who are unable to see her. Here, in this second dream, Rahel finds herself in a big and festively lit hall, and on its walls are hung "the portraits of all sculptors and painters who have ever lived or still live" (die Portraite aller bildhauer u Mahler die es je gegeben hat u giebt, 650). Painters and sculptors are forming crowds to look at these portraits and to evaluate them in "a kind of last judgment of art" (eine Art letztes Gericht der Kunst, 651):

> I saw men of every . . . age, from about 17 years on; . . . expression . . . of the face from all nations which art, imagination and reality had ever shown me . . . men with and without beards, with great ones and with moustaches, with moustaches without long beard; and again the other way around.

> Ich sah Männer jedes . . . Alters, etwa von 17 Jahren an; . . . Ausdruk . . . des Gesichts von allen Natzionen die die Kusnt, Einbildungskraft u wirklichkeit mir je gezeigt hatten . . . Männer mit, u ohne bärten; mit großen u Schnurbärten, mit schnurbarten ohne langen bart; u wieder umgekehrt. (651)

Rahel's attention is concentrated on the artists, not the paintings, and on the room itself. It is a ballroom that bears resemblance to a church:

> But also the large room I had to look at a lot, and I could not understand the light, it was very friendly in its *decoration,* above, with its pointed arches; and the many colors, of the many people and pictures, the colors of the room even above, the very light yellowish reddish light, all of this seemed to produce a crowd before the eyes, and gave the whole no cut up or petty look, but the impression remained large and joyful.

> Aber auch den Saal mußte ich viel betrachten; u die Hellung konnte /ich/ nicht begreifen, er war überaus freundlich in seiner *decoration,* oben in den Spitzbogen; u die vielfarbigkeit, der vielen Menschen u bilder, des Saales Farben noch oben ein, das überhelle gelblich röthliche Licht, welches alles ein Gewühl vor den Augen bildete, gab dem Ganzen nichts zerstükt-kleinliches, sondern der Eindruk blib groß-freudig. (651)

Rahel presses through the crowd of people, presses through their clothes—"carried dragged on between coats, dresses, backs and arms" (zwischen Mäntein, Kleidern Rüken u Armen getragen, u geschlept, 651)—and ventures forward, to see the Ideal, who has arrived, and who is greeted with awe by the gathered artists. The language of awe, that of the judging people who are present, is one of a silent hiss, like that of the seductive serpent itself:

> the Ideal some said quietly, silently hissing; and an astonishment moves like a quiver through the room where we are: I, however, center my glance on him, a young man of about 20 years, in common clothes, without a hat . . . who tries to suppress his laughter: the others do not see it; I, however, call, but he is a human being, he lives, he cannot refrain from laughter . . . I come closer and search directly for this person's eyes which he keeps covered, but he smiles more.

> das Ideal sagen noch manche leise zischelnd; u ein Erstaunen zukt gleichsam durch den Raum wo wir sind: ich aber sehe mitten auf demselben, einen Jungen Menschen von etwa 20 Jahren in gewöhnlicher Kleidung ohne Huth . . . [der] sich das Lachen verbeißt: die Andern sehen das nicht; ich rufe aber, es ist ja ein Mensch, er lebt, er kann sich ja das Lachen nicht enthalten . . . Ich gehe heran sehe diesem menschen recht nach den Augen, die bedekt bleiben er lächelt aber mehr. . . . (652)

Rahel is the only one who recognizes the joke and unheard laughter. And while she begins to waltz with "this human being" (652), and without any inhibition, the artists step back.

Blindness and sight, important for Rahel's description of her *confessions*, are thematic here as well. Now it is the Ideal who covers his eyes and needs Rahel to be properly seen. She is the only one who can recognize it as a young man and human being. While the audience looks on, Rahel can join with him in a dance. The reader, however, knows that she is the only one who would have been able to waltz with him. Despite the fact that some sculptors have freed their arms "like women" (651), Rahel is the only woman present. She reports, as a woman, that the ideal lives, laughs, and waltzes, that it is not only seductive, but can be seduced to dance as well; to a dance that asks those other artists, who know nothing about life, to withdraw. This ends the dream itself. And she reports this to Marwitz, who has chosen to read her letters, and whom she thinks of as an artist whose flattery she likes both to accept and to reject.

Waltzing is often mentioned in her early correspondence with David Veit, for whom she describes her dancing master and her lessons, and the education that is necessary for acculturation and *Bildung*, for example the French language of the *confessions*.[22] In all of these letters, waltzing becomes the metaphor of that seductive and dizzying common movement that she designs as an image to capture her writing, the movement of giving and withdrawing, as a linguistic dance. To dance happily with the Ideal: this indeed could be a proper alternative to the established judgment of art, whose criteria Rahel cannot fulfill in any of her letters, and certainly cannot meet with her own life.

IV

At the same time at which she records this dream, however, Rahel is engaged in a matter of aesthetic judgment herself. She exchanges with Varnhagen letters about Goethe's works. Varnhagen replaces the names of authors and addressees with letters, and transforms their exchange into an anonymous discussion. In this form he shows his and Rahel's letters to the master, Goethe, himself. Rahel, who idealizes Goethe, is curious about his judgment. Goethe answers, and his sentence is positive. In conferring his opinion, Goethe reads the letter that identifies Rahel's letters as the sign of a male author; and Rahel's letter is indeed a *G.* that corresponds to the beginning of his own name. Did Rahel want to be anything else but Goethe's well-meaning mirror? For her, Goethe's reaction is flattering, but it has disturbing consequences for her calculation:

> As much as this event pleases me, and flatters myself and my heart, I am so terribly sorry, that Goethe has to see now, which person of really no importance this G. is, in the world as well as in literature; and although he has probably never thought about it, he will not experience it as new that I love him, and in counting those who wish him well there will be one less now.

> So sehr mich das Ereignis freut, mir und meinem Herzen schmeichelt, so ist es mir doch äußerst leid, daß Goethe nun sehen muß, welche durchaus nichts bedeutende Person dies G. in Welt und Literatur ist; und obgleich er wohl nie daran gedacht hat, so wird's ihm nicht neu sein, daß ich ihn so liebe; und in der Zahl seiner Wohlwollenden geht ihm nun eine ab.[23]

Letters of flattery circulate here as well, and Rahel is again afraid of an exchange of judgment and affection. Her reaction to Goethe's reading parallels her reaction to Marwitz' response, and this is not accidental. Goethe is not only an object of Rahel's admiration and love, but also a constant theme in her correspondence with Marwitz. It is precisely in this movement of giving and withdrawing, exemplified by the exchange of letters itself, that the master of all *Bildung* and poetry can show himself. To Varnhagen Rahel writes about the instigation for her own words and correspondence:

> In *one* thing I have followed my innermost depth, I held myself in distance from Goethe shyly. God, how right this has been! How chaste, how safe from profanation, as if it would have been safeguarded throughout a whole, and unblessed life, I could now be able to show him the adoration in my heart. It passes through everything, that I have ever expressed, *every* written word nearly does contain it. And he, too, will be the one to take count of this for me, understanding how difficult it is to keep such loving admiration silently throughout one's whole life hidden in oneself. How embarrassedly I had to fall silent two years ago, when Bettina told me once of the object of her greatest passion, fiery and beautiful, in a Monbijou that turned shiny and silent in the autumn sun! I pretended that I did not even know him. This happened to me quite often; and, at another time, *I* am willing to talk. You know this. Now, Marwitz has to suffer it. All of our conversations begin with him, and end with him.

> In *einer* Sache hab' ich meinem tiefsten Innersten gefolgt, mich von Goethe scheu zurückzuhalten. Gott, wie recht war es! Wie keusch, wie unentweiht, wie durch ein ganzes, unseliges Leben durch bewahrt, könnt' ich ihm nun die Adoration in meinem Herzen zeigen. Durch alles, was ich je ausdrückte, geht sie hindurch, *jedes* aufgeschriebene Wort beinah enthält sie. Und auch er nur wird es mir anrechnen können, wie schwer es ist, solche liebende Bewunderung schweigend ein ganzes Leben hindurch in sich zu verhehlen. Wie beschämt schwieg ich vor zwei Jahren, als Bettina mir einmal als von dem Gegenstand ihrer größten Leidenschaft feurig und schön in dem von Herbstsonne glänzenden, stillen Monbijou von ihm sprach! Ich tat, als kennt' ich ihn gar nicht. So ging's mir oft; ein andermal schwatz *ich* wieder. Du kennst es. Jetzt muß es Marwitz aushalten. Alle unsere Gespräche fangen mit ihm an, und hören mit ihm auf.[24]

While Bettina von Arnim freely talks about her love of Goethe, Rahel hides her admiration. Pretense prevents any competition that also would presuppose that their positions are the same. Rahel denies her own confession the aesthetic scenery, moreover; no autumnal sun keeps shining on her words. Her confessions appear only sometimes, and they cannot always be expected. Goethe, and the confession of her admiration of him, form, on the other hand, the beginning and the and of every talk with that other partner, Marwitz. Her confessions about Goethe are a necessary part of her letters to him, of those special conversations that communicate her dreams as well. But as her letters to Marwitz deal with Goethe and—as *confessions*—with her own truth as well, Goethe's words themselves have to speak an ambiguous language, one that does not only tell a story, but can tell Rahel's life. The special relationship between Rahel and Goethe becomes thus understandable. It is a relationship that provokes Rahel's admiration of the master:

> You [Marwitz] were smiling the other day in such a way, when I told you that all of Goethe's words appear to me so totally different, when he is saying them, than when also other people have said the same: such as hope, faith, fear, etc. You smiled, judged my observation as correct, and proceeded to explain my words. But now, listen to the unheard of. It seems to be the same for me in regard to my own life. I always think, in the first sense, which is taken from the bloodiest and liveliest heart, that the other people do nothing. I think of this, if not quiet as clearly, since already a long time. And in this way I am telling you this, too. Therefore, I am able to recognize Goethe's words, and every truth of men.

> Sie lächelten neulich so, als ich Ihnen sagte, alle Worte von Goethe kämen mir ganz anders vor, wenn er sie sagte, als wenn auch andere Menschen dieselben sagten: als Hoffnung, Treue, Furcht, etc. Sie lächelten, gaben mir recht, und erklärten meine Worte. Nun hören Sie aber das Unerhörte. So kommt es mir mit meinem Leben vor. Mich dünkt immer, in dem ersten, aus dem blutigsten, lebendigsten Herzen gegriffenen Sinn tun die andern Menschen nichts. Ich denke so, nämlich noch nicht lange deutlich, und so sag' ich's Ihnen auch. Drum erkenne ich auch Goethens Worte, und jede Wahrheit von Menschen geübt.[25]

Rahel's letters are confessions that deal with herself and speak about Goethe; they are aimed at Marwitz, at herself, and Goethe. Goethe, on the other hand, writes a language that becomes immediate metaphor; he writes with the same letter differently. The metaphor sets Rahel's view in words. Goethe is able to write like this, because there is a truth in his writing, and this truth is offered by words that cannot be his own. Goethe, with his *Bildungsroman,* the masterful *Wilhelm Meister,* writes the unheard of because he can hear. Rahel, the reader, comments:

> Yes, I would be a real part of this book (as you [Veit] say: "as if this is a great loss!"). Although he may have invented everything, even Aurelie, the speeches that she gives he must once have h e a r d, this I know, this I believe. Namely, the princess of Tasso says the same; only in a different tone. How great is t h i s! But he must have heard it. The women nobody can argue with me about. Either one thinks this a s woman, or one hears it from a woman. One cannot invent this. Every other humanly possible thing I grant him. But t h i s I know as I.

> Ja ich wäre ordentlich in dem Buche vorgekommen (wie Sie sagen: "Ob das Verlust wäre!"). Wenn er auch alles erfunden hat, Aurelien auch, die Reden von ihr hat er einmal g e h ö r t, das weiß ich, das glaub ich. Es sagt's ja die Prinzessin von Tasso auch; nur aus einem andern Ton. Wie groß ist d a s! Gehört hat er's aber. Die Frauen laß ich mir nicht abstreiten. Entweder, man denkt so etwas a l s Frau, oder man hört's von einer Frau. Zu erfinden ist das nicht. Alles andre nur Menschenmögliche gesteh' ich ihm zu. D a s weiß ich aber als ich.[26]

By listening to a woman, and by writing Rahel's life in specific, Goethe finds words for a life that Rahel cannot describe but in comparison, in a paradox that is her truth. This truth, which appears unexpected, is unexpected because it always appears in another place. As a "thoroughly witty" similarity and likeness,[27] it can even appear in Goethe's letters themselves. Just "like this," Goethe describes her life. While Rahel is unique in comparison to him, she produces with her life a balance that is needed, not only for any comparison, but for any counting and calculation as well. She herself cannot appear differently but in the image:

> I am as unique, as the greatest appearance on earth. The artist, philosopher, poet does not stand above me. We are of the same element. We are of the same level, and we belong together. And he who wants to exclude one, is only excluding himself. I am, however, appointed to the l i f e; and I remained as a germ

until my century, and I am t o t a l l y   b u r i e d from
outside, therefore I say it myself. Because o n e image should
end the existence.

Ich bin so einzig, als die größte Erscheinung dieser Erde. Der
Künstler, Philosoph, Dichter, ist nicht über mir. Wir sind vom selben Element. Im selben Rang, und gehören zusammen. Und er den
andern ausschließen wollte, schließt sich nur aus. Mir aber war
das L e b e n angewiesen, und ich blieb im Keim, bis zu meinem
Jahrhundert, und bin von außen g a n z   v e r s c h ü t t e t,
drum sag' ich's selbst. Damit e i n Abbild die Existenz beschließt.[28]

With the statement of this comparison, the irony as well as the
"truth" of another dream becomes apparent, which Rahel, in her
dialogue about hearing and true silence, adds to her dream about
art and the Ideal. This other, shorter dream is older, but it is one
that she "loves still" (652). It is presented as an appendix to the
earlier one, and recounts a judgment of art. In this dream again,
Rahel is among men. Men visit her father, and refer, among other
topics, to the Duke of Weimar. Rahel provokes a smile, although
not suppressed laughter, because she herself knows the unheard of
this time:

The talk about war ended, and the men dispersed, at that point, I
asked somebody who came together with an officer, if Goethe is
with the Duke, and how he does. "Goethe?" says the man, "who is
this?" What? You don't know Goethe, I answered; our foremost poet.
Goethe is your foremost poet, this may not quite be the case; the
man smiled; this I have not yet heard. After a pause, in which I
could not confront the man, and could not find any answer, nor
any evidence; I said: listen! He *is* the greatest poet; because if
God would come down from heaven and tells me that this is not
the case; well I say, then I no longer understand His world.

das Kriegsgespräch verlohr sich, u die Herren gingen etwa ausein-
ander; u da frug ich einen der mit dem offizir gekommen war, ob
Göthe beym Herzog sey, u was der mache. "Goethe?" sagte der
herr, "wer ist das?" Was? Sie kennen Goethe nicht antwortete
ich; unsern ersten dichter. Goethe ist Ihr erster Dichter; das wird
wohl noch anders seyn; lächelte der Herr; das habe ich noch nicht
gehöhrt. Nach einer Pause, in welcher ich gar den Herrn nicht
stellen, u keine Antwort, u keinen beweiß finden konnte; sagte
ich: höhren Sie! Er *ist* der größte dichter; denn wenn Gott vom
Himmel kommt u sagt mir nein; so sag ich; nun, so versteh ich
seine Welt nicht. (652)

V

Bettina von Arnim published her memoirs of Goethe as a collection of letters that, while not without erotic impact, are entitled *Goethe's Correspondence with a Child.*[29] For Rahel, Goethe is a paternal figure who has to be worshipped, but who undergoes a peculiar secularization. Goethe's writings represent all that a German *Bildung* should strive for, the desired place and style that Rahel is unable to attain. In her dream, the uniform of military men gives entrance to the House of Weimar, and it is an entry that neither Rahel's person, nor any of her letters are ever able to obtain. Venturing from a native Yiddish, and trying herself with the established pen, her writing mirrors the military order as anarchy. She writes to the poet Fouqué:

> Something else! And something quite different! Quite! When I am writing myself into the Fouquéan writing house, it is quite honest and naive of me! I know very well, that I am writing things that are worthwhile reading; but my words and yours! Like exercised soldiers with beautiful uniforms everything of yours is standing there; and mine, they look like run together rebels with sticks!

> Noch Eins! Aber ganz etwas anderes! Ganz! Wenn ich so in das Fouqué'sche Schreibehaus hineinschreibe, es ist doch ganz ehrlich und naiv von mir! Ich weiß wohl, daß ich Ihnen lesenswerthe Dinge schreibe; aber meine Worte, und Ihre! Wie exerzirte Soldaten mit schönen Uniformen steht alles von Ihnen da; und meine, wie die zusammengelaufenen Rebellen mit Knittlen!—[30]

Neither Rahel, nor her writing wear the proper uniform, but this may not necessarily imply any deficiency on her part. In contrast to this men's world, it may simply be "something else." To be lacking properties, but to be of the same level, and to produce a balance by the absence of a proper place: Rahel's images designate a failure as well as a success. Unlike Bettina, Rahel is neither child nor daughter in her relationship to her male correspondents. While her writing lacks the uniform of Marwitz or Fouqué or, above all, Goethe, her Jewish mother tongue is the origin of more than an alternative discourse. Rahel can only write differently under Goethe's image. But Goethe's writings themselves are only true because they offer a metaphor for Rahel's existence.

This dialogue offers a peculiar paradox. To be able to liberate, to open one's powerful hand to let go, emancipation presupposes an established ownership. Goethe's paternal hand, however, can only offer emancipation by writing what is already not his own, the truth of Rahel's life and conversation. Far from being barred from any access to literature and aesthetics by her lack of social freedom, Rahel undermines in turn the structure of emancipation itself, and she does so with her writing. Neither the positions of master and dependent student seem stable, nor any delineation of gender that would conform to and confirm this configuration of power. Her letters, linking the dependency of life with art, give birth to a mastership that transgresses the relationships of mother and son, of father and daughter. Here, the search for any Jewish and feminist aesthetics has to begin.

4

The Sign Speaks:
Charlotte von Stein's Matinees

Katherine R. Goodman

The expression of classical humanism in the "Age of Goethe" reached its pinnacle in Goethe's play *Iphigenie auf Tauris* (1779 prose, 1786 verse). The "master" himself referred to it as "devilishly humane" ("verteufelt human"). Within the drama, the embodiment of this humanism and the personification of the ideal of German classicism is its heroine, Iphigenie. This character has been the subject of much scholarly attention. However, it is almost impossible to read secondary literature about Iphigenie without encountering the idea that she was loosely based on the person of Charlotte von Stein, a woman with whom Goethe carried on a liaison for about ten years, and the play itself on Goethe's own experiences when he first arrived at the court of Weimar in 1775. Charlotte von Stein therefore entered History, in Goethe's interpretation of her as a vital force in the production of *the* representative work of German "classical humanism". What is unknown about her character has sometimes been supplied by references to Iphigenie, or worse, when von Stein did not behave as an Iphigenie might have, she has been strongly chastized. In this sense she has been mistaken for the image, and the image has been used against the historical figure—and other real women. But Charlotte von Stein was a real person with a history of her own.

Charlotte von Schardt was born in 1742. Her father was the *Reisemarschall,* or superintendent of court travel, in the small duchy of Sachsen-Weimar. He was promoted to *Hausmarschall,* superintendent of household affairs, in 1743, and to *Hofmarschall,* superintendent of court affairs, in 1747. The family remained a fairly impoverished example of the lower nobility. Young Charlotte was educated at home by a pedantic student of theology.

Apart from the domestic arts, she learned reading, writing, math, the basics of religion. She also had special teachers for French, dance and music. Among her favorite readings were a translation of Young's *Night Thoughts* and Luise Adelgunde Gottsched's German translation of Addison and Steele's *Spectator,* suggesting personal tendencies in the direction of the enlightenment and sentimentalism.[1] From her mother, devoted to God, she learned that she should be servile to her superiors in order to survive and that the fate and duty of a woman was to care for others, to suffer, to go without and to endure until God raised the low (Hof, 34). From her father, devoted to the court protocol which it was his duty to oversee, she learned courtly manners extremely well.

This education would stand her in good stead when the seventeen-year-old Duchess Anna Amalia (1739–1807) chose the fifteen-year-old Charlotte von Schardt as her lady-in-waiting in 1757. Anna Amalia's husband, Duke Konstantin, died the following year. During the reign of Duchess Anna Amalia literary life became more lively than it had been at this backwater court. The Duchess introduced sophisticated culture. She was fond of concerts, and plays by Lessing, Molière, Diderot, Beaumarchais and Goldoni were performed. In 1772 the poet Christoph Martin Wieland (1733–1813) was invited to take charge of the education of the young Duke Karl August. This, as one scholar has stated, was the "birth of Weimar classicism" (Borchmeyer, I,59). In the most real sense, the monetary one, Anna Amalia was the founder of "Olympus." When her son, Karl August, ascended the ducal throne in 1775, Anna Amalia continued her active support of "Weimar's Court of the Muses" (Borchmeyer, I, 59), while the Duke, although tolerating these affairs, distanced himself from them.

Charlotte von Schardt therefore witnessed from close quarters this renaissance of court culture in Weimar under the reign of a woman. Although she married in 1763 the twenty-nine-year-old ducal *Stallmeister,* or superintendent of the horses, Freiherr Gottlob Ernst Josias Friedrich von Stein, at the age of 21, she retained her position at court. And when Duke Karl August married in 1775, she became especially close friends with his bride, the highly educated and refined Luise of Darmstadt. So her ties to the women of the court and to the exciting intellectual life there remained strong.

But if court life was interesting, Charlotte von Stein's domestic life was not all that she might have wished. To be sure, by all accounts, her husband was an attractive man and pleasant in company, but he is not reported to have been very stimulating. Perhaps as importantly, during the first ten years of their marriage she bore him seven children: four sons and three daughters; but all four girls and one boy died soon after they were born. From the beginning, childbirths were difficult for Charlotte von Stein, who took to her bed crying soon after her first one. She reportedly dragged herself from one day to the next, and letters tell us that she wondered why one sex had been given so much pain. Her sense of justice demanded that for such a burden, women should have just as much privilege as men: "Men earn fame and honor when they execute their duties well; women consume themselves in thousands of petty affairs that are not respected." (Die Männer ernten Ruhm und Ehre, wenn sie ihre Sache recht machen; die Frauen verzehren sich in tausend kleinen Geschäften, die für nichts geachtet werden, cited in Hof, 46). But her mother, who preached resignation to the burdens of this life, scolded von Stein when she cried about her second pregnancy. She insisted it was the fate of women, who must learn to bear it (Hof, 48). Charlotte von Stein, as we shall see, was not necessarily inclined to accept this advice.

To date the picture we have of Charlotte von Stein's early life is somewhat sketchy. This is about all the information we have. To be sure, hers was a privileged life, but it was not exceptional in any other regard. She was a woman with some intellectual interests, trained in and for both domestic and court protocol. However, her rebellion against the presumed "destiny" of women, even if it took no more active form than epistolary expression, strikes a modern reader, trained in the canonical literature of the period, as quite unusual. Moreover the nature of that particular expression suggests that von Stein's complaint was not merely a passing one, but rather one upon which she had reflected at some length. For now, little more can be asserted.

In 1775 the twenty-six-year-old Johann Wolfgang Goethe was invited to visit the court at Weimar. It is from this moment on that thirty-three-year-old Charlotte von Stein traditionally has been of interest to German literary historians. In her transfiguration as Iphigenie she has become the symbol of German classical humanism and, for many, the expression of ideal womanhood. But Goethe's representation of the issues in this character's life is not one she chose for herself. Two little-known dramatic writings of Charlotte von Stein suggest a different fiction and a different character, neither of which conforms to the ideal of German classical humanism.

I

As elsewhere in Europe, eighteenth-century German courtiers not only hired theater troops to perform for them, they also occasionally engaged in amateur theatrical productions themselves. In the small duchy of Weimar, the court also sometimes amused itself with amateur performances of plays. Upon occasion these matinees were written by someone in the court circle, regardless of his or her status as professional writer. Not infrequently such dramatic works concerned themselves with the lives and characters of people at court. The themes might even expand on those for traditional occasions (birthdays, weddings, coronations or anniversaries) and reflect more broadly on courtly events or situations.

Thus in 1776 Charlotte von Stein, then thirty-four and still a lady-in-waiting, wrote the matinee *Rino* about the arrival of a young poet at the court in Weimar. Johann Wolfgang Goethe is taken to be the model for this character. The young bourgeois author had but recently gained notoriety for his epistolary novel *The Sorrows of Young Werther* (1774). In the novel Goethe had allowed the hero to express severe criticism of the rigidity and exclusivity of courtly protocol. As the fates would have it Goethe would spend most of the rest of his life at the court in Weimar, but in 1775 he was something of a literary *enfant terrible* who apparently subscribed to notions of the natural aristocracy of individual genius, regardless of class. Such talent was not to be bound by social convention. Literary historians have made much of the beginnings of his friendship with the young Duke Karl August, describing somewhat wild adventures in which they hunted, caroused, and flaunted accepted courtly behavior.

In Charlotte von Stein's five page dramatic sketch we glimpse something of the nature of the impression Goethe probably made on the female members of the court. "Rino/Goethe" is introduced to four court ladies at a ball: Adelhaite/Duchess Anna Amalia; Thusnelde/Mistress Göchhausen (her *Hofdame*); Kunigunde/Frau von Werther; and Gerthruth/Charlotte von Stein. They are all curious to meet the celebrity and take a lively interest in him. Gerthruth/von Stein asks if he likes to dance. Rino/Goethe responds rudely that he sometimes does, but that usually "a sorrowful feeling about the ever-lasting troubles of the world" (ein trauriges Gefühl ueber das ewge Erdengewühl, Fränkel, I, 508) skulked around with him, and he leaves abruptly. Immediately the ladies loose interest in the ball. In the second scene Rino/Goethe is

dancing after all, and Gerthruth/von Stein opines that Rino/
Goethe likes to flirt with all the ladies. The other ladies, quite
taken with him, find her aloof unresponsiveness to him incompre-
hensible and a little offensive. In the third scene Adelhaite/Anna
Amalia awaits Rino/Goethe in her rooms and tells the other ladies
she will not leave him to any of them. He is hers alone. Thusnelde
and Kunigunde defer to her. Gerthruth admits he has made her
compliments and that, had she not reflected on the matter, he
might have turned her head. But she has observed that he contin-
ually seeks new conquests, leaving heart after heart in despair:
"And so he is not even master of himself / the poor soul I pity him."
(So ist er gar nicht Herr von sich, / Der arme Mensch, er dauert
mich, Fränkel I, 510). The other ladies are hurt, especially when
each discovers she has received a similar pile of epistolary compliments from him. So the vignette ends.

In fact, Goethe had been sending such compliments to von
Stein, and von Stein had responded. He had not been present at
the performance of the matinee, but von Stein sent him a copy. It
seems to have had little if any effect on their relationship. His diary for June 23, 1776 notes simply "Ryno". The following day he
thanked her: "Heartfelt thanks for your matinees, I enjoyed them
heartily. I have been thoroughly flayed, and I'm only glad it's not
really so." (Für Ihre Matinees dank ich herzlich, ich habe mich
herzlich darüber gefreut, ich bin weidlich geschunden, und doch
freut michs, daß es nicht so ist, Fränkel I, 37). The portrait of himself as unmannered and coquettish was taken in good humor.

Several things about this incident strike a modern reader.
First, Charlotte von Stein holds a mirror up not only to Goethe,
but to the court ladies as well. We are inclined to consider that
some instructional value was attached to this experience of reflection. Second, in today's society von Stein might be considered to
have made public certain private affairs (for instance of the Duchess), but not, apparently, then. No one is recorded as having taken
offense. At least at court the distinction between private and public sphere appears blurred. The matinee is, as it were, a family
affair, an appropriate literary form for a court lady. Third, Charlotte von Stein's self-portrait is the character who sees clearly and
speaks forthrightly. She values integrity and politeness. However,
while the vignette as a whole exhibits good-natured teasing, the
character of Gerthruth exhibits no such sense of humor. Fourth,
Goethe immediately accepted the similarity, but not the literal reality of the sketch. Such is the nature, apparently of matinees. For

certainly his comment to the effect that he was glad it was not really so refers to von Stein's real-life regard for Goethe. Based on recognizable characters and events the matinee may exaggerate or distort certain situations for effect.

II

If this category of dramatic writing is understood in a broad sense, then Goethe's famous, classical drama *Iphigenie* might fall within the bounds of such a definition. The prose version of this play was written and performed three years after von Stein's *Rino*, in 1779. It is usually assumed that *Iphigenie* reflects (in very general terms) Goethe's experience when he arrived at Weimar and quickly became a minister at court. His transformation, so the legend maintains, from a fiery, rabble-rousing young genius to a responsible court minister was in no small part the accomplishment of Charlotte von Stein, daughter of the master of court protocol, lady-in-waiting to the dowager Duchess Anna Amalia, friend of Duchess Luise, and wife of the ducal *Stallmeister*. No doubt the teasing and humor as well as the emphasis on integrity that she exhibited in *Rino* figured significantly in any such transformation. And we know from reports of her son and others, that von Stein did possess if not a ribald, then a hearty sense of humor.

In Goethe's play as in real life, so the legend, the noble-minded Iphigenie/von Stein, priestess of Diana, calms her troubled, nearly mad, brother Orestes/Goethe. (In his letters to Charlotte von Stein Goethe frequently referred to her as sister.) But in this context we are more interested in the transformation that Iphigenie undergoes.

In the course of the play we learn that Iphigenie now finds herself on Tauris, a land governed by the "barbarian" king Thoas. Just as her father Agamemnon had been about to sacrifice her by fire, Diana had secretly rescued her and transported her to the island. She has been living *incognito* among the "barbarians" for several years as priestess of Diana, but she longs for her Greek home. In her opening monologue we find a character not unlike some typically found in writings of the Storm and Stress, the literary period to which *The Sorrows of Young Werther* belonged, voices rebelling against social tyranny in the 1770s. In particular, however, Iphigenie bemoans the fate of women: "Woman's plight is the worst of all humans." (Der Frauen Zustand ist der schlimmste

vor allen Menschen, 102). In a virtual paraphrase of the passage
cited above in von Stein's correspondence, Iphigenie further opines
that, if a man desires glory he may fight for it in battle, or die a
hero's death. But a woman's fortune is narrowly prescribed. She
must thank others for her position, often strangers. And if destruction should reach her home she is carried from the ruins by the
victor (102). "To be useless is to be dead. Usually this is the fate of
women . . ." (Unnütz sein ist tot sein. Meist ist das des Weibes
Schicksal . . . 104). Goethe appears to have had Iphigenie utter the
words of Charlotte von Stein, to have lent her his voice. These gender complaints are one place where we know the character is close
to its live inspiration, and Goethe has done what we know him to
have done in other works as well: to have borrowed heavily from
experience, not only his own, but that of others as well. He speaks
in part for others. In the end, however, Goethe's working out of the
plot illustrates that he speaks, not for them, but for himself. He
has not lent von Stein his voice, he has appropriated hers.

Thoas desires the hand of Iphigenie so that he may sire an
heir. Iphigenie does not wish to wed him; however, she is indebted
to him for giving her a safe home and for allowing her to save the
lives of others who are cast upon the shores of this land. (Previously all strangers had been put to death.) Since Iphigenie refuses
his hand, Thoas is about to retract the latter privilege. Just then
two strangers are found, one of whom turns out to be Iphigenie's
brother. When Iphigenie cures Orestes' madness through her sis-
terly affection (thus breaking the family curse) he is determined to
rescue his sister, if necessary by subterfuge and violence. Iphigenie almost agrees. She longs, "O if only I had a masculine heart,
which when once it harbors a brave resolve closes itself resolutely
to every other voice." (O hätt ich doch ein männlich Herz, das,
wenn es einen kühnen Vorsatz hegt, vor jeder andern Stimme wi-
drig sich verschließt, 136). However Iphigenie's gratitude and integrity will not allow her to treat Thoas in this way: "If I begin
with deception and theft how can I bring blessings, and where will
I end?" (Wenn ich mit Betrug und Raub beginn, wie will ich Segen
bringen, und wo will ich enden? 137) The family curse will continue if she resorts to cunning and force, like men. Male minds, so
the logic of the play, become so determined on one course that all
means are allowed. Women, one infers, behave differently.

Iphigenie risks all and insists upon appealing directly to
Thoas' humanity. Taking this decision, she discovers: "I am as free
as one of you!" (Ich bin so frei als einer von euch! 140) A pure

soul does not need to resort to cunning. Against the violence of men women have only words, but they too can conquer.

> Do only men have the right to perform unheard-of deeds and to draw the impossible to their mighty breast? What is meant by great? ... if not that which was bravely begun despite its improbable outcome. ... Is there nothing left for us, and must a woman deny her sex, like the Amazons, rob you of the privilege of the sword, and revenge oppression in your blood?

> Haben denn die Männer allein das Recht, unerhörte Taten zu tun und an gewaltige Brust das Unmögliche zu drücken? Was nennt man groß? ... als was mit unwahrscheinlichem Ausgang mutig begonnen ward. ... Ist uns nichts übrig, und muß ein Weib wie eure Amazonen ihr Geschlecht verleugnen, das Recht des Schwerts euch rauben und in eurem Blut die Unterdrückung rächen? (141)

Iphigenie chooses not to behave like men or like Amazons, but still to wield her power bravely. She reveals the plot to Thoas. Ultimately her words persuade him to let them leave peacefully and in friendship. Orest's final words convey what we already knew: "Force and cunning, men's greatest glory, are put to shame by beautiful truth, by childlike trust." (Gewalt und List, der Männer höchster Ruhm, sind durch die schöne Wahrheit, durch das kindliche Vertrauen beschämt, 146). Thus in the course of the drama the dissatisfied and resentful Iphigenie has learned the power and superiority of women's more humane nature coupled with integrity and the talent to persuade with words. The rebellious voice of the Storm and Stress has become restrained and "humane"—in the character of a woman. In the play, therefore, Iphigenie no longer envies men, she discovers her power as a woman. She has become a harmonious individual, a classical heroine.

Charlotte von Stein shared many of Iphigenie's sentiments about gender differences. In a letter written May 1, 1813 to a male friend (Knebel), she once wrote: "As dear to me as you are as a true friend, it would be better if there were no men in the world. Then there would be no conquerors!" (So lieb ich Sie als einen treuen Freund habe, so wäre es doch besser, es wären keine Männer in der Welt: da gäb's dann keine Eroberer! Hof, 25) She believed that in every area, even government, women could be as good if not better than men. She may not have understood this to be *her* destiny, but while believing in gender differences, she clearly did not accept given gender relationships as "natural" (Hof, 12). Both von Stein's Gerthrut and Goethe's Iphigenie were based on the real von Stein, and portray her as possessing high standards of morality and integrity. In this quality they seem to agree.

Whatever its basis in reality, however, the character of Iphigenie was never intended as a realistic portrait of von Stein. Goethe was not a realistic writer in this sense. Any figure intended to actually represent von Stein, for instance, would have to exhibit her sense of humor, and this has clearly not occured in *Iphigenie* (or in *Rino*, for that matter). But Iphigenie is thoroughly imbued with Goethe's own ideals and illustrates well the "noble simplicity and quiet grandeur" which Winckelmann had claimed was characteristic of the Greeks and which became a model for Goethe as well. Iphigenie became the expression of Goethe's "humanistic" values, their sign. Years later in a conversation on October 22, 1828, Goethe would admit to Eckermann that his male characters were drawn from life, but that his female characters originated within himself—and that they were always better than the women he had known (Eckermann, 253). In the course of literary history, Iphigenie has also occasionally become a figure held up to readers as a positive example of women's cultural mission.[2] She was not only a "sign" for Goethe, she has become one for many Germans.

Whatever other incidents at court may have been alluded to in the drama, it seems probable that Goethe offered an instructional mirror to that side of Stein's personality which may well have been as rebellious, angry, and frustrated as his own upon arrival at court. For regardless of her calming effect on Goethe/Orestes, regardless of von Stein's avowed support for courtly manners and the prevailing social order, she also had the other side we know from letters: the side protesting the social role of women, the side critical of secondary gender traits of men, the side which manifested her humor.

Enhancing and elaborating on real events and characters Goethe exaggerated and distorted in order to edify by providing positive examples. Orest was transformed (Goethe gave von Stein credit for this), and Iphigenie was transformed (as Goethe wished for von Stein?), and Thoas was transformed. This last transformation, one too often overlooked, is crucial for the serene outcome of the plot. For if the barbarian patriarch, Thoas, had not been willing to listen to the words of the heroine, all would have perished. Tragedy is thus narrowly averted, not only by Iphigenie, but by

Thoas as well. The barbarian must *allow* himself to become "civilized." So the play is also instructive for reigning primitives, possibly Duke Karl August, who seems to have loved his horses more than his cultivated wife, the Duchess Luise, whom he sometimes offended with his boorishness. As crucial as Thoas' transformation may be for the outcome of the play, however, relatively little attention is given it. While we are privy to Iphigenie's thoughts about her transformation, we are not similarly privy to those of Thoas. As a consequence his motivation appears somewhat weak and his transformation carries less conviction than Iphigenie's. Moreover the very title of the play throws nearly all of its deictic weight in the direction of Iphigenie. Therefore, while it is Thoas who rescues the immediate situation, the credit/responsibility for change is actually placed on Iphigenie. It is the woman who must change, relinquish her anger at her social role—and then, miraculously, the man will accomodate her.

The harmonious ending of *Iphigenie* is a singularly idealist construction. It is predicated on the power of words—of literature—to effect change. In this sense it anticipates the more general call to aestheticism in German literature after the French Terror of 1792 (see the introduction to this volume). But in the process of erecting this ideal, it illustrates what happened to the discussion of the social role of women in society under the sway of aestheticism. As elsewhere in Europe, superficially women are accorded tremendous power, but in exchange for this verbal idealization they must relinquish claims to all real power.

Goethe's play was first performed at court on April 6, 1779. Goethe himself played Orest; Prince Constantin (brother of Duke Karl August) played Orest's friend Pylades (Duke Karl August played the role in the second performance on April 12), Karl Ludwig von Knebel (Hofmeister of Prince Constantin) played Thoas, king of the barbarians; Goethe's secretary Philip Seidler played Arkas, Thoas' advisor; and the actress Corona Schroeter played Iphigenie. Charlotte von Stein was not present at the performance, but Goethe must have given her his copy of the play. His letters to her record the fact that, when he wanted to show it to anyone or work on it, he requested it from her. Seven years later, and after consultations with other Weimar intellectuals, he completed the verse version of *Iphigenie* for publication in 1786. This bourgeois male author no longer restricted the public for his matinee to the court at Weimar, but rather, judging the issues to be of national significance, sought a broader one. Just what von Stein thought about the play in 1779 and its publication in 1786, we do not know. Her later response is affected by intervening events.

III

When he first wrote *Iphigenie* in 1779, Goethe was still sending von Stein almost daily letters affirming his devotion. He was also sending her flowers from his garden, his first asparagus, strawberries, radishes, poems, cakes, sketches, fabric, books, gloves, marzipan, artichokes, melons, carp, a desk. She responded, but we do not possess her letters to him, because she later burned them. We do know that she sent him cuffs, a vest, breakfast, chocolate, teacups, apples, cake, prepared dishes, a quill. We can assume that her integrity, her sense of humor, her quick wit, her concern for social form characterized her letters. Whatever happened in 1781 is not quite clear, but Goethe and von Stein reached some understanding and their relationship became even more intimate.[3]

However, this intimacy did not prevent Goethe from leaving Weimar in 1786. He left in the middle of the night. The court was not told. Charlotte von Stein was not told of his destination, and was left with the impression that he would be gone only a short time. Only the secretary who would forward his mail was told of his plans. During the nearly two years Goethe spent in Italy, he continued to write letters to von Stein, constantly assuring her of his love. But the relationship would never again be the same. Upon his return he began a relationship with his housekeeper, Christiane Vulpius, whom he eventually married in 1806. Charlotte von Stein, we know from reports of others at court, became rather bitter and somewhat sarcastic about Goethe and his choice of mistress. Around 1794 this bitterness eased somewhat, and it is just before this that she wrote *Dido*. Perhaps she used writing as a means to resolve issues for herself. Goethe had also acknowledged that his works often derived from inner turmoil, so perhaps it worked for von Stein as well.

Goethe scholars have not been kind to Charlotte von Stein in this phase of her life. Many imply she should have forgiven the great artist all his ways. And they particularly do not like the portrait of Goethe in *Dido*. But if we concern ourselves with the person of Charlotte von Stein, her reaction to Goethe's actions

appears justified. Moreover *Dido* can be read not only as her em-
bittered response to her personal history, but also as a woman's
angry response to the idealized solutions to tender bondage, like
that in which Iphigenie was held. Charlotte von Stein's tragic retort
contrasts strikingly to "humanistic" options envisioned by Goethe.

Given her own history and the title of the play a modern
reader is likely to conjure up images of Vergil's Dido throwing herself off the cliffs as Aeneus sails away. But Charlotte von Stein did
something far more interesting. She used a pre-Vergilian version
of the legend recorded by Justin.[4] In von Stein's play, Dido rules
the prosperous and cultured state of Carthage. Von Stein opens
the play with a monologue by Dido: "Everything around me is
blooming, everything is prosperous: my people, my navy, all under-
takings. No longer does any expression of need make its way to my
ear! . . . Even the arts and sciences . . . take root here . . . Everything is happy." (Es blühet alles um mich herum, alles ist im
Wohlstand; mein Volk, meine Seemacht, alle Handthierungen: es
dringt keine Stimme des Mangels mehr zu meinem Ohr! . . . Auch
Künste und Wissenschaften . . . schlagen hier Wurzel . . . Es ist alles glücklich, 3f.). Dido had fled her native Tyre, because its king,
her brother Pygmalion, had murdered her husband Acerbas; her
own life and wealth were in jeopardy. We recall that Charlotte von
Stein witnessed the renaissance of the arts in Weimar under the
reign of Anna Amalia, so that the general image of a woman rul-
ing an apparently blossoming and happy community was not far
fetched for her. There were also the contemporary examples of
Catherine the Great of Russia and Maria Theresia of Austria, both
generally esteemed for their progressive and enlightened states.
Only the economic situation in Weimar could not be said to be
nearly as prosperous at that portrayed in Carthage.

Conflict emerges in von Stein's play when Jarbas, king of the
neighboring barbarian state of Gaetulia, desires to wed Dido in order to acquire Carthage. There is no pretense of affection: ". . . in love
my beautiful African horses are dearest to my heart" (. . . in der
Liebe sind meine schönen Afrikanischen Pferde mir die nächsten
am Herzen, 17). Dido abhors the thought of this union, stating as
her reason her own personal vow of fidelity to her dead husband
that she would not marry again. Jarbas resorts to subterfuge and
violence to force Dido to agree. She must finally submit and re-
quests only to be allowed to sacrifice in the name of her husband.
As the sacrificial fire flames Dido stabs herself and throws herself
on the pyre.

It is difficult not to read *Dido* as von Stein's answer to *Iphigenie*. The basic situation in each in analogous. Regardless of significant differences, Dido and Iphigenie are each hard pressed by a barbarian king to marry him. Each heroine wishes to escape such a match, and each does: one through the persuasive power of words, the other only through death.

Moreover various themes are the same, most notably the association of violence and cunning with men and integrity and humanity with women. In both plays there is a family history of murdering relatives (Dido's brother had killed her husband), but in each case it is a history that belongs to the male side of the family. That deceit and cunning are associated with men by von Stein is emphasized by one of her deviations from Justin's version of the Dido story. According to Justin, Dido had secretly escaped from Tyre with the temple fortune of her husband, who had been priest to Hercules. This is an episode which parallels Orest's and Pylades' cunning plan to steal the statue of Diana and flee Aulis. Von Stein not only omits any reference to cunning on Dido's part, she has Dido's close friend Elissa opine:

> O destructive sex! without you the desire for war would be unknown. Why, Nature, did you give men this drive, this obsession for action, which adversely disrupts the peaceful course toward a better goal, for which your eternity has given us time.

> O zerstörendes Geschlecht! ohne euch wäre uns die Kriegslust unbekannt. Warum gabst du, Natur, den Männern dieses Treiben, diese Thatensucht, um den ruhigen Gang nach einem bessern Ziel, wozu deine Ewigkeit dir genug Zeit lässet, widrig zu stören. (28)

In Justin, Dido's cunning is exemplary, and so von Stein's rearranging of character attributes, to make the men bear the "objective" guilt for deceit and cunning, is clearly intentional. Within our parameters, we know (because of the statements in her letters) that this characterization of gender differences originated with von Stein. Given the emphasis she places on this distinction in *Dido*, it is also possible to assert that it was a strongly held conviction, which wielded considerable explanatory power for her.

On the whole Iphigenie and Dido are similar heroines. Each holds integrity to be a paramount virtue and each manifests valor in its defense. Each is also an inspiration to at least one man. (Dido finds a faithful admirer in Albicerio). As representations of von

Stein, however, neither shows her biting wit. Indeed, it is a little
ironic that Dido, unlike the Iphigenie who is priestess to Diana,
possesses a more religious inclination to resignation and death.

Just because of the plays' similarities, however, the differences
in the course of the plot and the resolution of the gender conflict
are all the more significant. They can be understood to represent
von Stein's own views on, indeed her response to, the gender issues raised in *Iphigenie*. Orest/Goethe came to rescue his sister,
Iphigenie/von Stein; but brother Pygmalion was a threat to Dido's
life. Except for mentioning the threat, however, von Stein did not
exploit this brother/sister aspect of the plot. Far more important is
the fact that von Stein's heroine is not a priestess and socially
subordinate to a king, but rather the successful ruler of a bountiful and cultured country that is the envy of the neighboring
barbarians. Iphigenie, priestess in the house of Thoas, never ques-
tioned Thoas' authority or power over her. Indeed in the end she
submits to it voluntarily when she submits her fate and that of
her brother to his decision. It is the voice of her "humanity" and
gratitude for the safe harbor he has given her which urge her not
to give in to the "male" cunning of her brother, Orest, and his
friend, Pylades.

Charlotte von Stein (as we know from the epistolary utter-
ances cited above) believed women to be even more capable of good
government than men, and this idealized queen Dido chooses not
to submit to the authority of any male. In the end, of course, she is
forced to do so by Jarbas' exercise of the very subterfuge and violence of which Iphigenie had been able to cleanse her brother (his
madness) with her words and integrity. This independent, powerful woman would rather die than submit to the rule of a barbarian
who has forced himself on her. She has no other option. Unlike
Goethe's Iphigenie, Dido's integrity causes her death, and her verbal skills are not able to alter the tragic situation.

In brief then, the flames for which Iphigenie had been intended by her father Agamemnon (and from which Diana had miraculously rescued her) receive the *self*-sacrifice of Dido. She does
not kill herself for some unobtainable love, rather the flames are
her only means of escaping the bondage of this barbarian king.[5]
Her brother has already killed her husband to obtain his throne,
so no help can be expected from that quarter. There is no deus-
ex-machina here. Dido's arguments to Jarbas fall on deaf ears. He
is no Thoas.

Goethe's faith in the persuasive power of words and in integrity to issue in an age of "humanism" is not shared by Charlotte

von Stein in 1794. Her view of gender relationships is more drastic, more pessimistic than Goethe's. In other words, it is less idealistic—dare we say, more realistic? Where Goethe had spoken in
glorious terms of ideal relationships, von Stein responds with bitter images. Goethe and von Stein present us with two ways of
viewing the world, views whose origins are not arbitrary in so far
as one issues from a privileged male position and one from that
of a woman, admittedly privileged in terms of class, though not in
terms of gender. It is not only a matter of aesthetics, it is also a
matter of real lives.

IV

It is not for her less harmonious views on gender conflict,
however, that critics have chastized Charlotte von Stein. Indeed,
perhaps not surprisingly, her differences with Goethe on this issue
have been ignored. It is rather her characterization of Goethe in
the character of Ogon that has distraught literary historians. But
precisely this represents her real achievement. For if von Stein
found her own, more "realistic" plot for the still idealized and exemplary Dido, it is only in the scenes between Ogon and Elissa
that von Stein reveals her real talent, her non-idealist, non-
classical, bitingly satiric humor.

The court situation in Weimar, to which *Dido* allegedly refers,
concerns reaction to the radical ideas with which the court associated the French Revolution. Critics identify the barbarians with
these ideas which, in the eyes of some, apparently paralleled those
represented by intellectuals at court. In the play the poet Ogon/
Goethe has just returned from Gaetulia with two other intellectuals: the philosopher Dodus and the historian Aratus.[6] They have
tired of female rule—even though it is to Dido that they owe their
comfortable existence at court. Dodus proclaims: "We have been
forced to bury the talent of our genius, which the gods granted us
for the benefit of all peoples, long enough under this regiment of
women." (Lange genug haben wir das Pfund unsers Genies, das uns
die Götter zum Wohl der Völker verliehen, unter dieses Frauen-
regiment vergraben müssen, 29). He sympathizes with the goals of
Jarbas. Indeed they aid and abet sedition among the Carthagin-
ians, for which they are eventually exiled by Dido.

However, for our current concerns, it is the relationship between the poet Ogon/Goethe and the queen's closest friend Elissa/
von Stein which interests us most. Von Stein incorporates many

paraphrases of Goethe's words (often from his letters to her) and some of his gestures into the character of Ogon—in a manner not dissimilar to the way Goethe incorporated fragments of reality into his works. However, if Goethe had appropriated von Stein's words in order to cunningly propound his own image of women, von Stein is very straight-forward in her satiric appropriation of Goethe quotations.

Ogon and Elissa previously had a love relationship. Now Ogon conspires to enlist Elissa's support for the marriage of Dido and Jarbas, and in this context they are given one scene to themselves. It is a scene which adds little to the dramatic action of the play, indeed which breaks the tone of the tragedy, so that we must assume von Stein included it for other reasons—probably personal. It is worth quoting extensively. The scene begins with Aratus trying to persuade Elissa to join the conspiracy. Suddenly, Ogon appears.

> Ogon: May I come in, beautiful Elissa? But I am probably unwanted here?
>
> Elissa: You're most welcome. The sun may have set in the heavens, but the brightest stars surround me.
>
> Aratus (aside, to Ogon): Help me! I cannot get to the point.
>
> Ogon: You are all like children. You don't know how to attack anything.
>
> Aratus: And you'll probably fall into the room with the door or knock so softly, no one will understand you. I have noticed that you always miss the right tone and falsely calculate your effect.
>
> Elissa: What kinds of recriminations are the sons of the gods making to each other?
>
> Ogon (to Aratus): You *are* coarse like a son of the gods. (To Elissa) Hear me, Elissa, with the trust you formerly granted me. Consent to follow our lead for a while, and advise the queen according to our guidance. She must become the bride of the King of Gaetulia.
>
> Elissa: She must? Have you forgotten the oath she swore the gods when we fled Tyre?
>
> Ogon: We make vows for ourselves and can free ourselves from them later.
>
> Elissa: Whoever fails to remain true to herself, cannot remain true to the gods.

Aratus (to Ogon): You know best how to work things out with women, I leave the task here to you and return to our friends at Albicerio's.

Ogon (looking around the room): You are a uniform creature. I have not seen this room for years, and everything is still in its place. It's true after all, women can endure a boring existence.

Elissa: Say rather a peaceful one, which the gods granted us in exchange for the more clever logic they granted men.

Ogon: And you probably make that into a virtue?

Elissa: Not like you, who appropriates the word virtue for what is most comfortable for yourself.

Ogon: You deceive yourself.

Elissa: Once I deceived myself in you, but now—despite the lovely styling of your hair and your well-shaped shoes—I see all too well the goat's horns and hooves, and the other attributes of the inhabitants of the forest. To these, no vow is holy.

Ogon: These false notions derive from a drink which is unhealthy for you, and for which I always reprimanded you. Indulge only in the true spiritual juices of the earth and you will soon learn to accept the beautiful image of me which you hold.

Elissa (laughing): I would not like to place my safety into your hands, since your morality depends on your cuisine.

Ogon: This is irrelevant to the point I wanted to bring up with you. You know that I once loved you. It is difficult to tell the truth without insulting you, but true human nature is like a snake: an old skin must be thrown off every few years. I have done this. Now let us enter into a political relationship. Work with me for the good of the queen.

Elissa: It is pointless to try to get me to do something out of non-love that I would never even have done for love of you. I do not strive for the honor of entering a political relationship with you, and I esteem the principles of the queen. Fare well.

Scene Three

Ogon (alone): She withdraws too quickly the presence which formerly she granted me so willingly, and I had no time to reason with her. But reason is of little use with that sex. The theatrical gestures with which I used to throw myself into picturesque poses at their feet, and drew their attention to me with an expression of silent passion, they never missed their mark. Only the queen never succumbed. And now that my inner wealth of spirit is matched by my outer girth, my formerly slender body is no longer so pliable. I have a great desire to cultivate my peace and quiet, for it is late. Even in the stormiest passion the thought of a beloved never robbed me of an hour's sleep; so political scheming won't do it either.

———

Ogon: Ist's erlaubt, schöne Elissa? Aber ich bin wohl hier zu viel?

Elissa: Sehr willkommen. Die Sonne ist am Himmel hinunter; die glänzenden Sterne gehen bei mir auf.

Aratus (zum Ogon, beiseite): Hilf mir! ich kann nicht zur Sache kommen.

Ogon: Ihr seid wie die Kinder, wißt nichts anzugreifen.

Aratus: Und du fällst vielleicht mit der Thür ins Haus, oder klopst so leise an, daß man dich gar nicht versteht. Ich sah dich immer das Rechte verfehlen, und meist deine Effekte falsch calculiren.

Elissa: Was machen sich die Göttersöhne für Vorwürfe?

Ogon (zum Aratus): Du bist auch grob wie ein Göttersohn. (Zur Elissa) Höre mich einmal, Elissa, mit dem Vertrauen, das du mir vormals gönntest, und willige ein, dich eine Weile unsrer Führung zu überlassen, und durch unsre Führung leite alsdann die Königin. Sie muß die Vermählte des Gätulischen Königs werden.

Elissa: Sie muß? Hast du das Gelübde vergessen, das sie den Göttern that, als wir aus Tyrus flohn?

Ogon: Gelübde thun wir uns selber, und können uns auch wieder selbst davon entbinden.

Elissa: Wer sich nicht treu bleibt, bleibt's auch den Göttern nicht.

Aratus (zum Ogon): Du kannst mit den Frauen noch am besten zurecht kommen; ich überlasse dir hier die Ausführung und will unsre übrigen Gesellen beim Albicerio wieder aufsuchen.

Ogon (der sich im Zimmer überall umsieht): Du bist ein gleichförmiges Wesen. Jahre lang sah ich dies Zimmer nicht, und noch ist alles auf dem alten Fleck. Es ist doch wahr, die Frauen können eine langweilige Existenz ertragen.

Elissa: Sag lieber eine ruhige, für die uns die Götter zum Ersatz dessen, was sie den Männern vorausgaben, einen geschicktern Sinn schenkten.

Ogon: Und das machst du wohl zur Tugend?

Elissa: Nicht so wie du, der sich zur Tugend anmaßt, was ihm am gemütlichsten ist.

Ogon: Du betrügst dich.

Elissa: Einmal betrog ich mich in dir, jetzt aber sehe ich allzugut, ohngeacht des schönen Kammstrichs deiner Haare und deiner wohlgeformten Schuhe, dennoch die Bockshörnerchen, Hüfchen und dergleichen Attribute des Waldbewohners, und diesen ist kein Gelübde heilig.

Ogon: Diese falschen Vorstellungen kommen von einem dir ungesunden Trank her, den ich dir immer verwies. Gönne dir nur von dem rechten geistigen Erdensaft, und du wirst dich bald mit dem schönen Bild, das du dir von mir machst, vertragen lernen.

Elissa (lachend): Ich möchte meine Sicherheit nicht in deine Hände legen, da deine Moral von deiner Küche abhängt.

Ogon: Dies gehört nicht zur Sache, die ich mit dir abhandeln wollte. Du weißt, daß ich dich einmal liebte. Es ist schwer die Wahrheit zu sagen, ohne zu beleidigen; aber echte menschliche Natur ist schlangenartig, eine alte Haut muß sich nach Jahren einmal wieder abwerfen: dies wäre nun bei mir herunter. Laß uns jetzt in ein politisches Verhältniß zusammen treten! arbeite mit mir zum Besten der Königin!

Elissa: Es ist vergeblich, daß du mich um deiner Nichtliebe willen zu etwas bringen willst, das ich nicht einmal um deiner Liebe willen gethan hätte. Nach der Ehre, in deinem politischen Verhältnisse zu stehen, strebe ich nicht, und ich verehre die Grundsätze der Königin. Lebe wohl!

Dritte Scene

Ogon (allein): Zu schnell entzieht sie mir ihre sonst so gern gegönnte Gegenwart, als daß ich ihr nur Gründe hätte beibringen können: aber was Gründe! die schlagen bei dem Geschlecht nicht an. Die Schauspielergeberden, in denen ich mich sonst bei ihnen in einer malerischen Stellung zu Füßen fiel, ihre Aufmerksamkeit mit dem Ausdruck stummer Leidenschaft auf mich zog, da verfehlte ich meines Endzwecks nie; nur mit der Königin wollte mir's nicht gelingen. Und jetzt, da mein innerer Geistesreichthum mir auch von außen anlegt, ist mein sonst schlanker Körper zu unbiegsam worden. Große Lust hätte ich alleweile meiner Ruhe zu pflegen; denn es ist zu spät. Mich brachte nie in der stürmischesten Leidenschaft das Andenken einer Geliebten

um eine Stunde Schlaf; so soll mich auch gewiß das politische
Getreibe da nicht darum bringen. (Geht ab.) (III, 2, 38–46)

These scenes are von Stein's major offense in the eyes of most
Goethe scholars. It is wonderful satiric writing, though a little out
of place in a tragedy. Throughout this dialogue we catch glimpses
of a possible one between von Stein and Goethe. There are many
allusions to Goethe, court intrigues, and to issues argued by
von Stein and Goethe. In his early years in Weimar Goethe sometimes drew his own analogies between himself and a son of the
gods. Elissa then refers to Ogon with great sarcasm as a brightly
shining star in the firmament. There are things we know Goethe
wrote and told Charlotte von Stein: not to drink coffee; that, like
snakes, human beings need to shed skins to grow. Probably he
opined after his stay in Italy that her rooms had remained the
same, like herself. They are thoughtless, condescending remarks
that had obviously pained von Stein. The satire is her appropriation of his speech for *her* own ends.

Intriguing in these scenes are also the similarities to issues
raised in *Iphigenie,* the juxtaposition of vows (integrity) and oppor-
tunism. Ogon attempts to persuade Elissa to follow his lead, as
Orest and Pylades try to entice Iphigenie into cunning and force,
i.e. to place herself under their guidance. Elissa notes that her
"boring existence," which she (sarcastically?) corrects to "peaceful",
is something for which the gods have given women a more skillful
awareness, in compensation for all the advantages they have given
men. In particular there is one exchange in *Iphigenie* which is ech-
oed here. Arkas (advisor to Thoas) tries to persuade Iphigenie to
accept Thoas' marriage proposal. She still has time to change her
mind.

Iphigenie: Even that is not within our power.

Arkas: You hold impossible what your will makes possible.

———

Iphigenie: Das steht nun einmal nicht in unsrer Macht

Arkas: Du hältst unmöglich, was dein Wunsch dir möglich macht.
(132)

Here as in *Dido* the man tries to persuade the woman to relinquish her integrity for the sake of something expedient in the
eyes of the man. In each case the woman holds out, though the
man ends up criticizing her for her inflexibility. The scene as a

whole is a stand off. There can be no resolution. Like the Dido/ Jarbas encounter the Elissa/Ogon scene convinces us that for von Stein, gender issues have not been and can not be so easily or harmoniously resolved as in Goethe's *Iphigenie.*

As different as the idealized Dido and the down-to-earth Elissa are, their actions are not to be viewed separately. According to Justin "Elissa" was "Dido's" real name, "Dido" merely an epithet given her after her death, meaning "valiant woman". It was the idealized designation given a real woman after her death. Dido and Elissa are, therefore, nothing less than two sides of the same woman: one, the noble side, similar to the one Goethe portrayed in Iphigenie, and another, the side he omitted, the down-to-earth wit also characteristic of Charlotte von Stein. It is not a connection which von Stein made explicit (would she have had to?), but, on whichever level and however unintegrated, she insisted finally on incorporating that other side of her. It is precisely this persona that critics have both chastized and sought to expunge from History.

Like Iphigenie, though somewhat later, Charlotte von Stein found her power in words. But the words in *Dido* do not resemble those of *Iphigenie.* They are angry, biting, pessimistic, and perhaps a little self-righteous; but, above all, they reject the image of women projected by Goethe. No one will claim that this play contains the mellifluous tones of an *Iphigenie,* but in *Dido* Charlotte von Stein wrests her own image of herself from the one given to her.

There was no performance of this play. Charlotte von Stein wrote it in 1794, but kept its existence secret until 1796. In that summer she gave it to read to Elise Gore, a former favorite of Duke Karl August, and she mentioned it in a letter to her friend Charlotte von Schiller. Charlotte von Schiller requested the play in November of 1796 and after returning it the following January, her husband, the author and friend of Goethe, requested a copy of the manuscript for his own. He wrote:

> I found it indescribably interesting, in every respect. Apart from the lovely, quiet, gentle spirit which breathes in it, and apart from much which is admirably conceived and expressed, it is dear to me—and principally so—because of the liveliness with which a delicate and noble feminine nature, with which the entire soul of our friend is drawn in it. . . . However, as individual and true as it may be, so that we may count it among the *confessions* which a

noble spirit makes to and of itself, it is as poetic in everything as
it is because it manifests a productive energy, the power to make
one's own sensibilities the object of a serene and peaceful play
and to give them an external body.

Sie hat mich unbeschreiblich interessirt, und in jeder Rücksicht.
Außer dem schönen, stillen, sanften Geist, der überhaupt darin
athmet, und außer dem vielen, was im einzelnen vortrefflich ge-
dacht und ausgesprochen ist, ist es mir, und zwar vorzüglich,
durch die Lebendigkeit theuer geworden, womit sich eine zarte
und edle weibliche Natur, womit sich die ganze Seele unsrer
Freundin darin gezeichnet hat.... Aber so individuell und wahr
es auch ist, daß man es unter die *Bekenntnisse* rechnen könnte,
die ein edles Gemüth sich selbst und von sich selbst macht, so
poetisch ist es bei dem allen, weil es wirklich eine productive
Kraft, nämlich eine Macht beweist, sein eignes Empfinden zum
Gegenstand eines heitern und ruhigen Spiels zu machen und ihm
einen äußern Körper zu geben. (in Stein, li)

It is difficult to recognize *Dido* in this description. Schiller was
more generous in his assessment than later critics; but he bends
the truth somewhat when he refers to "the delicate and noble feminine nature" he claims to have seen in the play. His reading of the
play obviously corresponded more closely to the reigning myths
about women than to our reading. Nevertheless he elsewhere correctly assessed von Stein's talent for comedy and encouraged her
to try her hand at one. He even suggested she might publish *Dido*.
To this von Stein replied to Charlotte von Schiller:

As happy as I am that it pleased Schiller, I still cannot agree to
have it published. If the comedy I have started succeeds, then,
with Schiller's approval, I would be more inclined to publish it. I
would make enemies with the other one.

So sehr mich's freut, daß sie Schiller gefällt, so kann ich mich
doch nicht entschließen sie drucken zu lassen. Wenn mir die an-
gefangene Komödie glücken sollte, so könnte ich mich eher dazu
entschließen mit Schiller's Beifall. Mit ersterer könnte ich mir
Feinde machen. (in Stein, liv)

Thus she considered this material too personal, too sensitive either for the court at Weimar or for the public at large. The tone
was too critical of her larger family, the court, and she feared
making enemies. Even in her family there were limits she was not
willing to risk transgressing, and von Stein, herself (nevermind

Goethe scholars), did not consider this degree of criticism appropriate for a lady at court. Nor was it appropriate for a lady to publish it for a broader audience—at least not without the approval of a man. That she wrote it at all is perhaps a sign of the times, for especially in the wake of the French Revolution, with which Charlotte von Stein otherwise had no sympathy, other women were beginning to write and publish.

Eventually the Schillers' daughter Emilie von Gleichen-Rußwurm gave the manuscript to the Freies Deutsches Hochstift in Frankfurt/Main, on the occasion of the 118th anniversary of Goethe's birth. On the title page of the manuscript Charlotte von Schiller had written "Unfamiliar manuscript", and on the reverse side "By a friend who wishes to be unnamed, not for publication. 1803." It was published in 1867 with the permission of Charlotte von Stein's heirs, but not without indignant disclaimers about her portrait of Goethe on nearly every page. The editor, Heinrich Düntzer, made continual reference to her bitterness and spite, but none to the gender issues she raised. Perhaps those were disqualified because of the perceived vituperative nature of *Dido*. And so Goethe's version of the "humane" resolution of gender issues prevailed.

5

Goethe and Beyond: Bettine von Arnim's *Correspondence with a Child* and *Günderode*[1]

Edith Waldstein

Bettine von Arnim first met Goethe in April 1807 in Weimar. From her own recollection of this occasion, one cannot infer much more than naive adoration on the part of the 22-year-old. In a letter to Achim von Arnim, dated July 13, 1807, she writes: "... in Weimar a single wish of mine was granted, the four hours that I spent there, I looked into Goethe's face, who looked back at me in such a friendly way, so friendly!" (... in Weimar ward mir ein einziger Wunsch erfüllt, die vier Stunden die ich dort zubrachte, schaute ich in Goethes Antlitz, der mich wieder so freundlich ansah, so freundlich![2]) In another letter to Achim a month later she describes this adoration more precisely: "When I think of him [Goethe], I would like to rove about him eternally, play with him tenderly like a cool wind in the summer heat, give him fresh water, warm and care for him in the winter, a tribute of my fulfilled heart." (Wenn ich an diesen [Goethe] denke, so möchte ich ewig um ihn herumstreichen, ihn zart anspielen, wie kühler Wind in der Sommerhitze, ihm frisches Wasser reichen, ihn wärmen und pflegen im Winter, ein Tribut meines erfüllten Herzens.[3]) After the meeting in Weimar, a correspondence between the two continued for four years, characterized by Bettine's unfailing devotion and a friendly, but paternal, attitude on the part of Goethe, which served to maintain the distance he desired from his easily excitable young friend. Bettine actually visited Goethe only a few times, and in 1811 an argument between her and Goethe's wife, Christiane, ended the friendship. She did not see him again until 1824, but even then he remained cool and not interested in reestablishing contact.[4] Bettine von Arnim's admiration, on the other hand, continued well after Goethe's death, the best expression of which

was the statue of him she designed, beginning in 1823, and which
Karl Steinhäuser completed as a commission in 1853.

Despite Bettine von Arnim's obsession with Goethe's personality,[5] she was also critical of him, primarily in political matters.
In 1850, reflecting on the struggles of 1848, she writes: "Schiller,
in his great human striving—would have contributed to the struggle, while Goethe may have stayed at home." (Der Schiller in
seinem großen menschlichen Streben—der hätte auch mitgestrit-
ten, wo Goethe vielleicht zu Hause geblieben wäre.[6]) Bettine and
Goethe would certainly have had political differences, had Goethe
still been alive in the 1840s. But shared political beliefs were not
the basis of their relationship, rather it was primarily von Arnim's
fascination with Goethe's personality and image. While one cannot
deny that Bettine von Arnim learned to recognize and appreciate
extraordinary literary talents and skills through her relationship
with Goethe and her familiarity with his works, Hermann Hesse's
claim that her writing "would not be without him [Goethe]" is too
simplistic in its implication of her complete dependency on Goethe
for her own literary production.[7] She enjoyed the stimulation he
provided her and hoped that he would see "his own worth so
deeply and firmly in the soul of another" (seinen eignen Wert so
tief und fest in der Seele eines anderen[8]), namely in her own. This
statement says something about Bettine von Arnim's belief in her
own creative abilities and in the exchange of ideas and feelings as
the driving force behind not only personal and political development, but also the creative process.

Bettine von Arnim's entire life and work reflect her commitment to such an exchange in the form of a dialogue. Her private
life and political activities, her salon and literary works all depend
on the exchange of feelings, ideas and experiences between herself
and others. She never pretends to be the sole source of that which
she produces, but always emphasizes in both form and content
that dialogue and communication are essential.

An example of a personal relationship that, in contrast with the
one with Goethe, is in fact reciprocal and successful in dialogue is
Bettine von Arnim's friendship with Karoline von Günderrode.
Günderrode was the second person after Clemens Brentano, Bettine's brother, through whom Bettine von Arnim became acquainted
with early romantic concepts. But Günderrode's knowledge of history was the key influential factor in Bettine's cultural development. Without Günderrode's insistence that without an historical
base, Bettine von Arnim's interest in contemporary issues could not

be developed or transformed into constructive action, von Arnim would probably never have developed an appreciation of the importance of a knowledge of history. As it was, her tendency toward ahistoricity remained a weak point throughout her literary work.

Günderrode's interest in revealing the world of history, mythology and the writers of antiquity to Bettine von Arnim was another expression of her desire to channel Bettine's energies, as Clemens had attempted to do earlier. What distinguished Bettine von Arnim's relationship with Günderrode from the one with her brother and with Goethe was that the conscious effort of creating and developing together through dialogue was the key to their friendship. The early romantic goals of free and equal conversational exchange, the poeticization of the world, a synthesis of the rational and the emotional, and an understanding of nature without the desire to dominate it, were all better realized in their friendship. They created their own love relationship and their own "suspended religion" (Schwebereligion), whose primary principles were courageous action against injustices, "sharing life," and developing wisdom and *Poesie* within oneself.[9] Christa Wolf's description of the relationship between Bettine von Arnim and Günderrode is one of the most accurate and beautiful.

> To think together out of love. . . . Love, to use longing as the means to knowledge; thinkingly, knowingly not having to neglect oneself; to make each other's "temples burn with hot zeal into the future". . . . To play with language, to find new words to call one another. . . . This book [*Günderode*] represents an experiment into which two women have ventured, holding each other, affirming each other, learning from one another.[10]

The friendship between these two young women was founded upon correspondence. Through an open dialogue in letters Bettine von Arnim and Karoline von Günderrode came to understand themselves and one another.

Before addressing the question of how Bettine von Arnim's relationship with Goethe and Karoline von Günderrode affected her literary writings, I will describe her works in general terms. Due to the untraditional technique of compiling and editing personal, documentary and fictional modules, literary critics have had difficulties placing von Arnim's works in established categories. Some sceptics have gone so far as to question whether or not her books can be called novels, while others, such as Waldemar Oehlke, specifically designate them as epistolary novels.[11] Debates over categorization limit the discussion of Bettine von Arnim's aesthetic techniques to defining and judging her works according to traditional forms. This indicates a misunderstanding of her literary intent.

To grow beyond that which exists was her personal motto, which found expression, among other places, in her experimentation with writing. Her personal letters are characterized by what appears to be sporadic punctuation, a disregard for grammatical rules, and an over-abundance of dashes and ellipses. These "experiments" in the private sphere served as the basis for the creative process of writing a fictional literary work intended for publication. The original letters were scrutinized and reworked; further experimentation finally resulted in one conversational and four epistolary novels.

None of Bettine von Arnim's novels are written in a closed form. They consist of any or all of the following modules: letters, conversations, diary entries and material from contemporary documents. Her primary interest in existing aesthetic theories and standards was to learn enough from them in order to transcend them, at which point the same process would begin to repeat itself. In her view, ideas and forms must be in a constant state of flux in order for progress to occur; rigidity will result in stagnation and possibly regression. Understanding this commitment to change and open literary forms is central to an interpretation of Bettine von Arnim's novels.

Goethe's Correspondence with a Child

Bettine von Arnim's first novel, *Goethe's Correspondence with a Child,* appeared in 1835, four years after the death of her husband. The timing and choice of topic, namely her relationship with Goethe, are not coincidental. Despite the fact that Bettine and Achim did not live together for extended periods during their marriage and were thereby able to develop individual interests independently, Bettine devoted much of her time, as is evidenced by their correspondence, to giving moral support to her sensitive and often depressed husband. In addition, she bore primary responsibility for their seven children. At the time of Achim's death, the two youngest were four and ten.

The loss of her husband saddened Bettine deeply. Yet she appears to have experienced a kind of rebirth around this time, almost as if bereavement had allowed her to become more aware of her own life. This "coming-to-herself"[12] expressed itself in two ways, both of which gave her more recognition in the public sphere. First, she began the very practical task of working with the poor and sick. Second, she began to define and "realize" herself and her own creativity through the writing of her first novel.[13] That she would try to take advantage of her correspondence and relationship with Goethe, the most celebrated writer of her time, makes sense.[14]

In the analyses of *Goethe's Correspondence with a Child,* critics have often accused Bettine von Arnim of arrogance in portraying a more positive relationship than the one that actually existed between her and Goethe. Others use it to point out that this novel is yet another piece of evidence to support the fact that Goethe was a legend in his own time.[15] Such interpretations, because they do not accept this novel as a work of art, but rather as von Arnim's sentimental toying with old letters, overlook its central theme, structure and purpose. While von Arnim's love for Goethe appears to be the focal point of the fictional correspondence, she herself made it clear that the emphasis was on "love" and not on Goethe: "I was not even so especially in love with Goethe; I just needed someone to whom I could vent my thoughts, etc." (So außerordentlich war ich gar nicht in Goethe verliebt; ich mußte nur jemand haben, an dem ich meine Gedanken usw. auslassen konnte.[16]) And this is precisely what she does in this novel. She comes to terms with her own self through the relationship with Goethe, which, while it had its origins in a real friendship, is ultimately fictitious. A fusion of the real and the fantastic for the purpose of articulating her own creativity is the goal of this love. In a letter to Clemens she describes the nature of the book in the following manner:

> . . . but precisely that which you criticize, that is the true foundation of everything holy and heavenly in this exquisite book, here the innocent soul does not need to hide, it can freely pronounce what is its greatest bliss, and it does not need to make the entire public believe that that which is true is not true. I, an eighteen-year-old child (for that I was a child, as I am today, you know very well), sat on Goethe's lap and immediately, out of

blissful peace, fell asleep at his heart and wrote it in drunken joy
to Goethe's mother, and that's it; what would there be to lie
about?—I want to tell you that the root of the entire trunk is full
of magnificent blossoms . . . without this occurence, my spirit
would not have blossomed through this love.

. . . aber just was Du tadelst, das ist das wahre Fundament alles
Heiligen und Himmlischen in diesem wunderschönen Buch, hier
braucht die unschuldige Seele sich nicht zu verbergen, sie kann
unbefangen aussprechen, was ihre höchste Seligkeit ist und
braucht dem ganzen Publikum nicht weis zu machen das was
wahr ist sei unwahr. Ich 18jähriges Kind (denn daß ich ein Kind
war wie heute weißt Du wohl) hab auf Goethes Schoß gesessen
und bin gleich an seinem Herzen eingeschlafen vor seliger Ruh
und habs in trunkener Freude an Goethes Mutter geschrieben,
und dabei bleibts; was wäre dabei zu verleugnen?—ich will Dir
sagen, daß dies die Wurzel des ganzen Stammes ist voll herr-
licher Blüten, der sich Leben, ohne dies Ereignis würde mein
Geist nicht geblüht haben durch diese Liebe.[17]

The significance of this love lies primarily in its direct relationship
to Bettine von Arnim's definition of herself in her creative capacities. She is, on the one hand, genuinely concerned with developing
her self as a distinct entity, while at the same time viewing
this process as one which is most productive through exchange
and reflection. She learned well from the Romantic Movement
in her attempt to transcend individuation, but the novel is also
filled with mirror motifs, a literary device signaling Bettine's
self-reflexiveness. The spontaneity of this creative process, which
is simultaneously a self-definition, strikes the reader throughout
the novel and is the result of von Arnim's concern with the construction of one's identity through a love relationship based on
reciprocity.

Yes, the human being has a conscience, it reminds him that he
should not fear anything, nor neglect that which the heart asks
of him. Passion is the single key to the world, through it the
spirit becomes familiar with and feels everything, how else shall
he [the spirit] come into it?—And thus I feel that I have just been
born into the spirit through love to him [Goethe]. . . .

Ja, der Mensch hat ein Gewissen, es mahnt ihn, er soll nichts
fürchten, und soll nichts versäumen, was das Herz von ihm
fordert. Die Leidenschaft ist ja der einzige Schlüssel zur Welt,
durch die lernt der Geist alles kennen und fühlen, wie soll er denn

sonst in sie hineinkommen?—Und da fühl ich, daβ ich durch die
Liebe zu Ihm [Goethe] erst in den Geist geboren bin. . . .[18]

To love is to know and to feel, to have greater insight into oneself
and the world. As a result of this at least two-sided and reflexive
view of the world and herself, Bettine von Arnim was able to write
a novel whose purpose was to express the ideal of authentic communication and mutual creative inspiration. For not only was
von Arnim discovering herself through her aesthetic creations, but
she was also hoping to inspire Goethe, as her many monologues,
on which Goethe reflects, indicate. Mutual reflection is the
key to the communication between the "I" and "you" in this
novel.[19]

The manner in which reflection and communication between
the two correspondents is portrayed, gives practical validity to the
theoretical conception of communication and creative spirit (*Geist*),
as defined by Goethe, his mother, and Bettine, in the novel. Ideas,
experiences and feelings take on a variety of tones and perspectives, depending on the particular context and location of the discussion in progress. Not only do the correspondents' moods change,
but so do the places (Frankfurt, Kassel, Munich, Landshut) and
the time (1807–1832). Everything is in flux and constantly under-
going reevaluation. The form of the novel itself is regularly transformed. Its superstructure consists of three main parts. First, the
correspondence between Goethe's mother and Bettine, followed by
the correspondence between Goethe and Bettine, and then Bettine's diary. According to these divisions, it may at first appear as
though only two forms of communication were employed, namely
the written dialogue typical of letters and the inner monologue
which characterizes diary entries. The novel, however, uses a much
broader range of communicative techniques. In the first two parts,
one finds not only dialogue, but music, poetry (often by Goethe),
tales, many of which are told by Frau Rat Goethe and then retold
by Bettine (II, 274–75), and the partners' stream of consciousness.

A good example of this literary technique is the exchange of
letters between July 24 and August 3, 1808. Between July 24 and
27 Bettine writes to Goethe every day, and on August 3 Goethe
responds (II, 127–33). The central topic of discussion is music, and,
more generally, aesthetics. In the letter of July 24 Bettine dis-
agrees with comments made by Goethe. At the beginning of this
epistolary sequence the correspondents, as well as the reader, are
involved in several conversations: first, the written exchange of

letters between Goethe and Bettine; second, earlier conversations
which had taken place between Johann Friedrich Heinrich Schlos-
ser (the nephew of Goethe's brother-in-law), Goethe and Bettine
and, third, Bettine's reflection on her own series of five letters (before sending them to Goethe). The exchange of ideas does not end
here, but is expanded to include the retelling of a conversation between Bettine and Goethe's mother, followed by an account of a
walk along the Rhine by moonlight, which von Arnim transforms
into a very poetic tale. Interjected between the retelling of conversations, anecdotes and experiences are dreams which are related
in such a way as to add yet another quality to von Arnim's unique
style—namely an enchanted, fairytale-like aura. Finally, after
many reflections on music and aesthetics, Bettine writes five mea-
sures of music with lyrics to wish Goethe a good night.

Although logical arguments are not lacking in these letters
(see, for example, the first quarter of the July 24 letter, on page
127), Bettine, as a partner in an exchange of ideas, is concerned
with becoming conscious of, and expressing, the more intangible
components of human experience. To experience life in the full
sense of the word is the goal of the Bettine portrayed in this novel,
and the letters are proof of this. As Goethe writes relatively early
in the correspondence: "Two letters from you, dear Bettine, so
rich in experience, just arrived one after the other. . . ." (Zwei
Briefe von Dir, liebe Bettine, so reich am Erlebtem, sind mir kurz
nacheinander zugekommen . . . , II, 120). This bombardment with
letters full of "experience" is maintained throughout the novel to
the extent that sometimes even Goethe feels he must read them
differently than one normally reads letters, in order to be able to
respond to her.

> I must forgo answering you, dear Bettine; an entire picture book
> gracefully runs through your fingers; skimming over it, one rec-
> ognizes treasures, and one knows what one has before one can
> master the content. I use the best hours to become more thor-
> oughly familiar with them and encourage myself to withstand
> the electrical shocks of your enthusiasms. At this moment I have
> barely read the first half of your letter and am too moved to
> continue.

> Ich muß ganz darauf verzichten, Dir zu antworten, liebe Bettine;
> Du läßt ein ganzes Bilderbuch zierlich durch die Finger laufen;
> man erkennt im Flug die Schätze, und man weiß, was man hat,

noch eh man sich des Inhalts bemächtigen kann. Die besten
Stunden benütze ich dazu, um näher mit ihnen vertraut zu werden, und ermutige mich, die elektrischen Schläge Deiner Begeist-
rungen auszuhalten. In diesem Augenblick hab ich kaum die
erste Hälfte Deines Briefs gelesen und bin zu bewegt um fortzu-
fahren. (II, 133)

Bettine von Arnim chose to portray the epistolary exchange between the characters in *Goethe's Correspondence with a Child* in
an untraditional manner for the purpose of highlighting her concept of authentic communication. The open form and interest in
articulating a range of experiences encourages simultaneous self-
definition, reflection and discussion with others, both internally
and externally. That is to say that not only the characters in the
novel, but also the reader are enabled to perceive, feel and understand a spectrum of thoughts, opinions, emotions and attitudes associated with the "primary" information conveyed.

The third part of the novel, the "diary," is much more staid
than the two preceeding it. Its tone is introduced in the last letter
of the second part in which Bettine, in great detail, describes her
sketches of the monument she hopes to have built in honor of
Goethe.

Goethe . . . deviates from the *straight path* of the sculptor, for he
bends imperceptibly to that side where the crown of laurel, which
has been neglected in a moment of excitement, rests in a limp
hand. The soul, controlled by a higher power, implores the muse
with outpourings of love, while childlike Psyche proclaims
through the lyre the secret of his soul, her small feet find no
other place, she must use your foot to climb to a higher site. . . .
The small geniuses in the niches along the edge of the chair . . .
all are working for you, they tread wine-grapes for you, they light
fires for you and prepare the sacrifice. . . . Mignon, at the moment on your right side, where she resigns (oh to proclaim this
song a thousand times and to sadly soothe the soul which again
and again becomes agitated), this allow, that I give up my love so
that this apotheosis may take its place.

Der Goethe . . . weicht schon vom *graden Weg* der Bildhauer ab,
denn er sinkt sich unmerklich nach jener Seite, wo die im Augen-
blick der Begeistrung vernachlässigte Lorbeerkrone in der losen
Hand ruht. Die Seele von höherer Macht beherrscht, die Muse in
Liebesergüssen beschwörend, während die kindliche Psyche das
Geheimnis seiner Seele durch die Leier ausspricht, ihr Füßchen

findet keinen andern Platz, sie muß sich auf dem Deinen den höheren Standpunkt erklettern. . . . Die kleinen Genien in den Nischen am Rande des Sessels . . . haben ein jeder ein Geschäft für
Dich, sie keltern Dir den Wein, sie zünden Die Feuer an und bereiten das Opfer. . . . Mignon an Deiner rechten Seite im Augenblick, wo sie entsagt (ach so tausendmal dies Lied aussprechen
und die immer wieder aufs neue erregte Seele wehmütig beschwichtigend), dies erlaube, daß ich dieser meiner Liebe zur
Apotheose den Platz gegeben. . . . (II, 299–300)

While it is certainly true that Bettine von Arnim was more resistant and uncompromising in her search for a creative identity
than her fictional counterpart, the Mignon of Goethe's *Wilhelm
Meister*,[20] the passivity and loss of sense of self that this character represents in Goethe's novel cannot be overlooked. The sacrificing of the self in order to glorify Goethe becomes obvious in the
last sentence of the above quotation. Love, the central theme of
Goethe's Correspondence with a Child up to this point, is now replaced by apotheosis. In addition, dialogue, as a form of reciprocity,
has disappeared. Although signs of communication, as defined in
the first two parts, exist in the third, the diary form eliminates
the partner's direct response. Despite the fact that the informal
"du"-form of address is regularly used, and some entries are even
labelled as letters, Part III of *Goethe's Correspondence with a
Child* consists almost entirely of a monologue in praise of Goethe.
Not only are conversational partners eliminated, but also less and
less self-reflection occurs, in spite of the first sentence of this part
which appears to continue the discussion of love, contemplation,
the intellect, etc.: "In this book I would like to write about mysterious thinking in lonely hours of the night, about the maturation
of the spirit, as a result of love, as well as of the noon sun." (In
dieses Buch möcht ich gern schreiben von dem geheimnisvollen
Denken einsamer Stunden der Nacht, von dem Reifen des Geistes
an der Liebe wie an der Mittagssonne, II, 305). Concern with the
self gradually diminishes, and an adoration of Goethe takes its
place. While the diary can be an effective aesthetic medium for
portraying the struggle with, or the development of, oneself, it
loses its potential impact in this novel. By substituting the epistolary form with the diary, the theme of mutual love is transformed
into Bettine's declaration of her love for Goethe, which culminates
in a recollection of the Goethe monument described earlier: "a radiant product of my [Bettine's] love, an apotheosis of my enthusiasm and his [Goethe's] fame. . . ." (. . . ein verklärtes Erzeugnis

meiner [Bettines] Liebe, eine Apotheose meiner Begeistrung und
seines [Goethes] Ruhms . . . II, 404).

Communication and love have been flawed, because the epistolary partners are not on equal footing. An indication of this is
already apparent in the title, despite the many positive connota-
tions of Bettine von Arnim's reference to herself as a child.[21] With
each part of the novel, this discrepancy becomes greater. The exchanges between Bettine and Frau Rat Goethe are fairly regular
and although Bettine's letters are almost always longer, Frau Rat
also responds at length. Their styles are quite similar in that both
employ simple and loosely coordinated compound sentences to
express their thoughts.[22] In the second part, the styles are quite
different in that Goethe's is much more traditional, formal and
distancing. Of significance, too, is the fact that Bettine's letters
predominate, since this reflects Goethe's disinterest in responding.
Finally, in the third part, epistolary or conversational exchanges
have entirely disappeared, with the exception of references to earlier conversations and letters.

In order to explain the discrepancy between the first two and
the last part of *Goethe's Correspondence,* one must look to the
actual correspondence between Goethe and Bettine von Arnim.
Because Goethe did not respond as she would have liked, mutual
love and true communication became impossible. Thus, von Arnim
created a fictional relationship which corresponded more to what
she envisioned, but was unable to transcend the fetters of reality
entirely. Therefore, her concept of communication becomes increasingly flawed. This is not to say, however, that the entire novel
is nothing more than a prosaic ode to Goethe. As has already been
pointed out, the general intention and message of the book is
far more complex. The content originated from a personal relationship, and personal, too, was Bettine von Arnim's need to "come to
herself" through the process of creative writing. In the public
sphere, her synthesis of art and life was reflected not only through
the publication of the novel, but also through the parallel activity
of hosting a salon where music, aesthetics, creativity and many
other themes which appear in *Goethe's Correspondence with a Child*
were discussed. The novel and von Arnim's salon illustrate her
concept of communication and the creative process: mutually inspiring communication which develops both the soul and the intellect
for the purpose of establishing and articulating a creative identity.

Goethe's ultimately distanced attitude toward Bettine von
Arnim must be interpreted as a kind of rejection of both her and

her work, despite the lengths to which she went to view their relationship as a productive one, and despite the positive effect it did
indeed have on her writing. One wonders whether this might not,
at least in part, have led to the fact that Bettine von Arnim
turned to her friendship with Karoline von Günderrode for the
source of her second novel. These two women shared the common
struggle to affirm themselves as women writers in cultural circles
for which Goethe shaped the standard for literary production.

Günderode

In 1840 Bettine von Arnim published her second epistolary
novel, *Günderode*. In general, she followed the same form she had
used in *Goethe's Correspondence*. Actual letters von Arnim and the
young writer Karoline von Günderrode exchanged between 1802
and 1806 served as the basis of this novel. Self-reflection and self-
definition through the establishment of harmony with others is at
its center as well.

> Isn't it the purpose of human nature to learn to produce it-
> self. . . . Think about it, Caroline—am I not right, I have vaguely
> in my mind that out of the spirit of one, the rebirth of all others
> must proceed.

> Ist's nicht der Zweck der menschlichen Natur, daß sie lerne sich
> selbst erzeugen. . . . Besinn Dich [Caroline]—hab ich nicht recht,
> es schwebt mir so dunkel vor, als ob aus dem Geist des einen die
> Wiedergeburt aller hervorgehen müsse.[23]

Both characters attempt to come to terms with themselves and
the world in which they live. Bettine's tendency to praise the one
she loves is apparent.

> You [Caroline] are simply the echo through which my [Bettine's]
> earthly life perceives the spirit that lives in me, otherwise I
> would not have, otherwise I would not know, if I did not proclaim
> it before you.

> Du [Caroline] bist der Widerhall nur, durch den mein [Bettines]
> irdisch Leben den Geist vernimmt, der in mir lebt, sonst hätt ich
> nicht, sonst wüßt ich nicht, wenn ich's vor Dir nicht ausspräch.
> (I, 299)

And yet there is reciprocation, a reflection in the other, in this
case expressed as an echo. Bettine's praise of Caroline is not an

apotheosis. Günderode is not beyond the reach of Bettine, and the two exchange opinions, experiences and emotions much more equally than the correspondents in *Goethe's Correspondence with a Child*. Love between the two is presumed, and not thematized and tested to the extent it is in *Goethe's Correspondence*. As a result, the epistolary dialogue between von Arnim and Günderrode serves the purpose of constructing new concepts appropriate to their experiences. In their search for a creative identity they sketch alternative concepts of history, reality and the individual.

Of primary significance in *Günderode,* especially in conjunction with von Arnim's later works, is the development of a philosophy of history. This would not have been possible without a character like Caroline, who provides the impetus for Bettine's initiation into thinking in historical terms. That the author, von Arnim, as well as the character, Bettine, openly disdain the study of history in favor of acting in the present becomes evident through anachronisms in the novel[24] and statements such as the following:

> When the teacher [history teacher] opens his mouth I see into it as though it were a boundless gorge which spews out mammoth bones from the past and all kinds of petrified stuff that no longer wants to sprout, to bloom, a place where sun and rain are not worth it.—Meanwhile the earth burns under my feet for the present, which I would like to court, without first having to lay myself on the anvil of the past and allow myself to be hammered flat.

> Tut der Lehrer [Geschichtslehrer] den Mund auf, so sehe ich [Bettine] hinein wie in einen unabsehbaren Schlund, der die Mamutsknochen der Vergangeheit ausspeit und allerlei versteinert Zeug, das nicht keimen, nicht blühen mehr will, wo Sonn und Regen nicht lohnt.—Indes brennt mir der Boden unter den Füßen um die Gegenwart, um die ich mich bewerben möcht, ohne mich grad erst der Vergangenheit auf dem Amboß zu legen und plattschlagen zu lassen. (I, 297)

However, due to her respect for Caroline's opinions, Bettine agrees to study not only recent history, but also the ancients and even philosophy. As she incorporates historical and philosophical discussions into the novel, Bettine von Arnim's ties to romantic philosophers become apparent.

As Gisela Dischner has pointed out, von Arnim's philosophy of history, as presented in *Günderode,* is closely related to ideas found in the writings of Novalis, Franz von Baader and Friedrich Schlegel.[25] She follows the early romantic tradition. While the past is a significant component of the philosophy of history described in the novel, a dialectic relationship exists between past, present and future. Caroline's and Bettine's reflection on the past leads to an appropriation of mythology and history with an orientation toward the present and future. This complex of ideas dealing with the path of history is introduced through Caroline's concept of a prehistoric world (I, 225), a primordial world of chaos, subconscious desires, dreams and, above all, unity.[26] In her first letter to Bettine, the young writer includes a fictional dialogue. Entitled "The Manes," it is a conversation between teacher and pupil about the relationship between past, present and future. Near the end of the dialogue the teacher summarizes the insights derived from it:

> From this capacity of the senses to perceive connections, which others, whose spiritual eye is closed, do not understand, originates the prophetic gift of connecting the present and past with the future, of seeing the necessary connection between causes and effects. Prophecy is a sense of the future.

> Aus dieser Sinnenfähigkeit, Verbindungen wahrzunehmen, die andere, deren Geistesauge verschlossen ist, nicht fassen, entsteht die prophetische Gabe, Gegenwart und Vergangenheit mit der Zukunft zu verbinden, den notwendigen Zusammenhang der Ursachen und Wirkungen zu sehen. Prophezeiung ist Sinn für die Zukunft. (I, 227)

And later Caroline addresses Bettine directly:

> ... history seemed important to me to freshen up the languid plant life of your [Bettine's] thought, in it lies the strong power of all education—the past propels forward, all seeds of development in us are sown by her hand. She is one of two eternal worlds which surge in the human spirit, the other is the future, from the one originates each wave of thought, and to the other it rushes. ... Your genius is indeed eternal in nature, but it comes to you through the past, which rushes into the future in order to make it fruitful; that is the present, the actual life; each moment that is not permeated by the past as it grows into the future is lost time which we must justify. Justification is nothing more than taking back the past, a means to reintegrate that which was lost, for with the recognition of loss, the dew falls on the neglected acre of the past and invigorates the seeds to grow into the future.

... [mir] schien die Geschichte wesentlich, um das träge Pflanzenleben Deiner [Bettines] Gedanken aufzufrischen, in ihr liegt
die starke Gewalt aller Bildung—die Vergangenheit treibt vor-
wärts, alle Keime der Entwicklung in uns sind von ihrer Hand
gesäet. Sie ist die eine der beiden Welten der Ewigkeit, die in
dem Menschengeist wogt, die andre ist die Zukunft, daher kommt
jede Gedankenwelle, und dorthin eilt sie.... Dein Genius ist
von Ewigkeit zwar, doch schreitet er zu Dir heran durch die Vergangenheit, die eilt in die Zukunft hinüber, sie zu befruchten; das
ist Gegenwart, das eigentliche Leben; jeder Moment, der nicht
von ihr durchdrungen in die Zukunft hineinwächst, ist verlorne
Zeit, von der wir Rechenschaft zu geben haben. Rechenschaft
ist nichts anders als Zurückholen des Vergangenen, ein Mittel,
das Verlorne wieder einzubringen, denn mit dem Erkennen des
Versäumten fällt der Tau auf den vernachlässigten Acker der
Vergangenheit und belebt die Keime, noch in die Zukunft zu
wachsen. (I, 295)

As the novel continues, the concept of change, which involves progression and transcendence, becomes the dominant factor in the
two women's discussion of history and the individual's role in it.

... in him [the human being] ... also lies time, and the work of
creation is nothing other than transforming time into eternity,
but he who does not transform time into eternity or who pulls
eternity down into time, is doing something evil, for all that ends
is evil.

... in ihm [dem Menschen] ... liegt auch die Zeit, und es ist das
Werk des Erschaffens nichts anders als die Zeit umwandeln in
die Ewigkeit, wer aber die Zeit nicht umwandelt in die Ewigkeit
oder die Ewigkeit herabzieht in die Zeit, der wirkt Böses, denn
alles was ein Ende nimmt, das ist böse. (I, 239)

Through the interaction of Caroline and Bettine, von Arnim creates an alternative philosophy of history in which past and
present, dream and reality, and mythology and history are synthesized for the purpose of giving the future a qualitatively different
direction. As Christa Wolf has described it, present and future reality are perceived and articulated from a viewpoint based not
only on classical sources, but also on more archaic, and sometimes
matriarchal, patterns. Teachings from India, Asia and the Middle
East made possible for Caroline and Bettine a new reading of
"mythology."

Eurocentrism has been infringed upon, with it the absolute sovereignty of consciousness. Unconscious powers, which search for
expression in drives, desires, dreams, are perceived in these letters, described, recognized. Thereby the circle of experience, and
the circle of that which is experienced as reality, is enlarged.[27]

Connected with Bettine's and Caroline's romantic philosophy
of history is a world view which incorporates non-rational elements. For this reason, qualities such as child-like naiveté, innocence, the ability to display emotions, the desire to become one
with nature and sensitivity are regarded as highly as the ability to
reason, to enlighten, to think or to be objective. In an essay, which
Bettine includes in a letter to Caroline, the younger friend articulates her thoughts about the nature of humankind. This essay explains in some detail the interaction of faith, thought, intellect
and "being" in the individual. Due to the intangible nature of such
concepts, discourses like this one are somewhat excursive but reflect an attempt at articulating spheres of existence and experience
which are traditionally viewed as inexpressible. In the process
Bettine creates a phrase that sums up the state she is describing,
"unconscious consciousness" (bewußtlose Bewußtheit, I, 230).

Just as Bettine acquires a certain level of historical consciousness through her friendship with Caroline, so does the latter become more aware of "a new life ... in which the soul may no
longer deny its higher characteristics. ..." (ein neues Leben ... in
dem die Seele ihre höheren Eigenschaften nicht mehr verleugnen
darf ... I, 318). The two women develop together and, to a certain
extent, realize, an utopian vision in which body and soul, sensuality and intellect, *Poesie* and "a higher life of action" (ein höheres
Tatenleben) coexist in a harmoniously functioning organism (I,
318–19). Their concept of history and reality, one which incorporates dreams and fantasy, has obvious implications for their concept of the individual. The ideal individual is one who can both
reason and fantasize at the same time.

One of the most important reasons for Bettine von Arnim's
success at painting such an alternative picture for her readers is
that she portrays two characters who not only discuss, but also,
more importantly, embody the romantic concept of *Poesie*. As
Christa Wolf, somewhat enviously, writes:

Should I keep silent the fact that something in me contracts in
envy and sorrow when I read and imagine how full of innocence—

which does not mean: casually and unencumbered—two young women . . . deal with one another; for *Poesie,* the actual humanity, flourishes only among the innocent; they had that; we have poems, but *Poesie* as a form of social interaction is not possible for us. . . .[28]

Von Arnim rejects the aesthetic norms passed down to her from the eighteenth century. Neither her characters nor the literary construct into which she places them adhere to existing systems and theories. The mixture of genres (poetry, tales, essays, letters, conversations) and the formlessness of this novel enable her to relate a panorama of experiences. In this sense there exist clear similarities to *Goethe's Correspondence with a Child,* and the influence of the early Romantic Movement is also quite evident.

What distinguishes *Günderode* from both von Arnim's earlier work and from other romantic literature, is the intense conversational nature of this second novel. "The spirit of talk who dwells in my [Bettine's] breast has always chatted with you [Caroline]. . . ." (Der Plaudergeist in meiner [Bettines] Brust hat immerfort geschwätzt mit Dir [Caroline] . . . I, 223). Thus begins the novel, and on the third page the letter is already replaced with conversational poetry, Caroline's "The Manes." Many of Karoline von Günderrode's writings are interspersed throughout the letters, and while much of this "fiction" within the novel is in the form of traditional poetry, pieces of conversational poetry are also included (See, for example, "The Wanderer's Descent" (360–63), and "The Franconian in Egypt" (534–36). Even the more conventional poetry is filled with the pronouns "I" and "you," which emphasize the interpersonal nature of her literary works, despite the occasional absence of the conversational partner in the poem itself.

Beyond the use of art forms as vehicles of conversational exchange, the letters also contain recorded conversations with third parties, which one woman wants to share with the other. Bettine, for example, had a conversation with her friend, the Jewish teacher Ephraim, and it functions as the basis for her own reflection, which manifests itself in one letter to Caroline as a conversation with herself on the interconnection between body, spirit and intellect (I, 498–500). This interior dialogue, in which the imaginary conversational partner are the stars, is sufficiently developed to provide the impetus for Caroline's response in the following letter. Similarly, letters from and to third parties are recounted. This self-perpetuating and vibrant conversational tone, in conjunction with the open form, allows the two main characters, as well as the reader, to participate in emotional and intellectual growth, a response which is determined and defined communally:

> It almost seems too crazy, dear Bettine, that you so solemnly declare yourself my student, I could just as well consider myself to be yours, but it makes me very happy, and there is some truth in it when a teacher is inspired by the student, so I can, with good reason, call myself yours.

> Es kommt mir bald zu närrisch vor, liebe Bettine, daß Du Dich so feierlich für meinen Schüler erklärst, ebenso könnte ich mich für Deinen halten wollen, doch macht es mir viele Freude, und es ist auch etwas Wahres daran, wenn ein Lehrer durch den Schüler angeregt wird, so kann ich mit Fug mich den Deinen nennen. (I, 230)

Such cooperation, mutual respect and reciprocal enrichment characterize the relationship between these two women and distinguishes it from all other friendships portrayed in Bettine von Arnim's novels. The two women reflect on themselves, each other, and they find themselves reflected in each other.[29] Christa Wolf goes so far as to suggest it may be unique in all of German literature.[30] The love that surfaces through the letters and poetry in *Günderode* comprises a distinct sense of community, self-awareness and spiritual growth.[31]

Although this novel did not enjoy as much popularity as *Goethe's Correspondence with a Child*, it was widely read by students, the younger generation to whom it was dedicated. It was an alternative to traditional works of literature, an experiment with a truly dialogic mode of perception and expression. Compared with her other epistolary novels, in particular *Goethe's Correspondence*, it is the most successful in reaching von Arnim's goal of authentic communication. The epistolary partners are women, and in that sense equal. They construct viable identities for themselves that are based in dialogue; they reciprocally affirm their artistic creativity and explore the means by which to construct alternatives to the society in which they live.

In both *Goethe's Correspondence with a Child* and *Günderode* Bettine von Arnim breaks with literary tradition. That the voice which emerges in all of her works is the result of gender-specific experiences becomes clear when one considers that she did not begin to write any of her novels until she was relieved of her "duties" as wife and mother, that is until after her husband had died and most of her seven children were grown. Moreover, she is most successful at fulfilling her own goals in writing when her partner in conversation is a woman. Both the form and the content of her novels are determined by close friendships. Karoline von Günderrode did not reject Bettine von Arnim, as Goethe did, and von Arnim could therefore include her concept of authentic communication in a novel based on this reciprocal relationship. Bettine von Arnim appears to have first looked to Goethe for aesthetic guidance but then ultimately created her own aesthetic which is driven by reciprocity in friendship and conversation. The best example of this aesthetic put into practice is *Günderrode*. Deviation from the standard, while simultaneously invoking the name of the standard bearer of modern German literature (Goethe), was certainly enough to deny Bettine von Arnim entry into the literary canon of the nineteenth and twentieth centuries. Her comeback over the course of the last fifteen years is long overdue and most welcome.

6

Caroline Schlegel-Schelling:
"A Good Woman, and No Heroine"

Sara Friedrichsmeyer

In 1789, after meeting the well-known Sophie La Roche, Caroline Schlegel-Schelling (1763–1809) wrote to her sister: "My room is scented with fragrant carnations provided by my devotees from the lower classes—not counts and lords—for me the people must suffice. . . . I have a laurel bush which I am cultivating for a poet . . . and a heavenly little mignonette bush—a momento." (Meine Stube duftet von gewürzreichen Nelken, mit denen mich meine Anbeter aus den niedern Claβen versorgen—keine Grafen und Herren—das Volk muβ mir auch dienen. . . . Ich habe einen Lorbeerstrauch, den ich für einen Dichter groβ ziehe . . . und ein himlisches Reseda Sträuchelchen—eine Errinrung.) As an explanation for her verbal excess, she added: "Haven't I caught the nuances of La Roche's style?" (Hab ich mich nicht ganz in den Ton der Roche geworfen? I, 193–94)[1] In part an expression of her distaste for the writer's popularity, it was also the cult of Sentimentality with its effusive and often dishonest emotionality, represented here in the person of La Roche, that she was rejecting. And she was just as critical of another dominant strain of eighteenth-century thinking. When she advised her brother to maintain a "sensitivity for the wide open world" (I, 174) and to avoid the narrow academic world "where knowledge alone makes one interesting" (wo Wiβen allein interreβant macht, I, 181), she was repudiating the sterile rationality of the late Enlightenment, as manifested in the person of her father, an acclaimed professor in Göttingen. Her over four hundred extant letters—spanning her life from the time of her fifteenth birthday—document her continuing criticism of these ways of thinking which, in her judgment, isolated art and knowledge from life. As a member of the German romantic circle in Jena, she worked to define a way of living and writing that understood the revolutionary power resulting from their combination.

Most of the monographs, articles, dissertations, and even biographical novels about Schlegel-Schelling have sentimentalized and idealized her life, or they have identified her through the lens of the male figures associated with Jena romanticism and have examined her letters for a reflection of that movement.[2] Several recent critics, however, notably Eckhard Kleßmann and Gisela Dischner, have begun to alter this focus. Although they have made conscious attempts to place her in the center of their investigations, some have been more successful than others. Sigrid Damm, for example, who is otherwise sensitive to Schlegel-Schelling's unusual accomplishments, nevertheless summarizes her life with the statement that she had "the rare good fortune" to have been associated with Friedrich Schlegel, August Wilhelm Schlegel, and Friedrich Schelling—the leading figures of early German romanticism—at the time of their most important work (67). Through a discussion of her life and letters, I hope to show that Schlegel-Schelling was an original thinker in her own right and a major contributor to romantic ethics and aesthetics, a woman, whom—to revise Damm's phrase—the male romantics were most fortunate to have known. That discussion will also document her importance for contemporary feminism.

As most other German women who began writing around 1800, Schlegel-Schelling grew up in a bourgeois family with the concomitant advantage of receiving at least a limited education, but with the disadvantage of being offered only a limited sphere for female activity. Her life, however, was hardly typical. Even her early letters demonstrated an awareness of the tension between the desire for independence and the pressure to adjust to societal demands. Her assurances to a friend in 1778 that her actions and thoughts were the "result of deliberations made, whenever possible, completely without emotion" (Resultat von meiner, wens möglich ist, bei kalten Blut angestellten Überlegung, I, 7) define the frame for her controlled challenge then and later. She had no role models to help her explore an alternative to the expected,[3] but as she wrote to another friend in 1781, if she could make her own decisions she would rather not marry "and try to be of use to the world in another way" (und auf andre Art der Welt zu nuzen suchen, I, 57). Shortly after, however, she acceded to the wishes of her father and brother and married the man they had chosen for her, accepting at least on the surface the values of the patriarchy.

The majority of the letters following her move with her new husband to Clausthal in the Harz mountains resemble diary entries, written as they were in an attempt to make sense of her new life. They are united by images of confinement and themes of loneliness, boredom, and renunciation. Most of all, these letters with their long self-reflecting monologs document the awakening of a woman who had hoped for more from life to what she saw as her unalterable future. "My lot has been cast" ([M]ein Loos ist geworfen), she wrote to her sister; and because she refused to devote herself to religion or domesticity, "the two spheres around which women's passions revolve" (die beyden Sphären, in denen sich der Weiber Leidenschaften drehn), she continued, "the wide world remained open to me—and it—made me cry" (die weite Welt [blieb] mir offen—und die—machte mich weinen, I, 153).

But her fate was not sealed. After almost four years of marriage—and three pregnancies—quite unexpectedly her husband died. After a brief period of mourning, her letters breathe a new independence and consciousness of self. As she expressed it to a friend, "There is so much brightness around me, it's as if I were alive for the first time" ([E]s ist so hell um mich geworden, als wenn ich zum ersten lebte, I, 176). That growing sense of freedom was manifested in her surprising rejection of a marriage proposal, despite reports that the prospective bridegroom had taken off his wig and looked ten years younger (I, 238–39). One of the main themes of this period is the monotony and rigidity of her society, "the deadening uniformity" (I, 185) of Göttingen, for example. This critique implies more than social boredom. Philosophically she also affirmed the concept of multiplicity: "Through diversity . . . good and evil are kept in balance" (Bey Mannichfaltigkeit . . . hält sich Gutes und Böses ziemlich das Gleichgewicht, I, 206). After several years of living with various relatives, she made the decision to live independently. Rejecting the security toward which she felt pulled by her "torpid nature," and heeding instead "the soul's pure and most inner flame" (I, 231), she moved in 1792 to Mainz. And there her life changed again, as did her letters.

She chose Mainz, hoping to have there more of the 'wide world' with her childhood friend Therese Heyne[4] and Therese's husband Georg Forster, who had sailed around the world with Captain Cook. She hoped for a diversity of experience there (I, 250) and was not disappointed, for in Mainz she became part of Forster's circle which sympathized with the French Revolution. Her letters from this period not only convey her excitement in being once again among people who gave her head "nourishment" (Nahrung, I, 256), but also document her embrace of revolutionary ideals. After only a short time there, her response to the possibility of a French invasion is telling: "We could still experience some lively scenes here if a war should break out—I wouldn't leave here if my life depended on it . . . we are truly at an extremely interesting political juncture, and that gives me . . . a great deal to think about" (Wir können noch sehr lebhafte Sceenen herbekommen, wenn der Krieg ausbrechen sollte—ich ginge ums Leben nicht von hier . . . wir sind doch in einem höchst interreßanten politischen Zeitpunkt, und das giebt mir . . . gewaltig viel zu denken, I, 250).

By choosing to remain in Mainz when the French took the city in October of 1792—a "traitorous" involvement many would never forgive—she became part of one of the most interesting experiments in German history, the attempt to create on German soil a republic inspired by the French model. Although many of her letters from this period are missing, perhaps intentionally destroyed,[5] those that remain leave little doubt about her support of revolutionary goals. By including one of her letters from Mainz in his work commemorating the French Revolution—the only contribution by a woman—Walter Benjamin offered additional testimony to her sympathies.

When she finally left Mainz, after Forster had gone to Paris and the Prussians were about to retake the city, her life took another unexpected turn when she was captured by Prussian soldiers and taken to a nearby prison. The letters she wrote from that incarceration reveal an undiminished support for the French. Even when she was most desperate for help and found it necessary to disavow the role of "proselytizer" (Proselytenmacherin, I, 297) for the Revolution, that disclaimer was subtly undercut by her choice of "this republican thou" (dies republikanishe Du, I, 321) as a form of address. There were no multiple layers of meaning when she recorded the fall of the Mainz Republic; a description of the flames shooting up from the beleagered city was followed with the hardly ambivalent: "Oh this unspeakable misery" (O dies unaussprechliche Elend! I, 300).

Her problems in prison were exacerbated when she discovered herself pregnant. From the correspondence of others, we know she sent many letters requesting assistance. To A. W. Schlegel, for example, she wrote for help in securing her release by the sixth month of her pregnancy or, if that proved impossible, for poison.[6]

After her release, Schlegel arranged for her to stay in Lucka, a small town near Leipzig, under the care of his brother Friedrich until her baby was born. When she was finally able to visit friends in Gotha, she discovered that she was no longer accepted by middle class society, and proclaimed herself desperately in need of a mirror "which does not distort my reflection" (der mich nicht entstellt zurückwirft, I, 318). Although the ostracization to which she was subjected was a direct result of her life in Mainz, it was not because of the "child of passion and night" (Kind der Glut und Nacht, I, 314) and his French soldier-father. Surprisingly, that portion of her life remained hidden from the public until long after her death. Nor was she overtly criticized for her political commitment. As Damm has recognized, society at that time was unable to think of women as political beings and was most comfortable judging a woman on moral grounds (35); in Caroline Schlegel-Schelling's case, that meant condemnation related to the alleged accounts of her sexual involvement with various men in Mainz.[7]

Partly to please her mother (II, 355), on 1 July 1796 she married August Wilhelm Schlegel, a decision that her letters recorded with at least a hint of resignation. "Now finally my life is . . . back on a straight track" (Nun geht es doch aber endlich . . . im graden Gleise, I, 390), she wrote to her life-long friend and correspondent Luise Gotter, echoing the phrase she had used in 1791 to explain her refusal of a marriage proposal: "You . . . wanted to bring my life back on track again" (Ihr . . . woltet mich auch wieder ins Gleis bringen, I, 230). Although she and Schlegel considered emigrating to America (I, 374), they instead moved to Jena where, as the histories of literature record, their home gradually became the meeting place for a group of young poets and thinkers who wanted to transform bourgeois society through a new kind of art.

"Since the beginning of the year I have hardly left Wilhelm's room," she wrote in 1799 to Novalis about her own literary activity (I, 499). Yet, as various critics have pointed out, we will never know exactly what she contributed to romanticism; in addition to her reluctance to write under her own name, the spirit of *Symphilosophieren* so integral to the group neutralized or made her contributions even more anonymous than those of the males. We do know that she helped her husband on his translation of Shakespeare and that she copied his manuscripts for him (e.g., I, 424, 426–28, 720). We also know that she helped Friedrich Schlegel, reading, editing, and commenting on his writings (e.g., I, 527, 529). In addition she worked on and wrote anonymous reviews for

Athenäum, the literary journal published from 1798–1800 under the names of the Schlegel brothers. She had come to Jena with an already developed critical appreciation for literature, and her activities there fostered an increased trust in her own judgment. This growing confidence speaks from her letters, and was reflected in another way by Friedrich Schlegel; she was, he lamented in the fall of 1798, "no longer so thoroughly maternal and tender" (I, 475).

Virtually all the figures associated with Jena romanticism either lived with or spent much of their time in the home of Caroline Schlegel-Schelling and her husband. Her perceptive, often witty letters tell us much about how they lived and worked and about their responses to contemporary culture. Her mocking report, for example, of their reaction to a poem by Schiller that glorified bourgeois values—" 'The Bell' nearly made us . . . roll on the floor . . . with laughter" ('Die Glocke' hat uns . . . mit Lachen . . . fast unter den Tisch gebracht, I, 592)—underscored their antipathy for the established order.[8] But her letters do not tell us as much as we would like, for they stopped abruptly in December 1799. Actually, she wrote very few after Friedrich Schlegel and Dorothea Veit, along with the latter's son, came to live in her house in the fall of 1799. Clearly the new living arrangement provided its own form of intellectual stimulation, but the gap in her letters also occurred because she was, quite simply, overworked. In October of 1799 she wrote to Luise Gotter that for the last three months she had had "not a moment's peace," often feeding fifteen to eighteen people for the main meal of the day (I, 560–61).

Shortly after arriving in Jena, Dorothea Veit reported to Rahel Levin, later Varnhagen, that Schlegel-Schelling was a "pleasant hostess, eager to please, and indefatigable" (angenehme Wirtin, gefällig, und unermüdlich), and that in addition she sewed her own clothes (I, 743). With the help of a cook and a young girl, she organized the cooking and cleaning for the entire group, worked on her own and the various projects her husband was involved in, and functioned as the social and intellectual center of the group. That she had little time for letters is no surprise. But her demanding schedule also led to a serious illness: by February 1800 she had developed what her daughter referred to as an inflammation of the nerves (I, 595). Still sick in May with what according to Kleßmann was dysentery or typhus (210), she and her daughter left for a spa. But as she recovered, the daughter she had treated as her "little sister" (I, 577),[9] the only one of her four children to have survived childhood, suddenly became sick and died.

When she finally recuperated from her own illness—she never did recover from the death of her daughter—there was no Jena circle to which she could return. The reason most often cited for the break-up of the group is the love between her and the philosopher Friedrich Schelling, which was known to the group even before her illness. But letters from the winter of 1799-1800 also documented serious differences in personal opinions and aesthetic judgments, and as Damm has pointed out, there were economic difficulties as well (54). In trying to chronicle and understand the disintegration of the group, it should also be acknowledged that Schlegel-Schelling's illness—caused at least in part by overwork—was a major factor. After she became sick in February 1800 and could no longer function as the center of the group, its members drifted apart.

She stayed away from Jena for a year, despondent over the loss of her daughter and unsure of the direction her relationship with Schelling should take. She returned to find her house in disarray, with many household items and dishes broken or missing (II, 125),[10] and had to rely on herself to find a structure for her life. Katja Behrens' claim that the women writers associated with romanticism were provided for by fathers and husbands (434) thus does not adequately describe Schlegel-Schelling's life. What she called her "instinctive propensity for independence" (instinktmäßige Neigung zur Unabhängigkeit) (I, 298) in fact placed her more than once in economic difficulties. A very real concern about money is evidenced, for example, in her letters to A. W. Schlegel between 1800–1803 after he had gone to Berlin, before their divorce and her marriage to Schelling.

Her life with Schelling in Würzburg and Munich was difficult because she had been divorced, but even more so because of her connections to Mainz. A ban prohibiting her from remaining in Göttingen, issued in 1794 and again in 1800, offers an example of the hostility she experienced then and for the rest of her life (Kleßmann 138, 289). Although her letters after 1800 expressed her continuing belief in the revolutionary power of art, they also contained more contradictions about her own independence, especially concerning her relationship with Schelling. Her letters to him during the first few years of their relationship pose a problem for feminist critics because they seem to refute her earlier and later assertions of personal freedom. But more important than these letters—and it should be remembered that they were written at a time of great emotional strife when she was questioning and reworking her own values—is the evidence that in her life with Schelling she continued to defy society's notions of gender roles. She began in 1805 to write reviews under her own name, but before she could do more, in 1809 she died unexpectedly, forty-six years old, after another attack of dysentery.

Caroline Schlegel-Schelling did not have time to reflect on her life as did certain other women associated with romanticism, like Bettine von Arnim, or to contemplate a published edition of her letters, as did Rahel Varnhagen. Her legacy is thus in her unpublished letters, letters that were carefully constructed—she acknowledged the difficulty of expressing in words her "long and clearly held convictions, put hourly into practice" (deutliche, lange gefaßte, stündlich ausgeübte Überzeugungen) (I, 221)—and exhibit a personal orthography and punctuation.

Recent scholars have analyzed for us the nature of letter writing around 1800 and offered explanations for its popularity.[11] Their work helps to explain why this brilliant woman—Friedrich Schlegel, for example, recognized "the superiority of her intellect over mine" (die Überlegenheit ihres Verstandes über den meinigen)[12]—began writing letters, but does not explain what she did with them or why she did it so well. And Schlegel-Schelling was good; she was recognized even in her own life-time as a gifted correspondent.[13] But rather than appreciate her epistolary writing, most critics have asked why she wrote nothing else. Dischner offers an explanation with her statement that public opinion around 1800 was so unambiguous about the horror of women's writing for a public audience that many, Schlegel-Schelling among them, confined themselves to letters and only in private helped their husbands who were working in other genres (92).

It should be emphasized, however, that her choice of letters as a genre also implied a conscious rejection of the other modes of writing available to women at that time. Her views on diaries can be gleaned from her comments, while still in Göttingen, about the efforts of a young woman whose handwritten entries were being passed around in secret. One need not read too intently between the lines to ground her suspicions of diaries on a conviction that their writers, by concentrating on a single personality, too often yielded to the temptation of forgetting or misrepresenting the larger world. What she found lacking in this particular example was a treatment of "people and things according to their true (unpoetic) nature" (Menschen und Sachen nach ihren wahren [unpoetischen] Gesichtspunkt, I, 69–70). She was no more favorably inclined toward novels, repudiating their distanced authorial stance and preferring instead a literature of real 'people and things' in which the author's voice could be heard. While in Clausthal she had often asked friends to send her books, acknowledging that she would read anything they could find, but expressing a clear preference for biographies, memoirs, or histories (I, 142–43), for something "amusing and true" (amüsant und wahr, I, 151). Her use of the adjective *romanhaft* as a pejorative meaning "fanciful as in a novel" documents her association of novels with what to her was a frivolous, fairy-tale like attitude toward life and a plot line focused on heterosexual romance (e.g., I, 27, 34, 56). Thus even though Friedrich Schlegel, among others, did urge her to write a "novelette" (Romänchen, I, 465), she chose not to, perhaps fearing that the effort would place her in the company of novelists whom she did not highly regard. When she mockingly suggested a conclusion to an ongoing relationship between acquaintances, she was implicitly identifying the novel with the literature of exaggerated sentiment and romantic escape that she scorned: "Perhaps he seduces her, loses his position, she flees with him, they go to Rome, become fervently Catholic, priests are allowed to marry, he becomes Cardinal—Pope—Prince of Heaven—farewell—farewell" (Vielleicht verführt er sie, wird abgesezt, sie flüchet mit ihm, gehn nach Rom, werden katholisch, die Priesterehe wird eingeführt, er wird Cardinal—Pabst—Himmelsfürst—Leb wohl—leb wohl, I, 153).

In 1799-1800 she did, however, write a short sketch for an autobiographical novel in which the central character was described as "an independent and . . . charming being" (ein selbständiges und . . . liebenswürdiges Wesen, I, 662–64), the latter a quality she had once linked to women's successful adaptation to bourgeois society (I, 157). The sketch documents what Elke Frederiksen has identified as Schlegel-Schelling's principle of *pro forma* adaptation (97), and helps at the same time to define the limits of that adaptation. The novel in the romantic program was linked in theory and practice to autobiography.[14] Women around 1800, however, were not accustomed to opening their lives to public scrutiny, even women whose lives inspired less controversy than Schlegel-Schelling's. Those bold enough to do so generally chose to express themselves in forms other than the novel. Yet she envisioned the novel as reflecting her own ideas and experiences. Although her heroine would exhibit a certain amount of "folly" (Thorheit)—a necessary bow to convention—that characteristic would be apparent only on first meeting, and would yield quickly to reason and self-sufficiency. Just as Schlegel-Schelling in this way distanced her main character from eighteenth-century Sentimentality, she also removed her from the values of the late Enlightenment. Her heroine, she stressed, would know how to value "the living world;" she would not appreciate "the sublime" (das Erhabene) only in books.

But in breaking off her sketch with the death of her first husband at the point where her own life had begun to diverge from the norm of female dependency, she was also demonstrating her inability or unwillingness to be the heroine of her own novel. On at least two occasions she declared summarily her aversion to functioning in that role, identifying herself rather as "a good woman, and no heroine" (eine gute Frau, und keine Heldin, I, 293; cf. 296). Such statements, and their literary proof in the unexpanded autobiographical sketch, demonstrate more than just a typical reluctance to confront centuries of prejudice. Sigrid Weigel has shown that women in the literature of this period became heroines by virtue of sacrifice, and Schlegel-Schelling had long ago and categorically rejected such a role for herself: "I do not believe in sacrifice" (Ich glaube an keine Opfer), she had written in 1791, dismissing those who did as people who had "gaps to fill—emptiness to hide" (Lücken zu füllen—Leere zu verbergen, I, 231).

Besides offering a means of expression not subject to the problems she believed inherent in diaries and novels, letters were her choice for more positive reasons as well. Epistolary writing offered her, for example, the desired opportunity for developing her own subjectivity. This same possibility exists in other kinds of autobiographical writing as well, but the letter writer, in taking cognizance of at least one intended reader according to the dictates of the form, could not fall prey to the same self-absorption she found so objectionable in a diarist's writing. As a response to different addressees, epistolary writing also offered opportunities for experimenting with, even constructing, various versions of a self. And Schlegel-Schelling presented us with many, including that of resigned wife, concerned sister, loving friend, non-authoritarian mother, and intellectual functioning in the literary world. One example will suffice to show that she was well aware of the potential in epistolary writing for controlling her image. From the time of her earliest letters, she had defined and redefined the concept of happiness, consciously presenting herself except during her Clausthal years as lighthearted and keen-witted. A letter from Dorothea Veit to Rahel Levin, however, indicates that the wit that sparkled from so many of her letters was a part of her self-construction; Caroline Schlegel-Schelling in her daily life, Veit had discovered, was "not as vivacious and cheerful as in her letters" (nicht so lebendig und lustig wie in ihren Briefen, I, 743).

She was also drawn to epistolary writing by its potential for transgressing the boundaries her society had erected between the relative anonymity expected of women and the public realm in which men could live and express themselves. She had long thought of letters as a way to escape the traditional sphere allotted to women, viewing them in Clausthal as the only thing "which . . . could occupy my mind" (welche . . . meinen Kopf beschäftigen könte, I, 208–209). Especially after moving to Jena and involving herself in the literary world, she could engage in an accepted exchange of ideas in epistolary essays directed to the leading cultural figures of the day, although her anonymous reviews document the limits of the kind of public acknowledgment she desired. Through her correspondence with Goethe, Schiller, Novalis, and the Schlegels, as well as with numerous less well-known figures, she could discuss issues usually reserved for males, such as literature and politics, thus participating in the public sphere while maintaining the pretence of offering merely private views. Because she could depend on their being read by more than the addressee, her letters were more than merely private messages.

That she was conscious of the power of epistolary writing to effect a bridge between the private and public spheres is clear from the review she published in *Athenäum* of a collection of letters written by the young historian Johannes Müller to a friend. What she found particularly praiseworthy in his writing was not just form, but his ability to present so many aspects of his being: not only did he open his soul to his correspondent about the joys and sorrows of his own existence, but he placed his own development in the context of a larger world and a future for which he was working. One of the main goals of this review, however, extended beyond the praise of Müller's letters; her intent was also to claim the epistolary form as a vehicle for more than private communication. Thus she recommended Müller's correspondence to others because, although it was directed to just one friend, other readers would be able to identify with, and benefit from, Müller's revelations, finding encouragement there for their own personal struggles (I, 664–66).

Just as importantly, letters were a form she could use to reflect the democratic principles she had absorbed in Mainz; they could provide a forum for the kind of genuine communication between equals she recognized as necessary for those principles to flourish. The thematics of her letters reflect her democratic values in a way other forms could not. Silvia Bovenschen's description of her letters as "true masterpieces of mixed aesthetic form" in which details of daily life and remembered conversations alternate with philosophical discourses, sometimes unkind gossip with literary allusions and criticism (47), attests to the non-exclusivity and interdependence of her epistolary themes. In consciously stressing the intertextual nature of her letters, by drawing for their content from the texts of culture and everyday life, Schlegel-Schelling was striving to establish the importance not only of the individual but of daily life. In emphasizing the importance of empirical reality, she was also consciously demonstrating her distance from the longing for a transcendental sphere that defines much of German romanticism. In rejecting a dualistic world view as a "magic caldron" (Zauberkessel, I, 496), she veered most clearly from what has come to be known as romantic thinking and proved herself at the same time more modern than the males of the movement. The "separation" (Scheidung) of which they spoke was for her a "merging" (Verschmelzung, I, 503).

Her choice of epistolary art was in the widest sense a function of her engagement in the world around her. Generally, the fragment has been considered the most intrinsically romantic form, and Schlegel-Schelling too recognized its value for philosophizing (II, 585). But her experience in Mainz had taught her to value social and political change even more highly than the abstractions of philosophy. In her 1801 parody of Friedrich Schlegel's dissertation, she articulated her commitment to political involvement, writing there: "Philosophical morality is to be ranked lower than the political" (Die philosophische Moral ist der politischen unterzuordnen, II, 584).[15] Two long letters to Therese Forster's second husband L. F. Huber, in which she placed his criticism of *Athenäum* and Friedrich Schlegel's novel *Lucinde* into a political context, convincingly document the extent to which she believed in romantic art in general, and in letters in particular, as the means for bringing about political change. Admitting that she was writing from a renewed sense of personal involvement because Napoleon was in power and meaningful political revolution now seemed more than ever possible, she rebuked Huber on the basis that his criticism of romantic art would serve to strengthen the conservative forces both in France and in her own country (I, 577–87).[16]

Despite the reluctance of many critics to credit her with any kind of political engagement because her efforts did not come in conventional ways, contemporary feminist theory linking the political with the personal provides us with the basis for valuing her contributions more positively—and more accurately.[17] Although she did not deal with political issues in a theoretical way, she believed that through her correspondence she was participating in the kind of public discussion of issues which could effect sociopolitical change. Except when emotional turmoil dictated the contents, political concerns were in fact often integrated into her writing, from her early criticism of a Hessian ruler's sending soldiers to America "so that he can build palaces in Kassel" (I, 62), to her remarks to her daughter in October 1799—"Buonaparte is in Paris. Oh my child, just think, everything is going to be all right again" (I, 572)—to her comments on the political alliance between Bavaria and France in some of her last letters.

The desire to engage in a public discussion of issues affecting her society also explains her interest in forming the Jena circle. Although it was not a typical romantic salon, in part because at the height of their creativity several members of the Jena group lived together in one house, it offered the same possibility for communication which defined *the* romantic salon. The conclusions of critics who emphasize the importance of salons for women as a place where they could partake of both private and public worlds thus apply also to Schlegel-Schelling.[18] In a debate over how to change the world—whether the individual is responsible for changing society or whether a given social order is the requisite for change—the romantics would clearly have argued the power of the enlightened, cultivated individual. And it was communication with others, oral and written, that they viewed as the greatest stimulus to that all-important personal development. In her book on Bettine von Arnim, Edith Waldstein summarizes the critical work on conversation to show its importance in the late eighteenth and early nineteenth centuries and documents the political implications of Romantic conversation for von Arnim's writings. Her novels, she argues, demonstrate the writer's conviction that an open exchange of ideas was the prerequisite for individual development, and in turn the catalyst for social and political change. The same conviction motivated Schlegel-Schelling's epistolary writing.

At least since the writer C. F. Gellert established the connection in 1751,[19] critics have recognized the letter as the written form of conversation. For the Jena romantics, letters were a valued form of art and the written form of "Geselligkeit," or romantic sociability, the kind of communication which took place in a romantic salon.[20] Schlegel-Schelling was adept at conversation—in

Schiller's careful judgment, she had "a great talent for conversation" (viel Talente zur Conversation, I, 712)—and in her own letters gave proof that she perceived them as substitutes for oral communication. Another tribute to her conversational skills came in one of the sections of *Lucinde* that critics recognize as a paean to Schlegel-Schelling. There Friedrich Schlegel praised his heroine for her conversational abilities, and went on to describe her as a woman who wrote letters "as if she were carrying on a conversation" (93).

Aware of the socio-political implications of personal communication, Schlegel-Schelling thus found in epistolary writing a structure whose form and content she could adapt to express the kind of non-hierarchical human interaction she believed the necessary stimulus to individual progress and thus to the creation of a new world order. In some of her letters she even developed a structure to underscore this emphasis. Because epistolary writing is practiced as a vehicle through which a writer addresses a reader, it is an inherently dialogic form. Contemporary critics associate the term with M. M. Bakhtin, for whom the relation between the author and character in a novel was its paradigmatic expression. Recent feminist critics, however, have documented additional ways of understanding the dialogic. Anne Herrmann, for example, who has focused on its potential for expressing sexual difference, uses the term to describe a "discursive relation between two subjects, understood as a dialogic in which the subject constitutes itself without the annihilation or assimilation of the other" (6).[21] Schlegel-Schelling's intensification of the normally dialogic nature of epistolary writing is an expression of her commitment to the romantic goal of self-development and to a belief that this was an ambition to be achieved not in isolation but through a non-hierarchical exchange of ideas with others. For her it provided a way of overcoming the monologic tendency of an authorial voice, of including diversity in a non-judgmental way, and of rejecting hierarchical patterns in human relations. In much of her correspondence, Schlegel-Schelling wrote from a subject position that granted to her reader the possibility of an independent existence as subject.

As is to be expected in any such correspondence, there is a great deal of variety in her letters, and some are more dialogic than others. She also chose a number of different partners for her dialogues. At times they were with herself, sometimes with one or more readers, and occasionally even with history. Whereas the dialogic element in some consisted in the exchange *between* letters, in others she found a way to include her reader in the writing process even more directly than is usually expected. Not only was her writing then a response to the imaginings of her anticipated reader, but the addressee's constructed questions, rejoinders, and even thoughts were incorporated into the letter. The dialogue, that is, was constructed not merely via, but within the letter. As a young girl she had also written letters that included the thoughts of her reader, but the constructed exchanges were more playful than issue-oriented. From those early breezy conversations to the more melancholy epistolary discussions with Schelling after 1800—"Your friend is all alone and comes to you. . . . Let us talk, my sweet friend, of great things—amiable conversation heals bitter pain" (Deine Freundin ist ganz allein und kommt zu Dir. . . . Lass uns reden, mein süßer Freund, von großen Dingen—liebliches Unterreden heilet bittres Weh, II, 56), for example—the dialogic pattern of much of her correspondence underscored her conception of letters as a written form of conversation. That message was carried even in the punctuation: long sentences were frequently composed of various thoughts connected by dashes.

By the late 1780s, she was beginning to formulate her epistolary dialogues for the purpose of clarifying issues through a democratic exchange of opinions with an intended reader. In contrast to the self-absorbed communications of the Clausthal years, many of the still-existing letters from Mainz, for example, were framed around constructed conversations between two equal partners in which she did not set herself up as an authority, and instead allowed the views of the writer and addressee to develop at least ostensibly in an egalitarian way. When the subject was political or literary, however, the conversational exchange at times was less a dialogue than a debate. Even when the discussion was weighted in her favor, the purpose of the letter was not merely to win an argument, but to help educate her reader and to sharpen her own views and reinforce her own convictions, that is, to help them both in the development toward responsible selfhood. She did not understand individual development as a gendered experience and thus saw no contradiction in undertaking the process through a dialogic with a masculine voice. She so often wrote to men presumably because she considered them more lively correspondence partners, given their access to the world of ideas. Gender was, however, a significant dimension of the dialogues, because through them she was exerting her claim to equality with the male intelligentsia of the day.

Schlegel-Schelling's dialogic form was especially well-developed in her letters to F. L. W. Meyer, a minor writer with whom she corresponded for several years in the 1790s. Frequently the comments prefacing those epistolary conversations emphasized their value to her. When trying to make the decision whether or not to move to Mainz, for example, she wrote in the summer of 1791: "I have many ideas in my head now that I would like to share with you in order to hear yours in return." (Jezt arbeiten manche Ideen in meinem Kopfe, die ich Ihnen mittheilen würde, um die Ihrigen dafür zu hören.) In the constructed conversation that followed, phrases such as "You are right in this sense," "but not your perspective either, my dear Meyer," "You are unjust like—a man! I won't listen to you!," "which you suggest," "as you . . . describe" (I, 222–24) identify his positions and provide the impetus for the articulation of her own.

The dialogues with Meyer were even more engaging when the topic was politics. Well aware of his royalist leanings, she consciously used his views as a foil for her own. A letter from 17 December 1792 offers a model of her form (I, 277–80). Through quotes from Meyer's correspondence, she established in the middle section of the letter his antipathy to events in Mainz. But after restating her knowledge that "[y]ou hold us *en horreur*" (Sie uns *en horreur* haben), she countered by asking where he had found "the right to mock us" (das Recht zu spotten). After once again taking his position into account, she stated her own, asking if he could "in all seriousness laugh when the poor peasant, who has given the sweat of his brow three days out of four for his masters . . . feels that he could be, that he should be better off" (im Ernst darüber lachen, wenn der arme Bauer, der drey Tage von vieren für seine Herrschaften den Schweiß seines Angesichts vergießt . . . fühlt, ihm könte, ihm solte beßer seyn). To this she added: "We start from this simple perspective" (Von diesem einfachen Gesichtspunkt gehn wir aus). The communal "we" included not only others already sympathetic to the Revolution but, by insinuating the impossibility of disagreement, her partner in the epistolary conversation as well. It also performed the equally important, if more subtle, task of assuring herself and her reader that she too was involved in cultural debates. This passage on politics was preceded by a conversation on Meyer's health and succeeded by a long section on Therese Forster, both of which were constructed to include the equally valid viewpoints of reader and writer.

The dialogic is thus one of the principal structuring elements in her correspondence; and its importance to her reached beyond its centrality in her letters to function as the general principle of meaningful human interaction. As her letters indicate, what she valued was not necessarily a frictionless intersubjectivity; Olympian harmony was not her goal. Her typical construction of an epistolary partner as antagonist reflects her attitude toward human relations in general. As she rather humorously lamented to Meyer soon after arriving in Mainz and before she had become a part of the Forster circle, she was getting fat, "because I am not allowed to get upset and quarrel" (weil ich mich nicht ärgern und zanken darf, I, 255). Her challenge in 1799 to a friend to come to Jena and discuss his differences with the group, "No revolution without factions" (Keine Revoluzion ohne Faction, I, 581), summarized her view of positive and purposeful human relations. Even in her literary criticism she abided by this principle; as Dischner has written, she formulated her opinions not to soothe, but to provoke argument (179). "Romantic sociability," as she practiced it in her life and writing, thus implied a dialogic relationship between individuals that could and should continue without the closure of a synthesis.[22]

Because Schlegel-Schelling wrote in a medium that critics traditionally have not credited with the prestige of other forms of writing, most have seen her importance for romanticism in what she transmitted to the men of that movement through the power of her personality. As might be expected, those critics who are able to appreciate the modernity and radicality of the Jena group are the ones most inclined to value that influence.[23] And quite simply, the revolutionary consciousness on which the circle's aspirations were based is impossible to imagine without Schlegel-Schelling, for it was through her that its members came into contact with the ideals of the French Revolution.[24] Even the redirection of Friedrich Schlegel's attention from ancient literature to the art of his own generation can be traced to their conversations in Lucka and the stimulation of her "brilliant insights into contemporary German poetry" (Eichner, 16). But she should be acknowledged as more than just an important influence on the male romantics. The evidence speaks for recognizing her as one of the original thinkers of the movement, as the one who not only infused it with the spirit of revolution but also the one who demonstrated in her own way the possibility of an egalitarian art which could serve as an incentive for social change. Further, she helped shape the romantic program to value one's own life and the dialogic communication through which it was developed as the essence of that art.

Without Schlegel-Schelling, there would have been no Jena circle, or a very different one, and romantic aesthetics and ethics would have taken another form. When she demonstrated through her letters that life with its infinite variety could and should be the subject of art, that an individual life as lived—not as imagined or idealized—could be its core, she was helping to revise long-entrenched concepts, as well as providing the movement with an impulse toward autobiographical art.[25] To be sure, without the Jena group she would have lacked a forum for her ideas, but the very existence of that forum was in part her own making: it was she who helped to create the circle according to what she thought important for her self and for society.

Not only did Schlegel-Schelling have a major role in defining the cultural revolution we call romanticism and its hopes for a new world order, she continued even after the demise of the circle to believe in the revolutionary powers of art. When others became disillusioned with political events and the inevitable rift between their ideals and empirical reality, they retreated to religion or mysticism, or to a preoccupation with an inner life. She, however, still considered herself in 1803 part of a literary and cultural revolution that was as "strong and fermenting" (stark und gährend) as the "tempests of a great revolution" (Stürme einer großen Revolution) in which she had earlier been involved (II, 356). The reviews she began writing in 1805—no longer anonymously—also attested to her continuing conviction; as Dischner has stated, those reviews were "masterpieces of literary polemics, full of romantic irony, in the tradition of the Jena group in its heyday" (160). Although she knew the Jena group could not be reconstituted, she continued even in 1808 to hope for the formation of a different romantic circle (II, 536) and frequently reminisced about her time in Jena. Shortly before her death, for example, she caustically remarked that Friedrich Schlegel—who along with Dorothea Veit had converted to Catholicism—was now "a fat and indolent voluptuary, like a monk" and then added with a hint of melancholy, "I knew them all in their innocence, in their best times" (II, 556).

To be sure, Schlegel-Schelling was not happy with her own world, but she was not trying to transcend it; she did not try to substitute for it a more spiritual realm, as did many others in the movement. Her choice was to work for a better future by doing her part to make her own present worthwhile. Her goal was not just the overthrow of a present system—in her case the bourgeois—but a better way of living than had yet been realized. If there is a utopian aspect to her thinking, it has to do with a very real human community of the future. Precisely that focus links her to much of contemporary feminist thinking, to its issues, its aesthetics, and its ethics. In part because hers was not a woman-centered kind of thinking and because she did not consciously work to advance the cause of women, she has attracted less attention from feminist critics than others among the romantic women. Her focus instead was to escape entrapment in the sphere traditionally allotted to her sex—to avoid letting "the purpose of a woman" (der Zweck des Weibes) become for her the "central purpose of a human being" (Hauptzweck des Menschen, I, 140). This does not mean, however, that she was trying to escape women's "sphere." Instead, her intent throughout most of her life was to combine what her society preferred to separate, to be a wife and mother as well as an active intellectual. Unfortunately she was not always charitable toward those women who did not share her goal.[26] Perhaps because of her experiences in Mainz, she did not distinguish between male and female emancipation, and instead believed in the dream of equality and freedom for all. And although she found a way to shape her own existence in conscious opposition to what she called her more conventional sister's "dream of eternal dependence" (Traum ewiger Anhänglichkeit, I, 214), she remained throughout her life sensitive to the problems encountered by other women, protesting in her own way against the restrictions her society placed on women's activities. From her blunt assessment as a young girl that intelligence was not valued in a woman (I, 55) to her resigning letters from Clausthal with their frequent images of the walls enclosing her,[27] to her wry comments from Munich, gender was in fact a major subtext throughout her writing. When she wrote from prison, "I laugh at the Greats and despise them, while bowing low before them" ([I]ch lache die Großen aus, und verachte sie, wenn ich tief vor ihnen supplicire, I, 293), she was defining the only way she had found to make herself heard in a patriarchal society. There could hardly be a more conscious statement of subversive intent.

Both the Schlegels and Schelling understood her challenge to bourgeois values in the context of overcoming sex-role divisions and used the language of androgyny to describe her.[28] Friedrich Schlegel referred to her in a letter as "independent Diotima" (selbstständige Diotima, I, 375) and found inspiration in her being for his essay "Über die Diotima" (I, 375), where he formulated his belief that "only independent femininity, only gentle masculinity" (nur selbständige Weiblichkeit, nur sanfte Männlichkeit) could be declared good and beautiful (*Kritische Ausgabe* I, 93). After her death Schelling described her as "this unique woman with a masculine greatness of soul, with the sharpest of intellects combined with the gentleness of the most feminine, most tender, most loving heart" (dieses seltne Weib von männlicher Seelengröße, von dem schärfsten Geist, mit der Weichheit des weiblichsten, zartesten, liebevollsten Herzens vereinigt, II, 578). They applauded her precisely because they *believed* she had combined the qualities their polarized society traditionally associated with masculinity *or* femininity. In others, however, her challenge to gender roles aroused great animosity. Kleßmann quotes the many epithets hurled at her from others associated with the romantic movement, especially from those in Schiller's circle, such as "Dame Lucifer" and the "Evil one" (Übel, 250–58). The antagonism exhibited by many with whom she came into contact is summarized by the remarks of an acquaintance in Würzburg: "The fool! It would be more useful for her if she knew how to cook a good soup!" (Die Thörin! Es wäre zweckmäßiger für ihre Lage, wenn sie wüßte, wie man eine gute Suppe kocht, II, 647). As adjectives such as the derisively intended "androgynous" that Tieck applied to her also demonstrate (I, 747), these criticisms were leveled at her largely because she challenged traditional structures of gender.

Even her much vaunted wit was frequently grounded in her awareness of, and antagonism toward, polarized sex-roles. In her early letters her humor was often self-deprecatory, chiding her sister, for example, for not answering such important questions as "should I have my white dresses ironed or not" (soll ich meine weißen Kleider plätten laßen, oder nicht, I, 158). But later as she became more confident of herself and of her place in the world, she directed her ironic wit at the activities of the well-known men with whom she came into contact, mocking a quarrel between the writers G. A. Bürger and F. Bouterwek, for example, as "noble deeds" (I, 254). And when her humor was not directly gender-related, it was often used to subvert patriarchal values. From Mainz she promised friends that during her upcoming visit she would not mention politics, then added as if in passing that her daughter was in the habit of shouting "vive la nation" (I, 281).

Although she did not have a sense of working together with and for women, her accomplishments were clearly the result of an attempt to created her own female space. And because she found a way to go beyond patriarchal definitions and models in her life and in her writing, she did help the cause of women, expanding their opportunities in both the social and literary worlds. She should even be recognized for her contribution in expanding the boundaries of autobiographical expression, for through her own letters she helped prove that women's epistolary writing need not be limited to the revelation of a "private self."[29] In many ways then, her concerns demonstrate her importance for the contemporary women's movement. Her belief in the political impact of personal actions, her embrace of diversity, and her rejection of a dualistic world view as well as of a linear direction to personal history (I, 214) all parallel concerns of contemporary feminism. In addition, other meaningful connections can be established through her art form and concern with ethics. If Christa Wolf is one of the clearest contemporary voices speaking for the same kind of reader involvement in literature that Schlegel-Schelling sought, it is in Carol Gilligan's work on feminist ethics where thematic parallels can be discerned. Many of the issues Schlegel-Schelling was concerned with—for example, her stress on the importance of relationships, her emphasis on process, her desire for a public airing of issues, and her concern with non-hierarchical communication—have been identified by Gilligan as components of feminist practice and as important concepts in women's moral development.

Gilligan's argument in *In a Different Voice,* that moral decisions based on a sense of shared responsibility demonstrate not a lower level of moral development, but merely a different one from the reasoning processes based on abstractions, helps to link Schlegel-Schelling to modern theory and also to find new perspectives from which to affirm her contributions. In her latest book *Mapping the Moral Domain,* Gilligan broadens her discussion to include the importance of communication for individual development, specifically the essential role of conversation. And as with Schlegel-Schelling, the kind of individual development she is interested in, it should be emphasized, retains an emphasis on relationships and has very little in common with the eccentric individualism often associated with romanticism. In concluding that our knowledge of ourselves and our sense of responsibility for our own lives, for others, and even for the world all come through relationships and are developed through communication, Gilligan is defining a position that Schlegel-Schelling affirmed with her life and her letters almost two centuries ago. Her writing demonstrated to the Jena romantics and still evidences to her readers today her belief that non-hierarchical communication between human beings, a process she once associated with "truth" (Wahrheit), can be a worthy subject for art, containing as it does all the "irresistible magic" (unwiederstehlichen Zauber) necessary for personal development and the consequent creation of a better world (I, 184).

7

Marriage by the Book:
Matrimony, Divorce, and Single Life
in Therese Huber's Life and Works

Jeannine Blackwell

I felt a pang in my heart—and became a bride.

Ich fühlte einen Stich in's Herz—und ward Braut.[1]

Therese Huber (1764–1829), a woman of great intelligence, private irony, irascible moods and disturbing passions, is a textbook example of the double standard in literary judgment and moral censure in the Age of Goethe. She stands between the old age of the sentimental ideal of mild, innocent womanhood and the brave new world of emancipated flesh: both politically, as a sometime proponent of the French Revolution, and emotionally, as a woman who had both a marriage of convenience and a love match. She was maligned by the enlightened paternalism of Schiller and Goethe as well as by the romantic sensualists, the Schlegels. The cause of their censure was her separation from Georg Forster, scientist and world traveler. She came of age as an unhappily married woman in late 1793, when she started divorce proceedings; they ended uncompleted at his death in Paris in early 1794. That same year, 1794, the *Allgemeines Preussisches Landrecht,* the civil code that eventually dominated most of Germany, went into effect. It made marriage a civil bureaucratic procedure, in addition to its being a traditional religious sacrament. The law required registration of all marriages with the state.[2] The new law also simplified civil divorce procedures, and took divorce out of the hands of the church. The decade of the 1790s even brought legal handbooks on divorce, as well as a heated discussion of the love match, sensual passion, and woman's true calling as wife and mother.[3] As participant and commentator, Therese Huber sheds light on the equivocal response of German women to their shifting dependencies between the patriarchal family and the state. This is particularly the case in her stories of the arranged marriage or love match gone awry.

Most literary historians of the period from 1770 to 1820 have considered the love match in the novel—particularly love across class, religious, or racial boundaries—to be a device for depicting social criticism or personal liberation from private-sphere oppression. The heroine reading *La nouvelle Héloïse* has been shorthand for this model of individualized protest in many women's novels; this tableau has also carried a second code, and that is the dangers of becoming the sexual prey of scoundrels who use the heroine's own sensuality against her, being "seduced" via the text. Whether she succumbs to a bad love match (with an tragic non-marital ending) or achieves a good one (reconciliation with some part of a restored family), we do not see the actions of the state in the novel at all—except in the veiled form of divorce proceedings.

I argue here that these two contradictory phenomena in the marital state of the 1790s go hand in hand: first, a secularized and centralized state bureaucracy and second, a passionate romantic love culminating in a romance-based marriage. I connect these two not merely by their chronological simultaneity, although the love match does begin to appear with greater frequency from the 1790s onward in Germany, when secular governmental control of marriage and divorce was instituted in France, England, and several of the German states. I see these two developments as mutually supportive social systems, in which control over women shifts from home and church to the state. The love match can be seen as bureaucratized upward mobility—a mobility which separates the young woman from her family and patrilineal class/estate, and causes her to shift her first allegiance to her husband and his class, to the exclusion of her own family, and to give her second allegiance to the state that condones and authorizes her love match (sometimes against familial wishes). Although this certainly has a liberating potential for the love match, as it chafes under the bonds of the patriarchal family, the state-regulated love match undermines its radical thrust toward personal liberation. The love match in effect makes patriots of women—or, as Johnnie Tillmon has described the American welfare system (a further development of women's dependency on the state in the twentieth century), women dependent on state welfare "exchange a man for The Man."[4] One might derive protection and support from the state, but only in exchange for ward-like loyalty and political passivity.

In novels of the late eighteenth century, we can sense some of the differences between the arranged marriage/mixed negotiation model, and the love match. We find significant shifts beyond the well-known personal and economic issues, such as dowry vs. lack thereof, the nature of contractual agreement, the identity of contract signers—fathers/families vs. individuals—, urban vs. rural settings, the age difference between partners, etc. I list below four shifts which I find occur more frequently than the previously mentioned ones: education, previous erotic exposure, plus her age at marriage, and the responsibility for failure of the marriage.

Negotiated Marriage	*Love Match*

1. Education:

Young girl is trained to run household, is sheltered, ignorant, her naiveté is source of appeal.	She is trained by reading books and by supportive relatives, and travels so she can participate in "male" conversations, ready for mixed society. She has experience in the world; her social grace is a source of appeal.

2. Previous erotic exposure:

None condoned, or it is seen as irrelevant to the marriage issue, unless pregnancy was involved.	There is limited exposure to eroticism in derivative forms such as *La nouvelle Heloïse, Manon Lescaut, La Vie de Marianne,* and German adaptations of these and similar works. This exposure better prepares her for emotional and sexual *HINGABE,* a kind of surrender that is a precarious balance of passivity and sensual receptivity. This passive passion is not full-blown active sensuality.

3. Her age: 15 or 16

She is older (18/19) to allow time for her education in passive passion.

4. Responsibility for failure:

Parents; husband/man   Wife/woman

Reasons for failure:

financial irregularities, usually having to do with loss of dowry to brother (career, education, debts) or father (gambling, drinking, debts). The girl loses her public reputation.	failure in personal traits of beauty, personal charm, gentleness, grace, social skills, finances, housekeeping, childbearing. Her charms are learned in books: Knigge, Schiller, La Roche, etc.
	husband/man frivolous loss of fortune, coldness or cruelty toward wife, desertion, keeping mistress, etc.

Women, in this review of the late eighteenth century German novel, are responsible for striking the precarious balance between erotic self-consciousness and the purity of innocence, while displaying themselves for examination as possible love match material. This shift in responsibility is an interesting one for the development of the *Frauenroman,* because it yields a more complex character than the long-suffering victim of unhappy arrangements in the simpler *Entsagungsroman* or novel of resignation, such as *Elise oder das Weib wie es sein sollte* (Elise or Woman as she ought to be). It is problematic, however, that much of women's literature has remained at this stage of development ever since— the heroine coming to terms with her own naiveté and the resulting bad romantic decision. In the catalogue given above, I have stressed that spontaneous eroticism, preparatory for the love match, is released by the literary model—or at least so it was perceived by several generations of moralists and women authors, who decried novels while writing them. I call this education toward controlled eroticism "marriage by the book," and it might explain the otherwise surprising lack of state censorship of women's reading material at the turn of the century, for controlled erotic fantasy on the part of middle class females was not at all in contradiction to the needs of the state. It might explain as well why fathers and ministers, the representatives of the patriarchal family and church, *did* object so vehemently to this material, and why they consistently associated it with the French and with court/ aristocratic life, rather than with a burgeoning book industry: it was indeed associated with emerging nation-state power, of which the best examples were still the established monarchies.

Therese Huber was one of the writers who showed most consistently in her *oeuvre* the disastrous yet informing effects of those hothouse erotic novels by Rousseau, the Marquis de Sade, and Marivaux. She is the only late eighteenth century female author I have encountered who actually cites de Sade's erotic novels. She shows in both her texts and her life the dangerous sides of learning "marriage by the book," and of learning the lessons too well. I will recapitulate the events in her life that made her an all-too-public model of the book-bred woman, who was forced by her notoriety into self-chosen obscurity, literary oblivion, and the protection of the state.[5]

In the very gossip-prone university city of Göttingen, where her father, Christian Gottlob Heyne, was a renowned professor, Therese was separated from peers and the community by her mother, who was suffering from some form of mental instability and who was alleged to have had several adulterous liaisons. Therese later described herself as a neglected child, and considered herself to be illegitimate, although she was born in wedlock. She received a haphazard education by listening to her father and his colleagues discussing intellectual matters, and was sent to boarding school for two years when her father remarried. Thus, the sentimental ideal set for a Sternheimian education—like that of La Roche's heroine Sophie who received a consistent training in the "feminine arts," was helped by a supportive set of educating males and a childhood maternal behavioral ideal type—was sorely lacking in Therese's family. Moreover, her family's transgression of the line between private and public sphere, as they became both famous and infamous in Göttingen, put her own reputation in jeopardy.

Although surrounded by erstwhile suitors in Göttingen who fit more closely the model of the sensitive sentimental ideal, Therese at nineteen chose to marry her father's friend and colleague, the natural scientist Georg Forster, a renowned world traveler who was thirty years old. It was not a love match and she was physically repulsed by Forster, yet she was attracted by his intellect. She was in love with a much younger man, an assistant to her father. Forster, a well-respected public figure with a reputation for kindness and intelligence, appeared to be different in his private life. At least according to letters from Caroline Schlegel, Forster forced sexual intercourse on his wife. On their return to Göttingen after two years in Vilna, Poland, Forster encouraged Therese to reestablish her friendship with her earlier love, F. W. Meyer, and suggested an intimate friendship between the three of them. Therese refused, and was relieved when they moved to

Mainz in 1788. There, too, the Forsters became involved with a mutual close friend, the diplomat, dramatist, and critic Ludwig Ferdinand Huber. Therese and L. F. Huber began an affair, and she asserted later in life that the last child born during her marriage to Forster was actually fathered by Huber. Therese wanted out of the marriage, but Forster again proposed a ménage-à-trois. During these hectic years, Caroline Michaelis Böhmer (later Schlegel-Schelling), Therese's childhood friend, moved into their home, and according to Therese had an affair with Georg. Georg Forster's heroic public reputation was contradicted by his private life, but Therese bore the brunt of censure for deserting him in his political crisis.

Political events in Mainz converged with the disruption of their marriage from 1790–1793, and the debts which Georg had incurred—unknown to Therese until this time—came to light. Economic, political, and sexual crises brought about their separation, as Georg left for Paris as the representative of the Republic in Mainz, while Mainz was retaken by the Prussian-supported anti-revolutionary forces, and Ludwig's collaboration with the Forsters jeopardized his position as a Prussian official. In effect, Georg left Therese with the debts and the children in a volatile and dangerous political situation. The family fled for Switzerland with the support of Huber in 1793, and they lived in neighboring towns to avoid gossip. They saw the ailing Georg again in a border town in late 1793; divorce proceedings began, but were not completed when Georg died in January 1794. Therese was condemned by many German intellectuals for having deserted Germany's "only" revolutionary and letting him die a lonely death in Paris. To the outrage and disapproval of the entire literary community in Germany, Therese married Ludwig in April 1794. Derogatory remarks came from both elite literary camps. Goethe, Schiller, and the Heyne family were shocked at the impropriety of her adultery and her public rejection of the marriage; the Schlegels as well as others were outraged at the desertion of the political radical for what seemed to them the comforts of bourgeois domesticity with a civil servant, who was also extremely critical of their writing. The Hubers lived in Swiss exile in poverty until 1798.

Because of this notoriety, and to support her family, Therese wrote anonymously or under her husband's name until 1819—that is, until all her children were successfully established in vocations or were married. Still today it is almost impossible to determine which of the Hubers wrote which essays, but all the prose fiction under his name is apparently hers. Even after his death in 1804, she continued to publish under his name, and supported her four surviving children alone for the next twenty-five years. Beginning in 1807 she was a regular contributor to the Cotta publishing industry in Stuttgart, and was installed in 1816 as the editor of Cotta's *Morgenblatt für die gebildeten Stände,* one of the most influential daily newspapers in Germany, which treated topics of artistic, political, and intellectual interest. She was, however, anonymous as editor, had no contract, and Cotta's name appeared on the masthead. Her salary was low; her deceased husband, who had also been the editor of a Cotta daily paper, had made almost twice as much as she—feminist scholars will appreciate the irony that she made only 57 per cent of his salary.

Given these periods of publicly censurable activity in Therese Huber's life, her rigorously defended anonymity suggests neither timidity nor a stylized sentimental pose. Therese tried to maintain propriety as best she could to keep gossip at bay—so that she would not jeopardize her daughters' chances for marriage. But what she perceived as her own faulty training and miseducation as a girl had already put her beyond the pale. She had already violated the invisible line of passivity in passion of the love match. Not *Hingabe* (surrender), but active sexual desire and concrete, rather than *literary,* erotic experience made her a warning example for others. By sheer determination, she was able to support her family and find jobs for her son (with Cotta) and one daughter (as a governess), and arrange marriages for the two others.

She was grateful to the Swiss state that gave her a brief refuge in 1793 in exchange for promises of political harmlessness, grateful to the Prussian government that allowed her to divorce Forster, grateful to the Swiss canton that approved her second marriage (although it required a testimony of agreement from Huber's father before the ceremony), grateful to the state that provided a pension for the education of Forster's children (since he was a University professor, and therefore a state official) and for her own pension as the widow of the state official Huber. Therese Huber was able to survive financially when no funds came from the families of Heyne, Forster, or Huber. Politically, she became "a harmless democrat," as Ludwig wrote to his father. Her lack of public criticism of the state after the Revolutionary period, I maintain, is *not* like the characteristic disillusionment of the German intelligentsia with the Terror and with a bourgeois revolution that threatened to become more than that. Rather, I see that

Therese Huber's personal life as a disenfranchised and disinherited woman reflected a shift in allegiances. Her life epitomizes the radical shift to the love match and its dangers, and the concomitant obligation to the state which makes individual mobility feasible.

Therese Huber's prolific writings—more than fifty short stories and novels—show the strain of the times, as the Napoleonic era and German nationalism dampened many burning questions; they reveal her real distress at the miseducation she received, and a certain political and emotional schizophrenia, all of which I find understandable under the circumstances of her notoriety.

I will not discuss here *Die Familie Seldorf* (1795–96), Huber's best known and most frequently analyzed work, a novel of the French Revolution in which sweet, innocent Sara Seldorf becomes an unwed mother and is driven to join the Revolution in search of the child's father.[6] Instead I center on the stories that directly address love, matrimony, and divorce: *Luise. Ein Beitrag zur Geschichte der Konvenienz* (1796), "Die Frau von vierzig Jahren" (1800), "Eine Ehestandsgeschichte" (1804), "Die ungleiche Heirath" (1820), and *Die Ehelosen* (1829).[7] The framing questions will be: what happens to all the women who are miseducated and cross the line of passive *Hingabe?* What is the fate of those who cannot, even with the best of intentions, keep eroticism at the literary level? What are ugly women, older women, women in unhappy marriages of convenience, to do with either their passive passion or their active sensuality? Do not expect from Therese Huber radical answers to these questions. But by their very formulation in her fiction, she, along with a few others like Isabella von Wallenrodt, Caroline Auguste Fischer, or Sophie Mereau, broke the taboo against imagining the failure of *Hingabe* for the sympathetic heroine, and thus called into question the validity of the love match as a totally liberating experience. Huber presents, for example, a case study of a woman gone mad in an abusive marriage of convenience, an emotionally deprived but beautiful older woman falling in love with her seventeen-year-old foster son, adultery narrated by a grandmother to her family, and a respected mother who had children out of wedlock. These literary countermodels to the successful sentimental heroine make use of the commonplace resolutions of sentimentality and even of the *Entsagungsroman,* but by the very tension of presenting "failed" women as positive figures, they undermine the universal validity of *Hingabe* as a moment of liberation for women. In addition, Huber problematizes *Hingabe*

by positioning these women in the underrepresented locales of women's work and passions: the kitchen, the nursery, in communal
living situations, and of course, in America.

Luise: The Madwoman in the Pantry

Already in the subtitle of this novel Huber indicates its analytical, rather than affective purpose: *Contribution to the History
of Marriage of Convenience.* The fictive introduction by a male editor—in its cautious belittling of Luise's case, her death, and the
female narrator's identification with and sympathy for Luise—
provides an almost clinically cool containment of a moving
tragedy.[8] Luise's story is similar to that of Elise's in *Elise oder das
Weib sie es sein sollte* by Caroline von Wobeser (1795). A naive and
self-sacrificing girl is married with her reluctant consent, but under family circumstances beyond her control, to an irresponsible,
volatile, and often violent military officer who soon lands them in
a financially and emotionally unstable household. In Luise's case,
as in many a *Frauenroman* tragedy, her dowry has been sacrificed
for the good of her brothers, and so she must marry quickly, be-
neath her station, or to a man of unsavory character. So the marriage she enters is superficially based on her husband's pursuit of
her in a mimicry of courtship, but is actually based on the older
principles of class standing and income. He and her family wran-
gle constantly about finances, loans, furnishing the household, and
her support when she is mentally deranged or physically ill. Eventually she acknowledges that neither her brothers nor her husband are dependable sources of income for herself and her
daughter, and she turns to the state, to the prince whom her deceased father had served. He gives her a marriage gift as well as a
yearly pension. The author stresses that this is a kind of liberation money that most women would use to escape a destructive,
oppressive life. Luise, however, not only gives the cash to her husband, but also transfers her pension to his permanent guardianship, trying ineffectively to buy his affection.

Rather than responding with noble resignation that is then
rewarded with a triumphant deathbed scene, as does Elisa, Luise
is overcome with massive depression, chronic respiratory and
other health problems, and hallucinations. The female stasis that
might be regarded in some *Frauenromane* as noble is portrayed
here as pathological *and* ineffective in accomplishing its end—

manipulation of the family for self-preservation. Noble self-sacrifice, naiveté, fragile health, submission to one's husband—characteristics of the sympathetic sentimental heroine—are pushed to pathological extremes, and she is indeed temporarily "insane," if a total absence of identity and self-worth is insane. Luise is kept captive as mentally deranged because she is unwanted by both her husband and her family. Significantly enough she is kept in the pantry/servant's room next to the kitchen, and is tended by coarse, rowdy, drunken servants. From this vantage point, she experiences hunger and abuse beyond the psychological suffering she has known before, witnesses the excesses of the "big house" from the bottom, and is not able to make the transition back to refined society and "mental health." She views the fundament on which the well-appointed, gracious table of her mother and brothers is built; the roughness of her husband's tastes is almost refreshing in comparison to the old patriarchal household, which she has experienced from the backstairs. Yet even after a partial recovery, her husband Blachfeld still rejects her and their daughter, to her great sadness, and she gradually slips into a deeper depression.

The open ending of this novel is uncharacteristic of the *Frauenroman,* which often imposes an artificial harmonious or sweetly resigned resolution to the heroine's problems. Here, the narrated time of Luise's story overtakes the narrative frame of the sympathetic female narrator: the ending is not told from the post-mortem perspective but from a narrative present. The immediacy of this opening is structurally formulated in a question in the last paragraph in the text, to which an emphatically negative, though speculative answer is given. The answer reaches out, however, into the undetermined future of Luise's daughter:

> Is hope still speaking in her tired heart, at the moment when she yearns longingly for health and fears the moment that Blachfeld must admit to himself, "The time for easing her pain has passed; the woman to whom I promised happiness at my side had to sink forsaken into her grave to find again the peace I had robbed from her." No! The black melancholy surrounding her mind, the fire that slowly dries her blood cannot postpone for long the time when every kind of succour will be too late. May all the tenderness, all the care, all the tolerance that Blachfeld denied his unhappy wife converge on his child, whom she raised to love and honor him!

> Ist noch Hoffnung, die in ihrem müden Herzen spricht, wenn sie wehmütig nach der Gesundheit sich sehnt, und den Augenblick

fürchtet, wo Blachfeld sich sagen müsste: "Die Zeit, ihr Unglück zu lindern, ist vorüber; der ich an meiner Seite Glück versprach, die musste einsam in das Grab sinken; um den Frieden wiederzufinden, den ich ihr raubte?" Nein! Die schwarze Schwermuth, die ihren Geist umhüllt, die Glut, die langsam ihr Blut auftrocknet, scheint den Zeitpunkt nicht weit hinauszuschieben, wo jede freundliche Rettung zu spät kommt. Möge dann alle Zärtlichkeit, alle Nachsicht, alle Duldung, die Blachfeld seinem unglücklichen Weibe versagte, sich auf sein Kind vereinen, dass sie, ihn zu lieben und zu ehren, erzieht! (*Luise,* 224)

The author sets her hopes upon a slender reed here—the very man who has helped destroy the heroine. The open ending makes problematic Luise's inculcated childrearing practices of honoring the father, no matter what the consequences. The absence of resolution forces readers to supply their own implausible happy endings, one of which obviously would be liberation through divorce, although Luise had rejected that earlier, as well as every other mechanism, in her stubborn insistence on retaining the world of the fathers.

A Woman of Forty: Sex in the Nursery

After thirty, the passions are no longer a game, no longer a summer shower followed by shining blue skies. They are autumn gales that shake the last leaves from the twigs, batter to bits the last blooms, and the bleached out sun fights in vain to revive Nature as she stiffens and dies.

Nach dem dreissigsten Jahre sind die Leidenschaften nicht mehr Spiel, nicht mehr Sommergewitter, nach welchen der Himmel schöner lacht. Sie sind Orkane im Spätjahr, schütteln gewaltig die letzten Blätter von den Zweigen, zerschlagen die letzten Blumen, und die gebleichte Sonne kämpft fortan vergebens, der erstarrenden Natur aufzuhelfen. (*Vierzig,* 181)

The painful, embarrassing, and potentially scandalous self-narration of the life of forty-year-old Amalie von Helm was written when Therese was 36, remarried, and the mother of two daughters in their teens. Set at the birth of her first grandchild and located in her daughter-in-law's childbed recovery room, Amalie's narration is told, orally and in a written missive, to her stepson, his wife with child at her breast, and an old admirer who still causes the grandmother to blush. Already at the outset this story relocates the sentimental center. Not the nubile girl, nor the young nursing mother, but rather the older woman is the subject and object of narration: a pseudo-warning example of the woman who has strayed from her true vocation as wife and mother. The narrative is told in three parts on different evenings, and halted each time by the overly intense emotion of Amalie, the narrator. The breaks, discussed below, are indicated by the following paragraphs:

A spoiled vain young girl, miseducated by her recently ennobled father to marry above her station, Amalie is later educated by the student Feldberg, who regards himself as her Pygmalion; they fall secretly in love, but Amalie is driven by egotism to marry the much older aristocratic minister von Helm, a widower with two children. Haughty relatives who disapprove of this *nou-velle riche* take away the two children, and the customs of high society—that she give her own child to a wetnurse—keep her from becoming a good mother herself. This child dies from an overdose of a tranquilizing drug given by the ignorant nurse. In her grief she refuses to take in von Helm's children, yet in casting about for a source of love, she finds a deserted child, the illegitimate daughter of an aristocratic officer. By spoiling the young Christine with praise and inadvertently encouraging her hypocrisy, Amalie contributes to her eventual ruin: Christine runs away to join the opera and dies, an unwed mother, of a miscarriage. Amalie meets and is perversely attracted to Christine's father, a dashing scoundrel and ladies' man who tries to seduce her by giving her de Sade and Rousseau novels to read. After a great struggle, and learning a lot from him, Amalie ends the relationship on her stepdaughter Julie's wedding day.

Amalie is still erotically vulnerable, even after this set of literary lessons. At a spa she meets the seventeen-year-old Victor, whose mother has died in her arms. Her maternal and sensual attraction to him drives her to accept him as a foster son. Years later she is shocked and disgusted to discover that she feels jealousy, erotic love, and envy as he tells her of his first sexual encounter with a peasant girl, and again when he seeks a bride. In the final erotic confrontation, she requires and forbids him to call her his mother, and he leaves to join the American Revolution, where he dies in battle.

After von Helm's death, Amalie finds an end to her destructive emotions in resignation and acceptance of her role as belated mother to Karl von Helm and his wife Gertrude, and as grandmother, through which she hopes to achieve equanimity and peace. To maintain that peace, she refuses the belated marriage proposal of her first love, Feldberg, who is present as a family friend for the birth of the child.

Amalie, then, misunderstands her role as daughter (her recent nobility is a detraction rather than asset), first love (she provokes Feldberg with jealousy), second mother (she raises "Rabenkinder" instead of the son and daughter that were her real responsibility), and wife (she falls in love outside the bounds of marriage). Although her figure is cloaked in the language of the sympathetic heroine—Karl, Gertrude, and Feldberg still love, honor and thank her—there is a definite tension between the sentimental ideal and what this woman actually does to herself and to others. Her type is well known to scholars of the *Frauenroman* as the villainous female figure: the unloving mother who refuses to nurse, the vindictive new wife who tries to spite her higher class in-laws, and the married woman who trifles with men's emotions.

Narrative breaks are the only mechanism by which the villain becomes the narrator/heroine. At the first break, Huber has the broken and ashamed grandmother leave the room overcome by emotion, and write the rest of the story by hand to be read aloud by the group. By removing herself at this narrative highpoint, she forces the family to recreate the story of her recovery and reintegration into the family circle, and removes herself from public view as an object of horror, pity, or disgust. Her absence is similar, to my mind, to Huber's own anonymity, which forces the reader to concentrate not on her notoriety, but on the story itself. The next break is initiated when Amalie interrupts the reading of her own written document with her reappearance in the nursery, ready to take up the present. Straightforward, she happily puts the past behind, refuses marriage to Feldberg, and settles into grandmotherly bliss. This drastic ending, where real and understandable emotions are violently bent into proper sentimental shapes at the end of the story, is not a real solution to her sensual desire; she simply denies herself a perfectly virtuous pleasure, and feels herself unworthy of her good children until she leaves sensuality behind. The only trace of her sensual transgression of boundaries is her constant blushing, which is both the sentimental code for continued youthful beauty and innocence, as well as for forbidden and repressed erotic desire. She is restored to ignorance/innocence by the end of the tale.

Yet in her erotically active stage, Amalie is also allowed editorializing comments on the state of women and their passions. The motto of this section, on the power of passions after thirty, is an explanation of Amalie's emotions after the death of Victor, her foster son, in the American Revolutionary War, and is one of the few personalized statements on destructive passion in women's literature from this period. More analytical is a second comment from Amalie to her stepson on the problems of marital economy:

> And yet—what usually determines our fate in marriage? The wisdom of our parents? That surely cannot move our hearts. Reason? What a sad matchmaker, when it is a question of joining two people in a union that is so serious, so earnest, so lasting that only love, which endures all things, can support it! So is it passion, then? And what happens when the flame dies, as die it must, because it burns from mortal flesh?—What can protect and save us, we who must place not only all our hopes, but our whole worth in this relationship? The unhappy husband can still be a friend, a citizen—even a father. We are nothing, if we are not happy wives: self-esteem, courage, tolerance—it all disappears and we sink into degradation, or else fight the destructive fight between conscience and heart.

> Doch, was entscheidet denn gewöhnlich unser Loos in der Ehe?— Unsrer Eltern Weisheit? Die kann unser Herz nicht bedenken. Vernunft? Welcher traurige Wahlmann, wo es darauf ankommt, zwei Menschen zu einem Verhältnisse zu vereinen, welches so schwer, so ernst, so dauernd ist, dass nur die Liebe, die alles trägt, es ertragen kann! Also Leidenschaft? Und wenn die Flamme verlöscht, wie sie verlöschen muss, weil sie aus irdischem Stoff entbrannt?—Was soll uns aber schützen, retten, uns die wir in diesem Verhältniss nicht nur unser Glück allein, sondern unsern ganzen Werth niederlegen mussten? Der unglückliche Gatte kann noch Freund, noch Bürger—sogar Vater könnte er noch sein. Wir sind nichts, wenn wir nicht glückliche Weiber sind: Selbstachtung, Muth, Duldung, alles verschwindet, und wir versinken in Erniedrigung, oder kämpfen den zerstörenden Kampf zwischen Gewissen und Herz. (*Vierzig,* 132)

This profound statement of the dilemma of marriage choices, and the particular quandary of women, whose *Bestimmung* (destiny) is so perilously defined, is immediately diluted in Huber's next sentence, in which she duplicates the *Gelassenheit/Entsagung* (serenity/resignation) model of wifely vocation:

And thus what can save us? Only one thing, my children; only the clear understanding of our duties as wives and mothers in their fullest meaning . . . duties not performed sporadically and in moments of passionate drama, but consistently, with a balanced eye on every step of life's path, not just the heroic, tragic duties alone, but all the trivial concerns of domestic living.

Was soll uns also retten?—Nur eines, meine Kinder; nur deutliche Ansicht unsrer Pflichten als Gattinnen und Mütter im ihrem ganzen Umfang . . . nicht stückweise und in Augenblicken leidenschaftlicher Spannung, sondern zusammenhängend, mit gleicher Aufmerksamkeit auf alle Schritte des Lebensgangs, auch nicht jene heroischen, tragischen Pflichten allein, sondern alle die kleinen Obliegenheiten des häuslichen Beisammenseins. (*Vierzig,* 132–33)

Thus a private solution in the domestic sphere is Amalie's answer to the malaise in gender arrangements. As the tension between critique and feminine acceptance of the status quo is shown here in Huber's editorial comment through Amalie, so too is all of Amalie's story diluted by the pseudo-happy ending with its grandmotherly bliss.[9]

America, Where the Personal is Political

In 1820 Huber again tackles the theme of the sexually active older woman with a younger man in *Die ungleiche Heirath* (The Unequal Marriage), asking how a woman can come to terms with her "unnatural" marriage.

After a quiet, domestic Pietist education at Herrnhut (the rural communal center of German Pietism), gentle Melanie St. Amand, an orphan, is given in negotiated marriage to an older aristocratic man who never awakens her passions and who dies when she is thirty. He leaves behind a nineteen-year-old foster son, Camille, for whom she develops a sensual yet idealistic mother-son love. When he is freezing to death in a snowstorm, she saves his life by holding his body next to hers for hours. For this and several other reasons of finance and propriety, they fall from mutual attraction into marriage. Although she blossoms into mature beauty and has a child, she ages prematurely after the birth; the baby is sickly and dies. Melanie blames herself for the child's ill health, for loving her "son," and for aging so fast. Camille flees, estranged from Melanie, and in the capital city falls in love with a sensuous young widow (based on Caroline Schlegel). He returns and proposes in vague terms that they have a ménage-à-trois, to which Melanie can only respond with a divorce. She begins proceedings, meets a group of like-minded idealists planning to establish a colony in America—Val du Gange, in Illinois on the banks of the Wabash. Here eventually Camille finds his way as a surveyor. Here, too, he rescues Melanie from the torrents of the Wabash. Yet before the final reconciliation can be enacted, the reunited mother/wife and son/husband agree not to reveal their "unnatural" marriage to the community as a whole. Melanie dies, and Camille marries one of the virtuous, hardy young women of the New World community.

In this story, as well as in "Die Frau von Vierzig Jahren" and "Eine Ehestandsgeschichte" ("A Marriage Story" 1804), Huber is at pains to show that such "unnatural" age spreads in marriage are a direct result of the arranged marriage system. Orphan girls and unprovided daughters are most susceptible to these bad arrangements in which love can play no role, yet the overwhelming power of sexuality drives them into love relationships with "forbidden" men—the ones closest to hand. Yet if she rejects these love matches between fairly sympathetic characters, how is marriage then to be organized ideally for Huber? The struggle for a satisfying resolution to all this erotic energy is won in one of two ways: a change in political program that creates free people, who can then make free choices in love, or a new social organization in which worrisome sexuality falls dormant.

For Huber, as for many a utopian thinker from the early nineteenth century, politically oppressive Europe could no longer generate such a radically new system. America was the only chance, both in this story and in "Eine Ehestandsgeschichte." The one concrete hope for eventual happiness and conjugal love for heroines married too young to older men is the New World. In "Ehestandsgeschichte," the heroine Julie is challenged by her true love (who emigrated to Virginia) to leave her unloving husband and Europe behind: "I demand, by all the rights of the oppressed, that you free yourself from your yoke, and put yourself wholly in my hands" (Ich fordre Sie auf, bei allem Rechte der Unterdrückten, befreien Sie sich von Ihrem Joche, und vertrauen Sie sich mir an, 77). He plans to flee with her "to a kinder stretch of heaven," to Virginia (78). Divorce is frankly discussed and even proposed by her husband, who suggests that her beloved move close to their home in

France, yet Julie sacrifices herself by staying with him in his last years. The pair are thus unable to realize the utopian dream.

Melanie is, however, to transform herself in America, as the maternal head of the community. Although the colony in "Die ungleiche Heirat," Val du Gange, does not have a religious basis, Melanie and Father du Gange are honored as its matriarch and patriarch, and much work there is done communally, such as fishing, hunting, and some food preparation. In that sense, it has similarities to the Amana community, some Shakertowns, and Pastor Rapp's Harmony; it is most, however, like New Harmony, Indiana, which was also situated on the banks of the Wabash, a secular communal ideal with equal authority and responsibility between the sexes. Melanie is teacher, midwife, healer, and arbiter of marriages in this earthly paradise. "Whoever joined this colony without bringing along anxious plans or fear of dire necessity, whoever came without bringing a tortured heart full of memories, that person would think that Val du Gange, this quiet little greening world, was the promised land." (Wer ohne ängstliche Pläne, ohne die Sorge, das erste Bedürfniss zu stillen, sich dieser Niederlassung anschloss, ohne ein von Erinnerungen gequältes Herz mitzubringen, musste Val du Gange, diese kleine, stille, grünende Welt für ein gelobtes Land halten, 291). By this geographic and consequent personal transformation, Melanie is able to change her consciousness: she can forget her past sensual self and rechannel her guilt-ridden and futile erotic energy into productive communal work. Camille, regretting his rejection of Melanie, takes years to work his way to join her in America. His rescue of her in America is the counterpiece to her rescue of him in Europe. Melanie ends by blessing her foster son and future daughter-in-law at her deathbed.

The shift in locale—from the stifling hothouse domesticity of the crowded European nursery and servant's kitchen to an outdoors American utopia, where the older woman is able to grieve and to reorganize her grief into work—makes it possible for a woman raised for the limited world of arranged marriage in a strict class structure to become the midwife of a new kind of love match. Camille's and Babette's love is the real and natural love match that is possible, to use Goethe's idyll from *Faust II*, only among free people in a free land; that is, only when free people join together on a basis of political and economic equality.

This parity of partners is a key to Huber's understanding of real marriage and of truly expressive femininity. As she describes it in an essay from 1802, femininity is a balance of nature, art (that is, social training and education), and society (that is, social necessity). Only when these three are in balance, only when women marry not out of financial need, for protection or support, or by social force, is marriage truly ideal.[10] In Huber's stories where divorce plays even a tentative role as an option, it is clear that deeper economic questions preclude it as a real solution to the social strictures of women in Europe. Divorce could work only if one has a safe place to flee to. Barring that, resignation to one's fate is all. In Europe, even the love match is problematic, and I know of no European-based resolution of the love match in Huber's *œuvre*.

So much for the conditions of the model love match. But what about women who want no flames of passion, or women who are ugly, old, unmotherly, unwifely, or who have a different agenda? Is marriage the only *Bestimmung* around for women? As Therese grew older and watched her children's struggles in marriage, she became more convinced that the entire educational model for girls was wrong, since so many girls and women never married at all, or were now being educated toward achieving a splendid love match rather than a financially lucrative arranged marriage. There were still tragic cases of young girls wilting on the vine, who could have had productive, even creative vocations beyond marriage. Again taking examples from her own experience, she addressed the problems of single women, for example in "Das Urtheil der Welt" ("The Judgment of this World") about a single foster mother in a Pietist community; in *Hannah, der Hernhuterin Deborah Findling* (*Hannah, the Foundling of the Herrnhuter Deborah*); and the short story "Die Hässliche" ("The Ugly Woman"). But not until she had literally lived out many of her own stories.

She gives us a painful example of life following art. First, she was herself a divorced woman, whose husband had an "avant garde" affair with a close friend, and who married the man with whom she committed adultery; a woman for whom escape to a more enlightened Switzerland was the solution of both a personal and a political crisis. She incorporated these motifs into a variety of works. But she was also an attractive and sensual woman who was widowed twice fairly young. In the 1810s, when she was in her forties, she took into her home Emil von Herder, the son of Weimar's famous author and collector of folklore, who was an old family friend. Both she and her daughter Luise gradually developed

affection for him. Therese corresponded with him in terms that
are unmistakable sexual passion—yet she was apparently unaware of her own feelings, and pressed her daughter and Emil to
marry. A hurtful interlude of Luise's infatuation with another
young man led to Emil's suicide attempt in Therese's home, and a
subsequent rushed marriage between him and Luise. Therese, at
this point traumatized, outraged, and jealous of the young couple,
goes to live with them for two months, and succeeds in bringing
about their divorce. Luise and Therese set up household together
in Stuttgart, but toward the end of Therese's life in the later
1820s, Emil and Luise reconcile without Therese's approval or assistance, and go on to have a happy married life. The bitter
Therese felt rejected by her children and realized that her own ill
humor and biting sarcasm contributed to her isolation from them.
She performed two last literary acts of resolution and reconciliation: she published the letters of Georg Forster (severely edited,
for which she has been sharply criticized by Forster scholars), and
she wrote a novel about her own children, and others, called *Die
Ehelosen* (*Unmarried Women*, 1829).

Die Ehelosen is an attempt to show how women who choose
not to marry can lead productive lives. Girls should be trained neither for the love match nor the arranged marriage, according to
Huber, but rather should be intellectually liberated through moral
and ethical training. Self-education is the key, so that the child is
raised to independence. The models she presents are teachers and
organizers of a young women's commune for welfare work; she suggests the resolution of couples' financial or emotional trouble
through the intervention of friends. I think of this collection of vi-
gnettes as Therese Huber's last definitive statement on marriage—even though she stated jokingly that far too many people
died of consumption in it. It may be surprising that a woman who
bore ten children, married twice, and was a happy grandmother
would advocate raising women not for marriage, but for independence. But as a woman who violently repressed her own sexuality
in later years and who felt all too keenly what the love match
meant in terms of social control, it is understandable that she
wanted this option for those who came after her. To my mind her
most important contribution to the discussion about marriage was
her placement of the love match in its political and social context:
that it can only be an ideal among people who are politically and
financially free, and who have been educated toward equality, independence, and autonomy. Although she achieved a love match

herself in life, it was at the high political cost of *Selbstverharmlosung,* of making herself harmless, and she never advocated the love match as a viable plot resolution in Europe—that is in locales where the state was identical with the abnegation of personal rights. Only in a vaguely conceived communal utopia, the vastly overrated new American republic, where women and men shared work and authority, could the love match be realized. So possibly Therese Huber was not such a harmless little democrat after all.

8

Escape to America: Social Reality and Utopian Schemes in German Women's Novels Around 1800

Ute Brandes

America! The land of milk and honey, the cradle of democracy, home of the noble savage, the symbol of freedom, the image of an unspoiled, natural way of living. We are still familiar with the lure of this myth.[1]

Without ever having set foot on American soil, German writers around 1800 frequently projected their ideals of freedom and justice onto the New World. Between the time of the American Revolution and the mid-nineteenth century, America became the primary focus for diverse social and political projections, ranging from the idealization of primitivism in a bountiful nature to Jacobine yearnings for equality and freedom in the American Republic. Far from showing realistic living conditions on the Frontier, some of these works portrayed alternative communes in idyllic natural settings. Their self-absorbed societies are intentionally designed to voice strong criticism over political terror, traditional class structure, or legal and social restrictions in Europe.[2]

When considering such 18th century literary visions of "America," the inherent emancipatory potential of utopian fiction immediately comes into focus. As Peter Uwe Hohendahl has demonstrated with Wieland's novels, eighteenth-century utopian thought is based on a "concept of reality in which the world appears to the individual as an unfinished field of operation that needs to be improved upon," (92). While older utopias tend to present more or less systematic political systems in the distant past or future or in a mythical place, eighteenth-century narratives put their utopian schemes into a realistic fictional context, either in the traditional genres of novels of travel, of adventure or, towards the end of the century, in the novel of development. After carefully establishing a fake authenticity of the epic context by providing exact dates, places, and documents such as letters and diaries, utopia is then placed in a geographically plausible, yet remote location. When the transition between the well-known world and the imaginary realm is gradual and smoothed over, specific features in utopia, such as innovations in education, religion, marriage, technical or economic institutions gain an immediate relevance. In activating their readers' sense of discrepancy between an ideally functioning social order and their own experience of reality, writers propose their utopian schemes as models for social change.

Such an emancipatory intent of utopian fiction clearly assumes special significance in times of rapidly changing social conventions. By the late 1700s, literary works had gained an increasingly important role as the mediators of moral values for the rising middle class. The development of a literary market oriented toward new readers and opposing courtly and clerical domination fostered a new emphasis on the potential of individuals as autonomous, self-directed personalities who, through their use of reason and morality, would enable themselves to unfold freely their talents and interests. Such a process of self-empowerment would set free productive energies and result in universal progress in culture, in the economy, and in overall social cooperation.

The fact that women were included as helpmates in this process of progressive self-improvement, but not as publicly autonomous, self-directed human beings, was initially not seen as a contradiction in the demand for egality, brotherhood, and freedom. The discussion about woman's nature and intellectual capabilities had assumed new vigor since the late 17th century. Early enlightenment reformers promoted the goal of education for women, whereas, at the end of the century, new cultural images of feminine naturalness and innate intuition were valued most. By 1800 a broad spectrum of contradictory goals for women existed side-by-side. In France, the Revolution had publicly formulated, and then rejected, legal and educational equality. In England, Mary Wollstonecraft responded to Edmund Burke's opposition to the Revolution by stressing the same rights for women as Thomas Paine had claimed in the name of all humanity.

In Germany, vigorous discussions about various appropriate patterns of ideal womanhood took place at this same time. The range of speculations extended from a congenital and never-changing *female nature* to highly energetic demands for education and legal rights—a change of *female conditions*. When confronted with such a broad variety of conflicting opinions, some writers, such as Goethe, Schiller or Hölderlin also portrayed more independent female figures, ranging from idealized images of woman as the ennobling and inspiring muse which would enable man to aspire to a new humanism, to woman as misplaced politician— scheming and powerhungry—or as an erotically demonic force. Yet the vast majority of German authors promoted ideal womanhood in a sphere of happy middle class domesticity: the pious, virtuous and passive mother, wife, and daughter. This latter cultural pattern, by far the most dominant, also matched the evolving division of labor between the female sphere of the home and the male's role of active achievement in the public realm of a business or a profession.

Yet the beginnings of a rift in the bourgeois concept of women's private and men's public spheres were already apparent. By 1800, women had become a large part of the reading audience without having the legal rights to participate actively in the public realm. This is also the time when female writers entered the literary market in greater numbers. Their acute sense of being outsiders in a well-established male domain is documented again and again.[3] When choosing to depict imaginary societies in their works, these authors do not focus primarily on comprehensive political or technological systems, as male utopian writers tend to do. Their attention is on a new social order and a redefinition of gender roles, which they assume will assure human happiness in a harmonious society. Their various formulations of women's social and cultural functions reflect the range of discussions about female roles around 1800 as much as they present individual attempts to transform an imperfect social order into a perfect one.

In the following, I will trace the relationship between diverse gender depictions and women's own reformist discourse about their situation. Since the discussion of utopian schemes merits a descriptive approach, I will set up a systematic comparison, measuring three novels on a narrative scale. Ranging from initial pre-utopian representations of an imperfect European reality to diverse constructions of utopian harmony in an American colony, my scale allows insight into particular points of cultural tension for women around 1800 and their specific proposals for the achievement of human fulfillment. It will also enable us to judge the measure of consistency within each novel's various proposals for social reform. I will consider three novels. The first is *Erscheinungen am See Oneida*[4] (*Occurences at Lake Oneida* 1798), one of the later works of the well-known enlightenment writer Sophie La Roche (1731–1807), the first successful woman author in eighteenth-century Germany, and the first female editor of a women's journal. La Roche was influenced by Richardson and Rousseau and highly regarded for her first novel *Die Geschichte des Fräuleins von Sternheim* (1771) which introduced the middle class sentimental novel as a genre to German literature. The second is *Das Blüthenalter der Empfindung* (*The Blossoming of Sensibility,* 1794) by Sophie Mereau (1770–1806), a prolific and gifted author and translator between the classical and romantic eras; central figure of a literary salon in Jena which attracted major writers, among them Schiller, Jean Paul, Fichte, Schelling, and the Schlegels. Mereau was one of the first economically successful women writers in Germany. The third, *Virginia, oder die Republik von Kentucky* (1820), by Henriette Frölich (1768–1833), a very little known author of short stories and a play, who published this only novel of hers anonymously.

These three works, written by women who represent two generations, voice very diverse views in their common theme of addressing the French Revolution and the colonization in America. Together they not only present a spectrum of women's responses to their own conditions of legal inequality, lack of access to education, and various degrees of consent or alienation about the division of private vs. public spheres. All three novels also understand their utopian impulse as a universal quest: the newly designed social reforms will be carried back to Europe in order to regenerate the old world.

In general, utopian narratives reflect a tension between the depiction of reality and the construction of a vision. In many cases, a protagonist experiences an imperfect reality, is uprooted by choice or circumstance from the familiar world, and arrives at or helps to build an ideal society. The narrative attention is first on the dramatic interaction of characters and circumstancial conflict; thereafter it shifts to the didactic exposition of a perfect community. Within utopia, only those situations, events, and figures are introduced which further our understanding of the doctrinal statement. Contrary to his or her character development in the pre-utopian phase, the protagonist ceases to serve as the focus of the

action and merely functions as a guide to the information about
the new society at hand.

When first considering the pre-utopian settings, all three novels point to alienation, tragedy, and severe political conflict within
their different situations in Europe. Mereau's heroine Nanette
experiences social persecution and inequality before the law. She
is manipulated by an older brother, her legal guardian and the
avaricious custodian of her inheritance. At first she must reject
his wish that she enter a convent, and then she flees from his
immoral demand that she become the companion of a lusty cardinal. With an elderly aunt she escapes from Genoa via Paris to
Switzerland. The experience of revolutionary enthusiasm in France
confirms her inner convictions of human equality and personal
freedom. Mereau shows us an unusually strong-willed young woman
whose social protest ranges from the rejection of female legal dependency to severe criticism of moral corruption within the Catholic church, bourgeois materialism, and philistine adherence to
arbitrary social barriers between the different confessions.

La Roche's novel, by contrast, derives its pre-utopian conflict
squarely from the psychological injury of a French aristocrat who,
with his wife, barely escaped the revolutionary mob. Initially resentful of the post-revolutionary American republic, his earlier life
in Europe now appears to him as a period of lost innocence: "In
America the seeds for the unfortunate revolution were fetched,
that troubled my soul.—America now was not anymore the place
of refuge for my angel Emilie and for my own heart, it was the soil
in which our distress germinated." (In Amerika ward der Saame
zur unglücklichen Revolution geholt, [das] beklemmte meine
Seele.—Amerika war nun nicht mehr der Zufluchtsaufenthalt für
meinen Engel Emilie und für mein Herz, es war der Boden, auf
welchem unser Elend keimte, La Roche, I, 119). In this situation of
reluctant exile, nature alone can re-establish the natural order
which was destroyed by the Revolution.

Emilie is the idealized model of a lady of sensibility.[5] As a devoted wife, she considers herself an extension of Carl. Careful not
to increase her husband's bitterness about their situation, she
weeps in private about their lost home and insists on maintaining
a cheerful politeness in their daily lives, even in utmost poverty
and seclusion. She listens to her intuitions and is certain that
Carl will overcome his political anger and that he will turn his
attention to her, the source of his strength. La Roche's protagonists' strictly defined gender roles and their nostalgic cultural

behavior point to a Burkean view of a well-ordered, patriarchal class-society which has been severely disrupted by senseless political chaos and crime.

In contrast to this anti-revolutionary stance, Frölich's novel, written twenty-one years later, protests the French Restauration's return to such conservative concepts as defended by La Roche. Frölich's protagonist Virginia is born into a family of French country gentry. Her father voluntarily institutes land reform before the Revolution. Virginia comes of age under the tutelage of an uncle who reclaims the estates, pressures his niece to marry for financial reasons, and orders her to forswear her Republican ideals. As a woman, Virginia has no legal recourse to defend what she considers her natural human rights. She is also forbidden to pursue her growing attachment to the republican-minded student Mucius. Since she fervently believes in the early, emancipatory goals of the Revolution, she escapes the restrictions of Europe and secretly heads for America, a most radical and unconventional decision for a woman.

All three novels begin at very diverse levels of critique of European reality—ranging from very specific demands for women's legal rights and public representation to a strong defense of the pre-revolutionary social order. At the same time, however, they set up similar idyllic realms of human fulfillment before they attempt to create a social utopia. In each case, this amounts to a personal compromise between a loving couple which removes itself from destructive societal requirements into a private bucolic setting. Yet these idyllic interludes cannot be sustained. Mereau's heroine Nanette experiences love and harmony in the seclusion and majestic beauty of the Swiss Alps. When she again happens to meet the narrator Albert, a Protestant, enthusiastic affection and alpine beauty bring about their happiness. This innocent interlude comes to an end with their increasingly erotic attraction to each other. Their marriage—a civil procedure—is made impossible by the legal authority of Nanette's guardian brother and by religious barriers. After various other attempts to solve their predicament fail, the couple's resolution is clear. There is no possibility of self-determination within the European context; only their escape to America will ensure personal fulfillment without legal and social restrictions.

La Roche's novel constructs a Robinsonade on a secluded island as her protagonists' apprenticeship for a utopian quest.[6] This interim period between their escape from the French Revolution and their integration into a commune within the post-revolutionary American republic is clearly shown as not truly befitting an aristocratic couple, yet it is the necessary first step towards psychological healing in nature:

> You want to live in solitude! Take me wherever you want, where only our love and benevolent nature will surround us ... My Carl! Your love alone can never be the foundation of my contentment, your own piece of mind, your own contentment must be connected with it.

> Du willst einsam leben! Führe mich hin wo du willst, wo nur unsere Liebe und die gütige Natur um uns seyn werden ... Mein Carl! deine Liebe allein kann nie der Grund meiner Zufriedenheit werden, deine Ruhe, deine Zufriedenheit müssen damit verbunden seyn. (La Roche, I, 123)

While Carl initially spends much time brooding over the destructive direction of human civilization, Emilie gladly takes on the basic tasks of survival. Then, in complete solitude, they learn to survive with the help of their *Encyclopedia* and their three-hundred-volume library. They stay committed to their self-perceived mission to ensure the survival of European culture and begin to transform the island into an idyllic paradise. Each basic task also acquires a gender-specific, artistic, and semi-religious dimension. Carl builds a dam to divert the rain waters, Emilie decorates it with an artful mosaic of shells; Carl works the fields, Emilie gathers wild flowers for the garden; together they build temples and resting places from which to watch the sun set over the lake, and they design neo-classical monuments for their murdered relatives. This idyllic isolation comes to an end with the imminent birth of their child. And only here, suddenly breaking out of her patient resignation, Emilie asserts her own will. She declares that with or without Carl, she will swim to the opposite shore to seek help from the neighboring Oneida Indians. Throughout the birth episode, Emilie remains a resolute and firmly determined woman. The idyllic spell is broken. The couple realizes that they must return to a social context.

Frölich's pre-utopian harmony is first sketched in retrospective, with Virginia's early childhood as idyllic interaction between the freed tenants and her family in the country. This sense of freedom and justice for all social classes, first introduced by her reformist father, later extends for Virginia also to social and legal self-determination which she can only hope to enjoy in the American republic. After her arrival, she eagerly sets out to explore her new country—a risky undertaking for a single woman. Her unusual independence is reaffirmed by the author through a wondrous happenstance. While she admires the Niagara Falls Virginia accidentally meets her French fiancé Mucius. The idyllic period which follows is also a busy time of planning for a happy and secure future. The couple assembles a group of like-minded immigrants and friends. Together, men and women first draw up and then vote on a democratic constitution. Next they buy machinery and provisions and head west to found their new colony.

While all three novels include such an interim, pre-utopian realm of idyllic existence, Frölich is the only author who does not limit her goals to the happy domesticity of a loving couple or a nuclear family in a secluded country setting—the eighteenth-century metaphor for an ideal life close to nature—a theme we find in so many novels influenced by Rousseau. From the outset, Frölich's attention is focused on the reshaping of economic and social structures which will then permit the individual happiness of men and women *within* the practical reality of legal and social contexts. Frölich's conviction that personal fulfillment must necessarily be rooted in a larger interaction with society comes only as an interruption and ex-post-facto realization to the idyllic harmony depicted by Mereau and La Roche.

Let us now enter their utopias. In Mereau's novel, Nanette and Albert do not actually set out for America. Instead, they envision a free republic where each person can determine his or her own fate according to their inner needs:

> In America . . . lives a free people, there the genius of mankind rejoices in all its rights, there the new fortuitous circumstances of a youthful state will preclude the restitution of adverse reforms for a long time to come. Let's go there!

> In Amerika . . . wohnt ein freies Volk, dort freut der Genius der Menschheit sich wieder seiner Rechte, dort lassen die neuen glücklichen Verhältnisse eines jugendlichen Staates noch lange keine widrigen Reformen befürchten. Laß uns dahin! (Mereau, 1920, 100)

Mereau's vision of unrestricted freedom in "America" is based on the various individual agreements between a loving couple rather than specific legislation for women's civil and legal rights. It is for

herself that Nanette claims equality and intellectual independence. Her desire for a separate realm of love and tolerance to
which the state has no access, her unashamed claim to erotic fulfillment, and her enthusiastic affirmation of the French Revolution place the author in distinct opposition to the moral and social
reality of women in 1794. Her poetic dream of America is voiced as
a Romantic longing for human completeness in a new Golden Age.
This utopian yearning does not include specific proposals for a new
social system:

> Why did so few nations discover the secret to the happiness of the
> individual in the well-being of society at large? These and similar
> contemplations became for me inexhaustible sources for [mental]
> pictures, sketched by an innocent heart and in which imagination
> happily was blending the colors.

> Warum fanden so wenig Nationen das Geheimnis, das Glück des
> Einzelnen im Wohl des Ganzen zu begründen? Diese und ähnli-
> che Betrachtungen waren mir ein unerschöpflicher Stoff zu Ge-
> mälden, die ein schuldloses Herz entwarf, und wozu eine lachende
> Imagination die Farben mischte. (Mereau, 1920, 16)

In such subjective visions, "America" stands for what is *not* to be
found in Europe: personal freedom, women's equality, and religious
tolerance.

La Roche's novel, on the other hand, imagines her utopia as a
patriarchally structured international commune. Her colony is
founded on the promise of its members to renounce all strife and
political passion. Each family must pledge its willingness to work
hard and live piously; only then will it receive a plot of land and a
cabin. However, in stressing the cultural superiority of those born
into the aristocracy, La Roche also sets up the beginnings of a traditional class structure. The narrator asserts

> . . . that the spirit of beautification, which . . . touches everything
> is an endowment of the aristocracy by birth. Some of the colonists
> are glad that he [Carl] now also has to share in the field work,
> but the best among them pity and admire him. I told the Wat-
> tines about this, both were glad, and slightly blushing and smil-
> ing to herself, Emily said: so the idea of nobility which has been
> eradicated in our fatherland, is germinating again in the wilds of
> Onatoga, surrecting itself in the souls of the new inhabitants.

> . . . daß der Geist der Verschönerung, welcher alles was er be-
> rührt, ganz eigentlich dem gebornen Adel gegeben sey. Einige der

> Colonisten freuen sich, daß er [Carl] nun auch Feldarbeit ver-
> suchen mußte, aber die besten von ihnen bedauren und
> bewundern ihn. Ich sagte es den Wattines, es freute beyde, und
> Emilie sagte erröthend und vor sich hin lächelnd: also keimte die
> in unserem Vaterlande ausgerottete Idee der Classe des Adels, in
> den Wüsten von Onatoga, in den Gemüthern der neuen Be-
> wohner wieder in die Höhe. (La Roche, III, 12)

Possessing this "natural" inclination towards beauty and order,
those born noble also have a natural right to establish themselves
as the privileged. Carl and Emilie are the only Oneida colonists
who hire a young couple, "who considered it as their duty of love
towards their good masters, and also as an honor, to work as in-
dustriously and as skillfully as they themselves," (welche es für
Pflicht der Liebe gegen ihre gute Herrschaft, und auch als Ehre
ansehen, eben so fleißig und eben so geschickt zu arbeiten als sie
selbst, La Roche, III, 11). Emilie is now freed from heavy work.
Chiefly occupying herself with needle work at home she functions
as a model for feminine virtue. Carl concerns himself with public
goals by designing a distinct work ethic to benefit other colonists.
He points out instances of industry and efficient organization;
communal coins imprinted with "work" and "blessings" are circu-
lated; under his guidance the village not only establishes itself
as an ideological unit within, he also deliberately plans it as an
ideal mythical model society for the neighboring Oneida Indians,
perceived as noble, but immature, savages. At the end, the narrator, our guide to this utopia, returns to Europe in order to promote Carl and Emilie as role models for the establishment of new
social harmony which will make obsolete the ever-present threat
of revolutions.

Frölich's "Eldorado" in Kentucky appears radically modern in
comparison. Her fictional commune is partly influenced by the
utopian thinker Gabriel Bonnot de Mably (1709–1785) who promoted the abolition of private property, and the French enlightenment philosopher Morelly about whose life and person is little
known today. His utopian model, based on the principles of natural law, the abolition of private property, and free love was referred to by Babeuf and intensely debated around the time of the
French Revolution.[7]

When Henriette Frölich reconsidered these revolutionary theories around 1820, communitarian ideas were intensely debated in
Germany. A number of utopian colonies had been established in

the American republic, among them the Shakers who in 1805 alone founded five new communities in Kentucky and Ohio, or the Harmony Society who had migrated from Southern Germany to a new settlement in Pennsylvania. In 1814, under the leadership of Georg Rapp, this group founded the new, highly successful community of New Harmony on the Wabash River in Indiana. Three years later, Josef Bäumler from Württemberg purchased land in Ohio. The members of his group insisted on their land in common rather than to divide it as originally planned. Based on egalitarian religious doctrines, these communitarian systems had a great impact on the German public; they were regarded as proof that egalitarian, utopian colonies could be economically successful (Bestor, 33–37).

There is no doubt that Henriette Frölich was influenced by the news of these religious groups. Her own fictional American colony, however, is based on secular, socialist principles. In her republic "Eldorado" in Kentucky each family owns no more than their clothing, house, and garden; all other material goods are pooled. Men, women, and children take their meals in dining halls where social contacts between young and old promote a sense of community and continuous learning. All members of her large multinational and multi-racial republic profess to a Deism which stresses nature as the God-given realm of human productivity and harmony. There are no social or legal differences based on race or class:

> We have arrived in the blossoming garden of Eden . . . A general shout of joy reverberated through the air; we all jumped up at the same time and ran down the mountain, exultated with open arms . . . This moment turned us into *one* people, all differences of color, of origin, of education were eradicated, we all became brothers, with equal rights and equal duties.

> Angelangt sind wir in Edens blühendem Garten . . . Ein allgemeiner Freudenruf tönte durch die Lüfte; wir sprangen alle zu gleicher Zeit auf und liefen mit ausgebreiteten Armen jauchzend den Berg hinunter . . . Dieser Augenblick machte uns zu *einem* Volke, aller Unterschied der Farbe, der Heimat, der Bildung war vernichtet, wir wurden alle Brüder, mit gleichen Rechten und gleichen Pflichten. (Frölich, 1963, 174f.)

Individual rights are based on social cooperation in Eldorado. Each adult chooses a particular trade or profession according to

personal inclination and communal need. There is a new interest
in learning: the better educated members teach the others, and
many of the women voluntarily enhance their less than equal
schooling by taking lessons in academic subjects. Childcare is a
communal effort as well. After a few months with their mothers,
babies are cared for in daycare centers; after work hours, fathers
and mothers both foster their development. Children are taught in
co-educational schools; girls receive additional instruction in domestic and community tasks, while boys are trained in para-
military sports. Yet the stronger young women are also encouraged
to fight alongside the men, if they so choose. Women initially have
only half a vote in the pre-utopian planning stage, and men a full
vote, but afterwards each family has one block vote in the public
decision-making process within utopia. By assigning equal public
and private space to men and women, Frölich optimistically asserts equal constitutional rights which predate those of German
women by one century.[8]

In the context of tracing women's reformist discourses about
their own situation in their novels it is interesting to note a number of inconsistencies in their utopian models. La Roche's work
is concerned with setting up Emilie as a cultural example for
women: a submissive and cheerful helpmate to her husband, pro-
moting happy domestic seclusion, pious trust in her intuition, and
silent suffering in order to heal her man. This idealization of feminine acquiescence does not lead her, however, to falsify genuine
female experience. When it comes to the survival of her child, Emilie's resolute decision against Carl's obsession with solitude is
common sense female behavior which breaks through the established fictional concept of cheerful feminine subordination and
passivity. Despite this interesting inconsistency, La Roche's retro-
gressive utopian concepts present an idyllic reaffirmation of the
past, yet enriched with new middle-class patterns of strictly polarized male and female attitudes. In this view, woman's voluntary
sacrifice of her legal and public rights will contribute to a harmonious, patriarchal society, dedicated to the aesthetic and moral
improvement of each individual whose personal and social goals
are defined according to what is proper of his or her gender. La
Roche's reformist impulse is carried by a strong pacifist conviction
which, so the author hopes, will be decisive in circumventing a
new plunge into terror and chaos.

In some ways, all three authors' concepts of marriage are similar, since all are preoccupied with affirming the bourgeois notion of the *certainty* of each partner's happiness within the context of a nuclear family. Such idyllic depictions of woman's greatest fulfillment in loving devotion to her husband can still be found to influence female consciousness in our time.[9] Yet the authors differ on how such mutual harmony is to be achieved. La Roche feels that a young girl's interest is best protected when her parents place her into a pre-arranged marriage, thus ensuring the similarity of cultural and financial backgrounds between her and her future husband. Mereau and Frölich—born thirty-nine and thirty-seven years later than La Roche—strongly reject such traditional matches of convenience for their heroines. Nanette and Virginia both rebel against their legal guardians and choose their husbands freely. Each bases her choice on the new middle-class values of personal agreement and erotic attraction between man and woman.

Other utopian schemes which these three writers present also result in divergent goals for women's self-realization and public competencies. La Roche, a well-known personality and successful writer, overstepped in her own life (as a publishing author) the social and cultural limits of the private female sphere while propagating a strongly idealized version of the new middle-class model of feminine submissiveness, quiet virtue, and legal dependency. Mereau, in contrast, openly questions polarized gender ideologies for men and women which in her view result in severe restrictions of the individual's talents and natural rights. Her demands for self-determination, social equality, and intellectual cooperation between man and woman, as well as her celebration of feeling and personal freedom over social conventions illustrate a yearning for human completeness which anticipates androgynous romantic concepts of love. Frölich's proposals for equal rights and duties for men and women purposefully transgress most gender definitions of her contemporaries.

While all three writers base their hopes for human happiness on love and cooperation within a nuclear family, Frölich's reform proposals specifically demand legal rights and economic independence for women and men. The communal structure of her utopia permits both partners private and public spheres of independence, but the family is still assumed to be a single patriarchal unit with one family vote in the public decision-making process. There are no single heads of households, neither male nor female, and the

possibility of disagreement between husband and wife, resulting in
a split family vote, is never considered. In spite of this truly utopian detail, Frölich's reordering of gender roles and of legal, educational, and social institutions point to a practical reformist
impulse. Her attention to the political and economic situation of
women most radically calls into question eighteenth-century cultural and literary images of an innate, ahistorical nature of
woman, such as the "eternal feminine," Goethe's Gretchen in
Faust; of woman as muse of sensibility and humanity, Hölderlin's
Diotima, Goethe's Iphigenia, the princess in Goethe's *Tasso;* or as
pious homemaker as depicted in Schiller's poem "Die Glocke."

Are these writers "in the shadow" or, even worse, "rejects from
Olympus?" A cautious "yes" is warranted, looking at the critical
response all three works received. But rather than arguing the explicit rejection and intentional subjugation of female authors
around 1800, I will point to the ambiguous nature of the developing bourgeois gender ideology which was formulated and propagated by men, primarily. The groping attempts of the middle class
at cultural and social emancipation resulted in hierarchical and
stereotypical categories—the effects of which all three authors experienced. Among the "Olympians," Schiller, for instance, liked to
encourage gifted women writers to contribute to the new image of
"the dignity of women" (die Würde der Frauen). Mereau enjoyed a
very supportive student-professor relationship with him and was
lauded: "I am really amazed how our women now, in a merely am-
ateurish way, have come to achieve for themselves a certain skill
in writing which comes close to art." (Ich muß mich doch wirklich
darüber wundern, wie unsere Weiber jetzt, auf bloß dilettanti-
schem Wege, eine gewisse Schreibgeschicklichkeit sich zu verschaf-
fen wissen, die der Kunst nahe kommt).[10] But she was hindered in
her work by the poet Brentano who, when he became her husband,
resented her intellectual independence. Ironically, her works survived because of the public's attention to biographical detail in
Brentano's life. La Roche was initially encouraged by the writer
Christoph Martin Wieland and her first work was widely read.
Then she was considered outmoded and was quickly forgotten, except by a faithful following of female readers. Frölich's work appeared in a limited edition only and, until its rediscovery in 1963,
never came to greater public attention. According to Gerhard
Steiner, only one review appeared in a literary journal, which resented a *woman* author envisioning a utopian society. All three
works fall into the large grey area of "ladies' literature," a quickly

consumed and always replenished fictional source of entertainment which, at that time, was not considered as fitting into any aesthetic category of literary works of art. The greater humanistic and emancipatory impulses reflected in these novels were therefore not registered.

Today we can approach all three writers in our attempt to understand eighteenth-century literary culture as conditioned by rapidly changing social, economic, political, cultural, and gender-specific conventions. In this broader context the three works provide a remarkably comprehensive and varied spectrum of women's views propagated around 1800. For us, it is important to note that their own goals for the improvement of their condition do not suggest a common direction, aside from reflecting the prevailing contemporary social order.

Among the three books, Frölich's utopian vision stands out as the boldest and most comprehensive. Undoubtedly, the author was influenced by her strong interest in alternative communes in America, such as the Shakers, the Rappites, and the Ohio colony of Josef Bäumler. Yet Frölich's thought was based on the principles of enlightenment reform, not on religious doctrine. In her attempt to shape an egalitarian society, she rejected the familiar patterns of religious discipline and celibacy as unnecessarily confining. In addition, her novel calls into question the supposedly *natural* social and legal restrictions for women around 1800 by first depicting the injustice suffered by them and then by advancing her own specific proposals for a just society. Written six years before the institution of Robert Owen's secular colony at New Harmony in Indiana, we can now recognize Frölich's work not only as a remarkably original contribution to the discussion about gender roles around 1800, but also as a highly original novel in German utopian literature.

9

Reconstructing Women's Literary Relationships: Sophie Albrecht and Female Friendship

Ruth P. Dawson

In the introductory poem to her second collection, the actress and writer Sophie Albrecht (1757–1840) addressed her friend Antoinette von Dalberg, writing, "Kühner sang ich nun / Ich wuste, / Daß *Du* mich gern hörtest" (More bravely I sang now, knowing that *you* listened gladly). Although Albrecht's boldest poetry, on the themes of love and of suicide, involves relationships with men, these poems are intertwined with the poet's relationships with women and with appeals of her lyric persona to women. Albrecht was able to write as she did because she felt supported by women in her efforts to write boldly; furthermore, she relied on women to help her sell her books, and before long she herself was being asked for a variety of forms of assistance by other women.

It is useful, precisely for the age that Goethe and his circle of male friends dominated and shaped, to look for and at the circles of support that women created. The frequency of references in mainstream literary history to Weimar as a cultural center indicates the importance in literary history of the human interactions which supported or rejected, praised or confused, redirected or reinforced a writer. The writer's circle provided the first readers and critics of new works; it often played a role in the conditions, decisions, and choices that affected the life the writer led, and the circumstances that promoted or discouraged further writing, that fostered or suppressed experimentation.

In the case of writers who were women, relationships with other women had further significance, for they shared certain problems that men did not face, or did not face in the same way, for example, of writing (especially of publishing), of economics, of

173

psychology, or of law. Not that all women would have agreed with each other. Society cast women in the role of social and cultural conservatives, but a women desiring to take unconventional steps might have found at least tentative support for her choices if her circle was broad enough. These thin but often important webs of connections women wove to each other were hard to establish, hard to support, and today are hard to trace. Yet there they are, indicating that literary women of the time supported each other, and that this mutual sustenance was important to the women themselves.

Albrecht repeatedly drew attention to the importance of women friends in her life. The unconventional poems on love and on death that make her an important, though still virtually unknown literary figure in late eighteenth-century German literature, are embedded in collections dominated by paeans to her women friends. She dedicated both her first and second volumes of poetry (1781; 1785) to women friends. The first volume also contained the only two plays that Albrecht wrote, one of them about a young woman who fled an unwanted marriage by committing suicide. The second poetry collection concluded with prose fragments from a fictitious diary of despair. Meanwhile Albrecht had also undertaken an unsuccessful effort to revive a seventeenth-century novel for eighteenth-century taste, *Aramena* (1783–87). In 1791 she published her third and last volume of poetry, after which she intermittently resumed composing in prose. She wrote a Gothic novella in 1797, eventually publishing the same work under altogether three different titles, the Gothic novel *Graumännchen*, (1799) which I have not seen, and nine years later a slim volume retelling legends of the early church. In the next decades she may have written some pieces for magazines before her final publication, a cookbook (1839). The following year Sophie Albrecht died.

Why she had stopped writing poetry well over forty years earlier is not known. In those days she had achieved a daring and distinctive voice, as in the poem entitled "Entschlus":

> Up, take death from your own hand
> Tear apart your fetters
> Your flowing blood is the dawn
> Heralding eternal day,
> Is the purple which in paradise
> Finally adorns you as a bride
> When, to him who rejected you
> An angel of God leads you.

Auf nimm von eigner Hand den Tod
Zerreisse was dich bindet,
Dein strömend Blut ist Morgenroth
Das ewig Tag verkündet,
Ist Purpur der im Paradies
Dich endlich bräutlich zieret
Wenn zu ihm der dich von sich sties
Ein Engel Gottes führet. (1785, I, 105)

Opening with a syntactically elegant first line, the poem transforms death into richly colored images of dawn, day, paradise, and
reunification with a mysterious lover. The stance of partial de-
tachment achieved by the second-person address increases the cer-
emonial quality of the poem.

The lover figure briefly evoked in the poem about suicide is of
course central to Albrecht's love poems, some of which are passionate, some playful, as for example, in her second volume "Nach Mit-
ternacht. Im November 1784." ("After Midnight, November 1784")

Ich muß mich los aus deinen Armen winden;
Noch diesen Kuß, nun eile schnell von hier!
Im Traume wirst du mich so glühend wiederfinden,
Und bis zum Morgen bleib' ich dann bei dir.

I must tear myself from your arms
Just this kiss, now hurry away from here
In your dreams you will find me as passionate
and till dawn will I then stay with you. (II, 181)

This one is followed by a poem to a woman friend.

Albrecht's intensive involvement with female friends is represented in the second volume by recurrent poems addressed to specific women, including Karoline von Dachröden, Frau Professorin
Reinhardt in Erfurt, Katharine Pipping, Henriette Froriep, Madame Tideböhl, Lörchen Bösenberg, Louise Pipping, and Minna
Lentin. Four of them were addressed more than once. By comparison, Albrecht wrote three poems of friendship here to designated
men. To be sure, the social sanctions against her naming men were
greater than those against naming women, but on the other hand
the social rewards for writing poetry to specific, mainly middle-
class women were minimal.

Despite the indications that women supporters were very
significant to her, it is nonetheless extremely difficult to retrace

Sophie Albrecht's female friendships. As usually happens in descriptions of women writers, the sparse biographical sketches of Albrecht stress her male relationships. They mention her father, a professor of medicine who died when she was fourteen, and her husband, a student of her father's whom she married when she was fifteen and who later became a novelist, dramatist, and director. The sources mention the male directors and dramatists with whom she worked after she took the uncommon step, for a middle-class married woman, of becoming an actress. They do not mention her friendships with women. These must be reconstructed today from scattered remnants of information.

One early friend, Henriette Froriep, is identifiable because of the poems in both of Albrecht's first volumes that are written to her. Froriep was also an author. Her single novel, *Amalie von Nordheim* (1783), published soon after her early death, centers on a sustaining friendship between the aristocratic mother, who is the title character, and a wise middle-class woman whom Amalie woos to be her friend; the female friendship at the heart of this epistolary and often satirical novel is given another dimension by the construction of the middle-class friend, Madame Laresche, as a portrait of the best known middle-class woman in late eighteenth-century Germany, the novelist Sophie La Roche, who offered assistance of many kinds to a large number of women writers. For Sophie Albrecht, Froriep was able to show support in a very practical way. She was the first woman to subscribe to Abrecht's first book. Especially in the absence of other documentation, subscription lists can provide hints about a writer's circle of support.

Most eighteenth-century German publishers were little more than local bookdealers or printers. To foster the wider distribution of a book and larger sales, a publisher could use two devices, the semiannual bookfairs and subscription lists. The lists, subscribed to before publication, had the special advantage of guaranteeing the publisher a minimum number of sales, and perhaps also helped him to determine what the total size of the printing should be. The subscription lists, which were usually printed along with the book and then bound in it, are invaluable documents but still seldom used for reconstructing important socio-literary facts, especially about women writers. When a writer's first book has a subscription list, it can be particularly revealing. Because a book being sold by subscription had not yet been published or reviewed and, as a first book, was by a little known or unknown author, its subscribers were likely to be mainly friends of the author or friends of her friends. A list from a first book registers the connections of that particular author, not drastically modified by the broader book market that was emerging in the eighteenth century and that was anonymous to the author. Of course a subscription list does not register the complete readership of the book, but it can be assumed to list many of the readers whom the author knew personally. Albrecht's first subscription list contained the names of 103 purchasers; thanks to the occasional subscriber who purchased more than one copy, the list indicates the initial distribution, in pre-publication sales, of 174 copies of her first book.

The number of copies sold is closely connected to the kind of place where the subscribers lived. Albrecht apparently had no connections with the metropolitan areas where larger numbers of readers were concentrated. She had no subscribers in Berlin, Vienna, Munich, Leipzig, or Dresden, and in Frankfurt and Hamburg only bookstores subscribed rather than personal friends (or even friends of friends). Most of Albrecht's subscribers lived in towns and villages that could have only a small number of subscribers, indeed only six places could boast five names or more. One was Erfurt, her home and the place where her first two volumes of poetry were published. The three most distant towns with five or more subscribers were Reval in the Baltic, where Albrecht and her husband had recently spent several years, Mainz on the Rhine, to which Erfurt was tied politically, and Schweidnitz, far to the east of Erfurt in Silesia. Two nearby towns where she had five or more subscribers were the market town of Langensalza and the neighboring princely residence of Weimar. The spotty geographical distribution of a woman writer's subscribers registers the relatively limited opportunities women had to cultivate expansive networks of literary acquaintances.

Even so, Sophie Albrecht, living in a town close to Weimar, was able to attract to her list a number of subscribers with readily traceable literary connections. Antoinette Dalberg, for example, to whom the second volume would be dedicated, had two brothers who subscribed to the first. One of them, Theodor Anton von Dalberg, is remembered as governor of Erfurt and a friend of Goethe. Friederike von Frankenberg in nearby Gotha is identifiable as a friend of Herder. Henriette Froriep of course was herself an author. Abraham Gotthelf Kästner was a professor and epigrammatist from Göttingen (and a frequent subscriber to the books of women writers). Magister Kranichfeld, in Langensalza, had been the mentor of the scholarly Friderika Baldinger in her youth and is praised in

her autobiography. The Countess von Stadion of Mainz is notable
for her connection, primarily through her father-in-law, with the
poet Wieland. Most of the subscribers however are unknown.

Nonetheless, the lists themselves contain in addition to geographical information another vital piece of data for each subscriber, gender. When Sophie Albrecht's first subscription list is
surveyed by this marker, a characteristic pattern emerges. Disre-
garding three bookstores on the list (one in Frankfurt and two in
Hamburg), one third of the people named as purchasers were
women. The percentage is high, for wives commonly disappeared
behind the names of their husbands. One of the poems in the volume, for example, is for "meine Freundin Wilhelmine Harpe, geb.
Kraft," but the only Harpe who subscribed is Herr Hofrat Harpe
in Reval; presumably this was Wilhelmine's husband. It was, after
all, not completely acceptable for a middle-class woman's name to
appear in print. Thus 40 percent of the women who subscribed in
their own names were unmarried and hence in some cases had no
man's name to substitute readily for their own. Several of them
partially concealed their identities by listing no place of residence,
a tactic occasionally also used by men. Furthermore the one subscriber identified only by a partial name was a woman, Demoiselle
Friderike H----l. Perhaps the five other subscribers labeled
"unnamed" were also women; Albrecht's second volume, with subscribers who knew that this collection too might contain remarkably open love poetry written from a woman's point of view, lists
seventy-seven who chose to remain anonymous. By then Frau
Harpe, however, was ready to appear in her own name, subscrib-
ing for two copies. In fact Albrecht had a remarkably loyal following. Of the named individuals who subscribed to her first volume,
almost 80 percent subscribed to the second also. The figure may
even be higher, since women who married in the intervening years
and changed their names cannot be traced in the second volume.
Any continuity to her third book of poetry in 1791 is untraceable;
by then Albrecht had a reputation as a poet, and her new publisher, Richter, operating from offices in both Dresden and Leipzig,
required no subscription lists from her.

With married women, their sisters and daughters often reading the books ostensibly ordered by their husbands, the number of
women readers was clearly higher than the number of women subscribers. Incomplete though the subscription lists are in this respect, they allow inklings of the female network that supported
Sophie Albrecht and also of the men who encouraged her. Indeed

the very fact that such lists were published constituted a kind of public announcement of a writer's network.

From her first subscription list, other more tentative information about how Albrecht recruited her subscribers can also be gleaned. Although it is arranged alphabetically, after the names are numbers that show the sequence in which subscribers enrolled, or rather the sequence in which their subscriptions were registered in Erfurt. When Albrecht's list is reconstructed according to this original order, Erfurt subscribers are scattered throughout, other places generally are listed together, suggesting the arrival of lists through the post from Mainz and Herborn, Schweidnitz and Frankfurt, Weimar and Gotha. If the sequence of names at a particular place reveals the sequence in which purchasers signed up, it is possible that individual recruiters can be identified, for they probably signed first, unless preempted by members of the upper aristocracy, who always got pride of place, and thus are listed first for that location. If this is so, Sophie Albrecht relied mainly on women to recruit her buyers, even though the buyers were, at least officially, mainly men. Thus Frau Hauptmann von Seydlitz headed the list from Schweidnitz; the other nine names from there are men's. Demoiselle Dumpf led a two-part list from Langensalza, Madame Tideböhl started off the list from Reval, and Frau Beust is the first name on the list from Naumburg. Of the two subscribers in Gotha, Baroness Frankenberg is second, but the name that precedes hers is that of Prince August von Sachsen, who ordered ten copies. From Lübeck came orders for five copies, all in the name of one subscriber, Madam Christoffersen. Considering the reservations that many women had about appearing on subscriptions lists in their own names, the frequency with which women's names lead the lists from particular places is even more striking. And perhaps some of the cases where men's names are listed first are again ruses for married women.

Yet it is also the case that men sometimes did not want their names (and by implication their approval) on a subscription list. Is it for example possible that Goethe was interested in the poetry of the professor's daughter from Erfurt? He did not subscribe to Sophie Albrecht's book.[1] His manservant did. In fact, Sutor subscribed again in 1785 to her second volume. The manservant's name represents the tantalizing unreachability of public approval from the Weimar Olympus.

After all, Sophie Albrecht had some connections to the powerful figures there. By 1795, she knew Goethe at least slightly, as indicated in a letter she and her husband wrote to him (Hahn, I, 381), and she knew Schiller well in the years before he moved to Weimar. Their relationship began at the onset of her acting career, when she took the leading female role in the premiere of Schiller's *Kabale and Liebe* on April 13, 1785 (Schiller 36, 2, 434). Three years later she played Eboli in the Leipzig premiere of *Don Carlos*. The friendly terms of her connection with Schiller are suggested by a casual letter he wrote to her from Dresden (partially published in Hoffman, 72). At the same time, Schiller's attitude from the start was ambivalent toward Albrecht's artistic ambitions. In a lengthy message to a male friend written soon after he met the young actress, Schiller acknowledged that Albrecht might have the talent to become a great actress (she did), but he nonetheless planned a strategy for persuading her to leave the stage; he had decided that this life, which after all was almost the same as the one he had chosen for himself, would jeopardize the woman's good "heart" and was thus wrong for her (Schiller 23, 137–38). Albrecht's admiration for Schiller, which was extensive, must have been tempered by such campaigns. And although he at least once wrote favorably about her poetry, he evidently did not turn his words into deeds. As far as can be detected he did not subscribe and did not elicit subscriptions from his friends. Practical support of that kind was more likely, as has been seen above, to come from Sophie Albrecht's women friends.

But any effort to demonstrate this brings us again to the original problem of the scholarly neglect of women's writings and lives. In Sophie Albrecht's case, the record of her life is not only slim but also uncertain, even on major points such as whether she had any children, and whether she was divorced. Only one of the several nineteenth-century biographical sketches of Albrecht mentions children (Schröder). Two accounts by a writer who claimed Albrecht herself as his distant source—he drew his information from the daughter of a servant with whom the aged Sophie Albrecht frequently discussed her life—never mention this subject (Neumann-Strela). None of her poetry refers to children of her own. None of the preserved letters makes any clear references to them either.

On the other hand, several accounts mention a divorce in 1798, usually adding that it was amicable (Alberti, Friedrichs, Pies, Schröder). The others are simply silent on the matter. None of the letters to Sophie Albrecht in any way confirm this claim. Several of them, written after the divorce was supposed to have occurred, refer to J. F. E. Albrecht as though he had still been her husband until his death in 1814. In one of her own letters from 1809 she sends his greetings (see letter 3 below).

A reluctance, first of her correspondents and then of her biographers, to mention unconventional aspects of her life may contribute to some of this uncertainty. Perhaps this explains two other discrepancies in the accounts. Most sources state explicitly that Albrecht's decision to become a professional actress was made only with her husband's permission (Lübker, Jördens, Schröder). But one writer, claiming access to Albrecht's own version of the matter, says she decided without any discussion with her husband (Neumann-Strela 1907, 390). Again, several sources have her making the long move from Leipzig to the Hamburg/Altona area with her husband (Jördens, Schröder, Pies). But the account based on her story contends that she went to Hamburg by herself and that she was surprised at her husband's unexpected later arrival (Neumann-Strela 1907, 392). Perhaps neither of these discrepancies can be resolved—although external evidence seems to fit the version that she first went north alone.[2] In addition to the possibility that an unconventional woman's life has been revised along more conventional lines, the discrepancies draw attention to the boldness of Sophie Albrecht's behavior—with or without her husband's approval. Might she not (also?) have had support in her decisions from other sources, such as women friends?

Few records have survived of relationships among women, and little scholarship has been published about the subject. For Sophie Albrecht, the total preserved correspondence with both women and men is extremely meagre: altogether sixteen notes and letters to or from her (see Appendix). Seven of these are to or from women (two of whom are unnamed) and another two are to unidentified persons with no clues as to their gender. The five letters to and from identifiable women are published here, beginning with a note from the poet and essayist Elise von der Recke.

Countess von der Recke was from Mitau, the capital of Courland (now divided between Latvia and Lithuania). Although the Albrechts had also lived in the Baltic, the difference in their social class makes it unlikely that von der Recke met them there.[3] Yet she may well have heard of them, for in 1779 and 1780 they published that region's first *Musenalmanach*, called *Ehstländische poetische Blumenlese* (*Poetic Bouquet from Estonia*). Von der Recke, as a woman with literary interests, would probably have been aware of this. So, in December 1784, when she and her travel companion, Sophie Becker, met the actress and poet Sophie Albrecht in Erfurt, Becker's brief diary note sounds as though Albrecht were a known person with whom Becker had now become acquainted (84). The letter to Albrecht, which von der Recke wrote four months later, is a request that she receive and assist a young painter. It shows the writer in a typical female role, as intermediary. It shows the addressee in much less familiar role, as a literary and theatrical woman whom people were eager to meet.

None of the other remnants of Albrecht's relationships with women is so straightforward. One concerns a dispute over the responsibilities of parents for childrearing. Another addresses a woman apparently seeking a divorce. The third, spread over two long and desperate letters concerns an aging woman's effort to earn a living and still keep up the facade of propriety. All of these letters refer to money.

The letter from Sophie La Roche is unique in La Roche's large correspondence: it is an apology. That much is clear. It is also clear that this apology had been preceded by at least two other letters. In an initial angry epistle to Albrecht, whom she had probably never met in person, La Roche had evidently defended herself against the impersonal and minimalist philosophy of childrearing that had been, as she says in the surviving letter written later, "preached" to her in Albrecht's name. Sophie Albrecht had evidently written a heated reply, disclaiming any belief that parents were responsible only for the basic physical care of their children, and denying that she thought La Roche greatly exaggerated the role of parents. She must then have attacked La Roche for believing such things of her. La Roche, in her apology, the one extant letter of the entire exchange on this subject, tried to explain how a visitor who claimed to be speaking on Albrecht's behalf had baited her with the other woman's alleged views. At the same time, La Roche expressed her relief in the preserved letter that she and Albrecht did not hold irreconcilable positions. And at the last moment, in a postscript, she thought of another action she had taken which Albrecht might misconstrue. She had asked someone to help her get money Albrecht owed her, probably money collected from subscribers to La Roche's *Pomona*. Perhaps Albrecht's subscription to *Pomona*—and she is on its list (Hutten)—is an indication that she had a daughter, since *Pomona* was a magazine for girls and their mothers. Albrecht's subscription to a work by another eighteenth-century woman writer adds plausibility to this speculation. In 1787 (when she had been married for fifteen years) Albrecht purchased the children's book *Neujahrsgeschenk für liebe*

Kinder by Philippine Engelhard (née Gatterer). Yet the total absence of references to having children, or experiencing motherhood, in Albrecht's letters and other writings counteracts the interpretation of the lists as indicating that she had children and leaves the question as open as before. The one point clearly made by her subscriptions is that Sophie Albrecht's purchases were acts of support for other women writers.

There is a gap of twenty years before the next preserved letter between Albrecht and another woman. Performing meanwhile in Dresden and Leipzig, Sophie Albrecht had become the leading actress for one of Germany's most important troupes, led first by Bondini and later by Seconda. Then, after she and her husband briefly ran Altona's National Theater together (following which they divorced, if the majority of biographers are right), Albrecht evidently spent long years on tour. In 1809 however she was back in the Hamburg area, for it is from there that she wrote to a young actress and mother about the woman's interest in what appears to be a divorce, although that word is not used in the letter. While offering cautious moral support, Albrecht nonetheless indicated her desire that Herz and her husband, who had been one of a succession of men to take over the Altona theater (Hoffmann, 17) would reunite.

The final set of correspondence with an identifiable woman also concerns an actress, Henriette von Montenglaut née von Cronstain (1768–1838). Her letters are long, inconsistent, and devious, but they give an idea of the struggle involved in a life similar to Sophie Albrecht's. Daughter of an officer and raised in Holland, the young woman had married and then divorced twice (first Gonsdruch and then Müller) before going on stage as Henriette Müller. Through her acting career, she had been able to meet and even marry one of the many aristocratic French emigrées in Hamburg and Altona, but the comfortable living that she expected to follow was aborted by her new husband's bankruptcy and then sudden death.

Those events, however, were in the distant past when the letters to Sophie Albrecht were being written. Albrecht had initiated the renewed acquaintance, as the opening lines of Montenglaut's first letter indicate. Yet aside from expressing her joy at receiving Albrecht's correspondence, Montenglaut responded to nothing her friend wrote. Considering the sensitivity that the next letter demonstrates, this lack of reference suggests that Albrecht's letter had been short and not particularly informative. The fifty-one-year-old

Montenglaut believed her older friend—Albrecht was then sixty-two—was in a favorable and influential situation.

Montenglaut, who had known both Albrechts at the beginning of her stage career in the late 1790s, tried in her first letter to summarize the events of the nineteen years that had elapsed since last the two women were together. Much revolves around her sons. The eldest, under pressure from an abusive father, had shot himself; the second had died in one of the Russian campaigns; the youngest, her child with the Frenchman, had died in infancy. That left two sons by her second husband, Fritz, who had become an officer, and Franz, who was still a minor.

Montenglaut referred constantly to money. Despite an attempt to appear painstakingly accurate and scrupulous, she seems mainly to be desperate. Her heiress mother had willed money to Montenglaut's sons but annual payments to Montenglaut only while the children were still minors. Considering her anxiety about giving the young men their money, it is possible that Montenglaut had spent some or all of the principal. Financial concerns, she wrote, had sent her back to the theater, even for a while directing her own troupe, one of the rather few women who undertook such a job. More recently she had attempted her luck with another of the limited choices available to a woman who needed to earn money, pedagogy. Her report of this is characteristically inconsistent. At the beginning of the letter she describes herself as merely vegetating through life "without a wish and without hope." A few pages later she claimed to have a wonderful posiion as a governess. Yet she was looking for another job and especially hoped that Albrecht could help her set up a declamatory performance; then she hastily added a long list of places where either her own reputation or her family's made a public appearance impossible.

She also seemed to believe that Albrecht could assist her with her literary career. Montenglaut wrote for money. For Sophie Albrecht, however, who at this time was also struggling to earn a living, there is little evidence that money motivated her to write; otherwise one would have expected, for example, more fiction in the Gothic mode that she had so quickly mastered before.

Montenglaut's letters are full of signs of the psychic fragmentation she experienced from wanting to be conventionally acceptable while still doing unconventional things, from being born into the aristocracy, yet without the means to live in an aristocratic fashion, from being attracted to the stage and claiming devotion to art, yet desperately needing money and work. At one point, for example, she blamed her brother and son for narrowmindedly forcing her to leave the stage; a few sentences later she considered them victims under pressure from the ignorant officers corps to which they belonged and which would have hounded out any member whose sister was an actress. In another passage she explained that her brother had lost all his money and could not help her; a few lines later she denounced him for his stinginess. Altogether, she tried to present a conventional image of herself as a caring, selfless, providing mother, a devotee of art, a hardworking woman who, however, would have been best served if she could have led the quiet aristocratic life to which she had been born.

The inconsistencies of the first letter are still present in the second but diminished, and Montenglaut seemed to feel more confident that Albrecht would approve of her as she was; she allowed herself there to indicate the somewhat tawdry devices that she had recently used for getting by.

Useful as the first letter is as a record of the difficulties an independent woman such as an actress faced, the second letter shows more about Sophie Albrecht herself and about her skid into poverty in her old age. This letter, written thirteen years after the preceding one, registers several of the ways in which Montenglaut was now assisting her friend. First, she had persuaded various groups and individuals from the theater world to contribute a small monthly pension for their aged colleague (Montenglaut explained that the woman in Hamburg responsible for the payments to Albrecht was Betty Herz, to whom Albrecht, in a letter mentioned above, had years ago sent a greeting when the child's mother had been considering a divorce.) Second, Montenglaut was sending Albrecht some used clothing that she could either wear or sell. Albrecht's old web of connections still helped to support her.

Meanwhile Montenglaut herself was also struggling to survive and remain optimistic. She wondered about coming to live with Albrecht, discussed the financial side of this possibility, and announced that she could earn money now by making artificial flowers or teaching this skill to others. Six years later, in 1838, Henriette Montenglaut died. Sophie Albrecht lived until 1840. At the very end of her life, she had resumed contact with one of her husband's old publishers, who brought out her last work, the cookbook.

The friend whose financial assistance to the aged writer and actress is sometimes noted in the biographical entries is Clemens

Gerke, but the letter from Montenglaut shows that in her last years of need, Albrecht also got help from her women friends.

Examining the record of female friendship can change the emphasis in literary history. The interaction shown among women in the fragmentary documentation of Sophie Albrecht's work and correspondence points less to intellectual stimulation and more to practical help that women asked and received from each other (often with complications and miscommunication along the way). How, Montenglaut asked Albrecht bluntly, could one make money by writing? The answers women gave to each other enabled them to find subscribers (and thus to get their work published), to reach a wider circle of readers, to learn from each other. The feeling of support, even when it came with reservations such as those Albrecht expressed to Herz about her divorce, could give a talented woman the courage to try bolder ways, to risk disapproval, to survive in the foothills and even the flatlands far from Olympus.

Appendix: The Correspondence of Sophie Albrecht

The numbered letters are reprinted in the Supplement at the back of this volume.

DATE		WRITER, PLACE, RECIPIENT	LOCATION OF MANUSCRIPT
29 April 1785	1	Elise von der Recke, Halberstadt, to Sophie Albrecht	Hamburg
13 March 1785		Theodor Anton von Dalberg, Erfurt, to Sophie Albrecht	Hamburg
23 ? 1785		Sophie Albrecht, n.p., to Unknown	Weimar
3 May 1786	2	Sophie von La Roche, Speyer, to Sophie Albrecht	Hamburg
17 April 1787		Friedrich Schiller, Dresden, to Sophie Albrecht	Hamburg
n.d.		August von Kotzebue, n.p.,[a] to Sophie Albrecht	Hamburg
after 1791[b]		Sophie Albrecht, n.p., to Unknown	Hamburg, TS
21 Feb. 1795		Sophie Albrecht, Dresden, in album (Stammbuch) of Unknown	Hamburg, TS
6 April 1795		Sophie Albrecht (Postscript), Leipzig, to Johann Wolfgang von Goethe	Weimar

n.d. (after 179–)		Siegfried August Mahlmann, Gohlis, to Sophie Albrecht	Hamburg
[1809]	3	Sophie Albrecht, Hamburg, to Madame Herz	SBPK Berlin
n.d.		Sophie Albrecht, Hamburg, to Friedrich Ludwig Schmidt	Hamburg
April 1816		Sophie Albrecht, n.p., to Daniel Schütte	Marbach
29 Jan. 1817		Salomon Ludwig Steinheim, n.p., to Sophie Albrecht	Hamburg
3 July 1819	4	Henriette Montenglaut, Stade, to Sophie Albrecht	Hamburg
18 Jan. 1832	5	Henriette Montenglaut, Braunschweig, to Sophie Albrecht	Hamburg
n.d.		Sophie Albrecht, n.p., to Friederike ?	Frankfurt
22 April 1839		Sophie Albrecht, St. Pauli, to unknown woman[c]	Frankfurt

Manuscript Locations:
Berlin = Staatsbibliothek Preußischer Kulturbesitz
Frankfurt = Freies Deutsches Hochstift
Hamburg = Staats- und Universitätsbibliothek
Hamburg, TS = Bibliothek der Theatersammlung
Marbach = Deutsches Literaturarchiv im Schiller Nationalmuseum
Weimar = Goethe und Schiller Archiv

---

[a]Internal evidence suggests a place not too distant from Weimar, perhaps Erfurt or Leipzig.
[b]The letter is a request to borrow a copy of *Egmont;* 1791 is when *Egmont* was first performed.
[c]Probably the Friederike of the above letter.

10

The Vanished Woman of Great Influence: Benedikte Naubert's Legacy and German Women's Fairy Tales

Shawn C. Jarvis

We servants at the altar of the muses—... wear the cloak of our ordination not like an everyday dress, we are good girls in our homes, quiet, domesticated women, pleasing, dedicated wives, patient mothers, cooks, seamstresses, spinners. We're easy to get along with, and a more elevated sentiment stirs only in the sanctity of solitude or with a friend who understands us.

Wir Dienerinnen am Altar der Musen—... tragen das Kleid unsrer Weihe nicht wie ein Alltagskleid, sind in unserm Hause gute Mädchen, stille häusliche Frauen, gefällige ergebene Ehegattinnen, geduldige Mütter, Köchinnen, Nätherinnen, Spinnerinnen beiher. Es läßt sich recht gut mit uns umgehen, und eine höhere Stimmung beginnt nur im Allerheiligsten der Einsamkeit, oder dem Freunde, der Freundin gegenüber, die uns versteht.

Benedikte Naubert to Louise Brachmann
Leipzig, October 22, 1805[1]

Christiane Benedikte Eugenie Hebenstreit Naubert, according to Manfred Grätz "one of the greatest German popular writers of all times," is both typical and untypical of women writers in the period dealt with by this volume. Born on September 13, 1756 as the sixth child of the daughter of a councilman and a professor of law and the son of a professor of medicine, she enjoyed an extraordinarily broad education for a woman of her times. Through the efforts of her brother and her own autodidactic endeavors, she received training in disciplines ranging from the classical languages, philosophy, and history, to her favorite subjects: mythology, medieval history and French, English and Italian. Yet while she benefited from an education generally only accorded men in her times, she maintained the proper level of propriety for a woman. Naubert also achieved "the highest degree of skill" in needlework and mastered the piano and harp (Touaillon, 342–43).

Her professional career was prodigious; she was, in fact, "one of the most prolific writers of the Goethe period" (Dorsch, jacket cover). Naubert's first novel, *Die Geschichte Emmas, Tochter Kaiser Karls des Großen, und seines Geheimschreibers Eginhard,* appeared in 1785. From 1786–1797, she produced at least one novel per year, and often more. In 1787, for example, two novels appeared, totaling almost 1150 pages. One year later she published three novels comprising 1500 pages and a major translation from the English. By the time of her death, Naubert, in 33 years and despite a five-year pause beginning in 1797, had penned over 50 novels, plus numerous novellas and fairy tale collections.[2] Even when already blind and almost deaf, the writer continued to dictate her works, until a rheumatic lung disorder ended her life in 1819.

Like many other women of this first generation of German women writers, Naubert chose professional anonymity, "the much more felicitous seclusion, ... the vestal veil from praise and reproach!!" (die viel glücklichere Verborgenheit, ... de[n] vestalische[n] Schleyer vor Lob und Tadel!!, letter to Friedrich Rochlitz, 1805, Dorsch, 23). Until 1806 her novels appeared only as "from the author of Walter von Montbarry" or of another of her novels, despite numerous attempts to encourage the writer to lift the veil of secrecy. A reviewer in the *Allgemeiner Litterarischer Anzeiger,* for example, encouraged the author of *Walter von Montbarry* to give up his incognito because "[the] writings of this anonym ... *belong without a doubt to the better products of our literature"* ([die] Schriften dieses Anonymus ... *unstreitig zu den bessern Produkten unserer Litteratur ... gehören,* Dorsch, 227; emphasis added). Such praise notwithstanding, Naubert's first concession did not come until almost a decade later, when she published *Eudocia, Gemahlinn Theodosius des Zweyten, Teil 1,* "by the authoress of Walter von Montbarry" (von der Verfasser*inn* des Walter von Montbarry).[3] After K. J. Schütz exposed her incognito in the *Zeitung für die elegante Welt* early in 1817—against her express wishes eighteen months before her death—the novel *Rosalba* (1818) appeared with the full name of its author. Once the reviewers knew with whom they were dealing, the critical reception of her œuvre could begin in earnest.[4] The gender of the author has played a role in the reception of her works and the perception of her importance to German letters.

A Woman of Great Influence: The View of Naubert in the Critical Literature

The reception of Benedikte Naubert falls into two distinct periods which roughly coincide with the period of her anonymity and the unveiling of her identity. While she remained anonymous—throughout her lifetime as a writer—she was well-received by her contemporaries *because* she went to such great lengths to create a male persona. One component of this male persona was her erudition in subjects uncommon for women—history, philosophy, and classical languages—in a time when female literacy lay around ten percent; (one reviewer of *Eudocia* commented, for example, that if speculations about the female authorship of the novel proved true, "then the great erudition (of the author) must certainly be admired" (so muß allerdings die große Belesenheit [der Verfasserin] bewundert werden, Dorsch, 171). The other component was her application of her readings to her writing, her attention to what Touaillon summarizes as

> the joy of action, the partiality to portraying events, the avoidance of sentimentalism, the preference for male heroes, . . . the connection to history, the rejection of familial subject matter, . . . the precision and energy of the tone, [and the rejection of the] habit of female writers of the time, in that love played only a secondary role. (435)

Her writing style and choice of topics pointed, for contemporary readers and critics, to a male writer, to works which reflected the dominant discourse. Naubert succeeded in convincing her readers, even discriminating ones like Körner, who wrote to Schiller in 1788: "All these works appear to be from a man, and not a mediocre one" (Alle diese Produkte scheinen von einem Manne, und von keinem mittelmäßigen Kopfe zu sein).[5] Undoubtedly Naubert realized this masquerade was necessary to insure a modicum of critical attention. Female writers had not come into their own in Germany, and, perhaps because she was not part of the protected class of women of the Goethe generation who belonged "to the

periphery of one (or more) great men, as a friend, muse, onetime
financée, lover, wife, grandmother, daughter, or simply as a pro-
tégée" (Becker-Cantarino, 71), Naubert's only chance for critical
reception came from appearing to be a man. Her estimation of her
vulnerability as a woman writer has proven true.

Today Naubert's oeuvre—from her historical novels to her
fairy tales—is rarely considered in its own right. The reception of
Naubert changed dramatically with the revelation of her gender.[6]
To read of Benedikte Naubert in modern literary histories—the
validated arbiters of authors and texts we should read—is to encounter the legacy of patriarchal canonical practices and strategies. In this century, two tendencies are apparent: Naubert, the
imitator and, paradoxically, Naubert, the influencer. Naubert the
imitator stands in the shadow of men she was like or whose texts
she presumably emulated. Her work with the historical novel is
generally situated into the literary climate of the times—the
growing interest in things German, stretching from Klopstock's
Hermann dramas, Jakob Bodmer's rediscovery of middle high German poetry, Herder's "Volkslieder" collections, Möser's "Patrio-
tische Phantasien," Goethe's *Götz von Berlichingen* (Greiner) and
Johann Christoph Gottsched's "Beyträge zur critischen Historie
der deutschen Sprache" to articles on the German past as a literary motif or subject for philological study in Wieland's *Teutscher
Merkur* and Boie's *Deutsches Museum* (Schreinert). Although
Christine Touaillon champions Naubert as "the path-breaking creator of the historical-rationalistic novel in Germany . . . in literary
status equal to La Roche, Sophie Mereau and Dorothea Schlegel,"
critics like Rudolf Bauer conclude: in the years 1789–95 "Ben.
Naubert obviously adjusted to the work methods of her male colleagues (Veit Weber, Schlenkert, Heinse); at the very least she
picked up the use of the medieval 'costume' from them" (39). Martin Greiner places Naubert's work, along with Leonhard Wächter's
(Veit Weber) in the context of a trend begun with Goethe's *Götz
von Berlichingen:* the need of bourgeois readers in the eighteenth
century to escape into a " 'free-German' bourgeois past" ('frei-
deutsch' biedere[n] Vergangenheit).

Paradoxically, canonical history also presents another view
of Naubert: the not-so-great woman behind all the great men in
German letters, the quintessential woman of influence. Although
Schreinert suggests that her indisputable contribution was her
reclamation of German national history for the novel (97), that
contribution has become the source of one of the longest influence

studies in *Germanistik*. Reading modern literary histories, we find a dizzyingly long trail of Naubert running through much of nineteenth-century, and even twentieth-century, German literature. We discover her works influenced everyone from the German and English romantics to Thomas Mann. For example, Friedrich de la Motte Fouqué was inspired by Naubert's *Velleda* for his rendition of the Undine tale, and by *Walter von Montbarry;* Gustav Freytag drew on *Velleda* in his "Ahnen;" Ludwig Achim von Arnim's *Kronenwächter* contains "several echoes of Naubert's historical novels" (Schreinert, 100); two of Naubert's fairy tales served as an important source for Adam Oehlenschläger, who combined "Die weiße Frau" and "Die Sage von der Ludlamshöhle" in his play "Ludlam's Höhle;" Franz Grillparzer was probably influenced by "Die weiße Frau" to create his "Ahnfrau;" Friedrich Schiller's *Wallenstein* and Conrad Ferdinand Meyer's "Gustav Adolfs Page" both were inspired by the characters in Naubert's novel *Thekla von Thurn* (which Tieck read with great pleasure); Heinrich von Kleist's *Käthchen von Heilbronn* was influenced by *Herrmann von Unna*. Naubert's influence on *male* writers extended even into this century, all the way to Thomas Mann's *Buddenbrooks,* for she is perhaps the starting point for a new literary form: "the family chronicle as the symbolic case study of the generative and destructive forces of an era" (Bauer). Naubert's influence was even felt across the Channel. In England many of her novels were translated, *Unna* was made into a drama, the fairy tale "Die Fischer" inspired Matthew Gregory Lewis of *Tales of Wonder* fame, and Sir Walter Scott, calling her novels *Herrmann von Unna* and *Alf von Dülmen* "excellent romances" (Schreinert, 101), began his own endeavors with the genre of the historical novel.[7] But not even Madame de Staël, despite reproaches from Isidorus Orientalis, included Naubert in her works about Germany. For an author whose main body of work has now conveniently been consigned to the nether realms of "trivial literature" (*Trivialliteratur*), a category created by bourgeois critics to exile certain writers from the canon, the extent to which Naubert was received, reviewed and emulated is astounding. The few scholarly studies dealing with Naubert suggest a broad and far-reaching influence; yet the list of the influenced suggests only men read her works, or at very least that only their re-workings of her texts deserve mention.

The fact is that, as she became a source of broad inspiration, Naubert was unable to defend herself against the broad, outright appropriation of her intellectual property.[8] Before copyright laws existed, no author could be sure his or her works would not be purloined, but the unabating tide of works by men based on texts by Naubert leads to the speculation that her lack of Olympian status made her more susceptible to what modern histories have called "influence," but which actually amounts to plagiarism. While Naubert's works were serving as "inspiration" to every writer from Arnim to Scott, Naubert herself was victim of a double standard of which she herself was aware. A case in point: in the foreword to her "Felsenjungfrau" (1818) she noted her source as an "old Nordic lay." Her friend Friedrich Rochlitz warned her repeatedly about borrowing too heavily from Friedrich de la Motte Fouqué, on whose *Der Held des Nordens. Drei Heldenspiele,* Rochlitz claimed, Naubert's work was based.[9] Rochlitz's warnings generated this somewhat irate response from the author:

> Fouqwet[10] adapted my Ida Münsterinn ten years ago already, and Oehlschläger wrote a Ludlams höle which, I have been told, is based on one of my fairy tales. This is no dipping into a common well open to everyone. All characters in Ida Münsterinn are children of *my own peculiar imagination,* and my Ludlamshöle is based on an old English saga and it would surprise me very much if another author found it anywhere other than by me. . . . In addition, I have been prudent in my invasions into foreign territories; I carried my lamp only to places where Fouqwet let his torch burn low, and took care not to pick any of his leaves, so that at the most I took in a few places a blade of grass in order to bind together the wild flowers I tended on the barren patches.

> Fouqwet adaptirte schon vor 10 Jahren meine Ida Münsterinn, und Oehlschläger hat eine Ludlams höle geschrieben, die, wie man mich versicherte, auf eins meiner Volcksmärchen gebaut ist. Hier ist kein Schöpfen aus gemeinschaftlichen Brunnen, der jedem offen steht. Alle Personen in der Ida Münsterinn sind Kinder *meiner eigenthümlichen Phantasie,* und meine Ludlamshöle gründet sich auf eine alte englische Sage, von welcher es mich wundern müßte, wenn sie dem neuen Bearbeiter irgendwo als bey mir zu Gesichte gekommen wäre. . . . Uebrigens bin in bey meiner Invasion in fremde Gebiete bescheiden zu werke gegangen; ich trug meine Lampe immer nur dahin, wo Fouqwet seine Fackel dunkel brennen lies, und hütete mich so sehr etwas von seinen Blättern zu pflücken, daß ich höchstens nur an einigen Stellen mir ein Grashälmgen ausbat, meine Wiesenblumen, die ich auf den leergelaßnen Stellen gepflegt hatte zusammen zu binden. (Dorsch 97–98; emphasis added)

With justifiable indignation, Naubert resisted, and yet bowed, to her subordinate role. She carried the flickering candle to dark corners where Fouqué's torch did not burn bright. Where he foraged, she carefully gathered up the few remaining blades of grass. This is the leitmotif of Naubert's and other women's work: histories of the chaff, tales by and about women.

Naubert and the German Fairy Tale Tradition

As early as 1787, in the midst of her historical novel production, Benedikte Naubert began publishing texts she entitled *Märchen* (fairy tales): *Amalgunde, Königin von Italien, oder das Mährchen von der Wunderquelle. Eine Sage aus der Zeit Theoderichs des Grossen; Neue Volksmährchen der Deutschen* (1789–92)[11]; *Velleda, Ein Zauberroman* (1795; second edition 1797); and *Almé oder ägyptische Mährchen* (1798). Later in her career, when she began to shift away from novels and more toward novellas, she continued to write and publish fairy tales like "Die Minyaden, in drey mythologischen Mährchen" (1808).

Naubert's various tales were well-received while the author's identity remained undisclosed. Contemporary reviews of the *Neue Volksmährchen*, for example, lauded the author with comments like: "Thus someone was ready to assume the position on the German Parnassus which became vacant upon Musäus' death. This new voice from the folk is truly not a hapless successor of the deceased" (So hätte also geschwind einer sich der Stelle bemächtigt, die durch Musäus Tod auf dem deutschen Parnass erledigt worden! In der That ist dieser neue Volkserzähler kein unglücklicher Nachfolger des Verstorbenen... Grätz, 233). The German romantics were especially drawn to her *Märchen*, as the list of the "influenced" above indicates. Achim von Arnim commented about her *Neue Volksmährchen* that he remained "inexhaustable in the praise of this book [. . .] which brightened for him very sad nights" (unerschöpflich in dem Lobe dieses Buchs..., das ihm sehr traurige Nächte erhellte," in the *Zeitung für Einsiedler* 20 July 1808, 256); he found in them "the true foundation of all poetic gifts—imagination" (das eigentliche Fundament aller Dichtergaben, die Erfindung); "Talent," and "a naive sentiment" (ein Kindergefühl). "And the book is forgotten! What's to become of it?" (Und das Buch ist vergessen! was soll daraus werden? Arnim to Brentano, May 1807; Touaillon, 439). Jacob Grimm mentioned in his foreword to a saga anthology that he wanted to include "Ottilie" (from the *Neue Volksmährchen*) in a German legend collection, and even called Naubert in a letter to his brother Ferdinand "a very talented and creative female writer" (eine sehr begabte und phantasiereiche Schriftstellerin). In that same letter, however, Grimm jealously guarded what in the German tradition became male terrain, the domain of the canonically approved book fairy tale, or *Buchmärchen*. To his letter he appended the caveat: "it's too bad that she wrote so much and so fast, which often makes her style deficient. Musaeus, who has an outstanding style, will survive longer for posterity" (es ist schade dasz sie zuviel und zu schnell schrieb, weshalb ihr stil oft schlecht und fehlerhaft wird. Musaeus, der sich im stil sehr auszeichnet, lebt darum bei der nachwelt länger, Grätz, 234). Musäus, the male fairy tale writer, reigned supreme.

While in modern times Naubert has received some limited critical recognition for her work with the German historical novel, her contribution to the German *Märchen* tradition goes completely unnoticed. This phenomenon is partially explained by Olympian categories. When we think of fairy tales, our critical apparatus has been determined by models formulated by the Olympians of folkloric studies in the late eighteenth and early nineteenth centuries: Herder,[12] Wieland,[13] the Brothers Grimm. In the German tradition, fairy tales may be from the mouths of nursemaids and old wives, but they must be mediated for us by male editors and writers. We also expect German fairy tales to chronicle the adventure out into the world, to document the establishment of connections outside the family, to teach us about dominance and mastery and the rites of passage to wealth and stature for men, to marriage and passivity for women. Any author or text which did not confirm and corroborate such narratives has been excluded from validation. The literary canon had little place for texts like Naubert's which do not chronicle the Odyssean journey toward mastery over others, but instead the journey within. Or for texts of hers which treat the establishment, confirmation and celebration of women's relationship with other women.

Canonical literary history ignores that Naubert's work with *Märchen* establishes her relationship to another tradition outside of Germany, that of the *Muses françoise* of the late seventeenth-century salon culture who were actually responsible for the genesis of the modern European fairy tale tradition in print.[14] Madame

d'Aulnoy, Mlle Lhéritier, Mlle Bernard, Mlle de la Force and Madame de Murat poked fun at the rise of classical literature by returning to the archaic and "pre-logical" world of the middle ages,
of nursemaids and of children, producing literary fairy tales (contes de fées) as an outgrowth of their activities. The women were
drawn to the fairy tale as an exploration of alternative realities,
as a vehicle for creating an ideal world which could only exist
within the imagination, and as a way to engage in the intellectual
discourse of the day, the battle of the ancients and the moderns
(Querelle des Anciens et des Modernes) from which they were officially excluded (see Baader, 231–33). Benedikte Naubert knew,
and responded to, tales from the French tradition (she makes
overt references in Velleda, for example, to Madame d'Aulnoy). She
also, with later generations of women writers in Germany, explored other female realities through the fairy tale.

In her historical novels, Naubert focused on stories of great
men; in her fairy tales she explored the forgotten histories of
women, both mythical and real. Rather than establishing, as canonical history has done, how Naubert has been co-opted by men—her
fairy tales, like her historical novels, were also used as a source,
specially by E.T.A. Hoffmann and Tieck—I am more interested in
demonstrating how Naubert's tales, rarely if ever mentioned in canonical histories of the German Märchen tradition, anticipated and
framed many of the themes and motifs of later German women's
fairy tales. Naubert's Märchen, from the Neue Volksmährchen der
Deutschen to Velleda, Ein Zauberroman, echo through German women's texts like the strains of a familiar, but now forgotten, melody.

A Paradigmatic Text: Velleda, Ein Zauberroman

Velleda, Ein Zauberroman (1795), a collection of loosely connected tales, followed the last volume of Naubert's Neue Volksmährchen by a short two years. Like many of her other fairy tales
in that earlier collection, e.g. "Die Legende von Rübezahl" and
"Die weiße Frau," the tales in Velleda reflect characteristics common to Naubert's general work as well as to the fairy tale literature of the times—the interest in subjects from ancient and
medieval Germanic history, the use of chronicles and legends as
source material, and (like her French models) the experimentation
with medieval narrative forms and motifs. Naubert's use of these
subjects and motifs rewrites the patriarchal narrative.

Schindel claims that Naubert paged "with enthusiastic zeal" in dusty old chronicles (Schreinert, 38), especially those concerning Roman and medieval history. This may have been where she came upon Velleda, an historical figure mentioned in Tacitus' narration of the war with Civilis (*Hist.* III, IV and VI) and P. Papinus Statius' *Vilvae* (1.4). Tacitus, who claims he and his comrades "actually saw Vespasia's Veleda" (*Vidimus sub divo Vespasiano Veledam*) describes her as a highly esteemed soothsayer and arbitrator. A powerful maiden of the tribe of the Bructeri, Velleda sat at the tables of the most influential men of her times as arbiter of various treaties. Before her capture by Rutilius Gallicus in about AD 77, she foretold the successes of the Germans and the destruction of the Roman legions. The histories do not tell of her fate at Roman hands.

Naubert clearly makes use in her two stories "Voadicea und Velleda" and its sequel "Der Riesentanz" of the figure Tacitus described, but she goes beyond canonical history to explain its context. This is the kind of literary legerdemain at which Naubert is so accomplished: while appearing to write the story of a figure from Germanic history, Naubert actually rewrites the patriarchal narrative. She contextualizes the life of Tacitus' Velleda by illuminating the circumstances of her development, her passage into history. Velleda appears in two incarnations in the work: in "Voadicea und Velleda" as the prognosticating sorceress and then, in "Der Riesentanz," as the princess Velleda (Tacitus' figure) who follows in the footsteps of her mentor and achieves magical status. Velleda embodied the image which fascinated Naubert (and women after her): "a memory of that . . . which we once were, what heights our powers can reach without losing true femininity" (eine Errinnerung an das . . . was wir einst waren, welche Höhe unsre Kräfte erreichen können, ohne wahre Weiblichkeit zu verlieren, letter to Friedrich Rochlitz, Naumburg, prob. early summer 1806; Dorsch, 46). Velleda is not only the figure Tacitus knew, but a legacy of women's power and connectedness.

Just as Naubert rewrites the patriarchal narration of history, she also rewrites the parameters of the medieval redemption fairy tale (*Erlösungsmärchen*)[15] when she creates in "Voadicea und Velleda" a generic amalgam of historical novel and medieval redemption fairy tale. By using the well-known and time-tested motif of the *Erlösungsmärchen,* in which a hero (usually male) sets out to rescue a captive damsel, Naubert drew on specific reader expectations regarding the outcomes of such narratives: the helpless captives, unable to save themselves, must be rescued to marry their "redeemers." The writer's solution to the dilemma, however, deviates sharply from literary conventions. In her framing of this issue "freedom" vs. "captivity," she charts the course for an entire series of tales which were to follow from female pens, as in her narrative of "Voadicea und Velleda":

> The Romans, occupying the lands of the Icanian king, have begun decimating its indigenous populations and shipping the captive children off to the Empire. Without consulting his wife, Voadicea, the king flees with his nine daughters, bringing them for protection to the secret island of the sorceress, Velleda. He dies on the trip home, and Voadicea knows nothing of her daughters' whereabouts.

> Left to her own devices, the queen defeats the Romans in several skirmishes and affects a temporary truce. Divining that her daughters are still alive, Voadicea sets out on a perilous journey to find them. When she finally does, they reject her offer of "redemption" and, with the exception of the oldest daughter Bunduica, they remain with Velleda. Bunduica is killed by the Romans on the journey back to civilization with her mother, and Voadicea takes a poisonous sleeping draught, "to still all her suffering."

> When the two young Romans Flavius and Julius appear on the island seeking refuge from the ravages of war, the princesses Velleda and Voada (in various animal transformations), befriend them. Seeking fire, Flavius and Julius stumble upon the temple ruins inhabited by the sorceress and her eight charges. They receive fire from the enchantress and an offer to assume responsibility for eight deer (the transformed princesses) in the cave with them. Before awaiting the Romans' response, six princesses commit ritual suicide, plunging themselves into a fiery abyss. The remaining princesses, Velleda and Voada, leave with the Romans. All that remains the next day at the temple is a smoldering pit and the petrified stone statue of the sorceress at the entrance to the cave.

> The Romans go on to great feats and are often seen in the company of white eagles or milky white maidens. Voada is fatally struck by a lightning bolt when she consummates her relationship with Julius; Velleda maintains her platonic relationship with Flavius.

In the sequel, "Der Riesentanz,"

the princess Velleda, in possession of some of the sorceress' visionary powers and longevity, mourns the passing of her family and her dependence on her Roman protector. On an evening walk she discovers a new temple. After reading the inscription at the entrance, she enters, and then exits as a truly magical woman. Upon her return to Salisbury, she scorns her male admirers and, when this world no longer pleases her, she goes on to other domains, leaving behind reading material she had used to amuse herself in her lonely hours.

While one could examine these texts from the standpoint of their reflection of the overall Enlightenment agenda—their concern, for example, with issues of "virtue" (Tugend), and "depravity" (Laster), "fate" (Schicksal) and "destiny" (Bestimmung)—or of their relationship to other German fairy tales of the time (as Anthony has done), this synchronic approach does not reveal the agenda Naubert set for later generations of female writers. "Voadicea und Velleda" and "Der Riesentanz" frame themes common to Naubert and to subsequent women's fairy tales: the creation of a female community outside traditional society; the mediating role of the magical wisewoman; the rites of passage for females, and the rejection of patriarchal "redemption." These interrelated and overlapping issues map out a yet uncharted fairy tale terrain which traditional scholarship has overlooked. Looking at the *Märchen* produced by women over a sixty-year period, from Naubert to Gisela von Arnim, we find these themes re-worked, and re-defined in ways that have yet to be explored by canonical history.

1. The Female Community Outside Traditional Society

In "Voadicea und Velleda," the Icanian princesses escape to the island with Velleda to find refuge from the "masters of the world" (Herren der Welt). Precisely because it is a domain outside that of the patriarchal rulers of the world, it is also a place where a kind of transformation can take place. The nine daughters, "accustomed to blind obedience to parental orders" (zu einem blindem Gehorsam gegen älterliche Befehle gewöhnt), follow "where paternal love and paternal authority led them" ([w]ohin Vaterliebe und Vatergewalt [sie] leiten, 10). Yet once they leave behind the world of their mother, who leads a life "not very different than that of common housewives" (welches nicht viel von dem Leben guter gemeiner häuslichen Frauen verschieden war) and of their father, they are transformed—in the literal and figurative sense. Under Velleda's tutelage, the nine Icanian princesses achieve an independent stature, leading most of them to prefer death over life with men, bewitchment to domestic entrapment.

It is significant that this realm is separate from domesticity, i.e., separate from the realms women traditionally occupied. Whereas their mother, Voadicea, tends hearth and home, the daughters pass their days on the island in various transformations, as doves, swans, lambs and butterflies; as deer and eagles—creatures of the elements of water, air, and land. Their only home is the temple of an ancient religion. They are content with their solitude and their transformations; life outside of traditional society has established their intimate connection to the creative forces of nature. The interlude on the various islands under Velleda's protection transforms them not only into swans and doves, but also into independent creatures seeking more (or at least other) than the outside world of female domestication has to offer.

In nineteenth-century German canonical fairy tales (by definition generally male-authored), a separation from home most often heralds the start of the female protagonist's greatest trials, her humiliation and degradation on the path to marriage.[16] Benedikte Naubert's text, like those of other women who followed her, shows how a separation from home can lead to the discovery of the true home of women's experience and desires, a refuge from the constraints of traditional society and an opportunity for women to develop their connection to nature.

The image of the island as the site of a utopian political state was already familiar to eighteenth-century European readers who voraciously devoured the Robinsonades and Amadis novels. Islands likewise figure prominently in a number of Naubert's works, e.g. in *Walter von Montbarry, Elisabeth von Toggenburg, Konradin,* and *Barbara Blomberg,* less, however, as a focus of political debate and more as the site of female religious communities. This island/convent imagery as the refuge for a female community also connects Naubert's work to an entire tradition of European women's literature, from the female-penned Robinsonades,[17] to the fairy tales of George Sand,[18] in which women explore other realms of human interaction and personal realization on island refuges. While islands function both as punishment and paradise in later women's fairy tales, in the overwhelming number of instances, they are the site of positive developments in the female character.

In two notable examples from the female fairy tale tradition, Agnes Franz's "Prinzessin Rosalieb. Ein Mährchen" (1841) and

Gisela von Arnim's fairy tale novel *Das Leben der Hochgräfin Gritta von Rattenzuhausbeiuns* (1844), the island plays an important role. In Franz' work, perhaps some of the least emancipatory of all female-penned fairy tales I have read, the disobedient Rosalieb is whisked away to an island tower[19] by two emissaries of the fairy godmother Amaranth. There she spends her hours spinning her daily quantum of flax. The reward for her diligence is a fully set table and food for thought—access to a book which tells the evolving story of her own life. Each day she successfully completes her tasks, albeit menial and traditionally female ones, another page to the story magically appears. While Franz is often almost sickeningly conservative in her insistence on prescribed gender roles, her imagery is insofar important as the island is the place that the female child writes her own story. Sequestered from the seductions of the material world, Rosalieb determines her own fate.

Gisela von Arnim, writing *Das Leben der Hochgräfin Gritta von Rattenzuhausbeiuns* (with her mother Bettine's help) almost fifty years after Naubert and combining the plot frameworks of *Märchen* and Robinsonade,[20] revives Naubert's combination of island and convent and demonstrates the difference between positive and negative female communities.[21] Twelve girls escape the oppressive clutches of the nuns in a convent on the mainland, only to be shipwrecked on a semi-deserted island while effecting their getaway. On the island they establish a new kind of convent, one dedicated to halcyon group activity. They tend sheep, harvest their own crops, and fend for themselves without male protection. They become the rescuers of various hapless males, Gritta's father and a young prince among them. One of the girls, like Velleda, even goes on to discover the secrets of nature and becomes a homeopathic healer. The female community established on the island is a place of refuge and self-realization. While *Gritta* is more whimsical than anything Naubert produced, the novel re-works the imagery developed in *Velleda* and other texts.

In *Velleda, Ein Zauberroman,* the island is a sanctuary where women connect to sources of strength and power. While the passage to this domain is generally due to cataclysmic events (in Naubert by flight from the Romans, in Franz by the transgression of a prohibition, in von Arnim by shipwreck—in other words, it was initially not a place consciously sought), the island serendipitously becomes the locus for personal development impossible in traditional society. Only in this separation do women achieve the full measure of their abilities. Outside of traditional patriarchal society, the protagonists seek spiritual rather than material wealth, wisdom rather than earthly possessions.

2. The Female Triad: The Magical Wisewoman, the Biological Mother and the Daughter

In "Voadicea und Velleda" Naubert pits the biological mother Voadicea, who represents traditional society, against the spiritual mother Velleda, who represents another world of female experience. In terms of pages, Voadicea's story plays the most significant role as she ascends to power after the king's demise and sets out to "redeem" her daughters. The sorceress Velleda, on the other hand, is the last character to be introduced and the number of pages she occupies are small.

There is a major split both between the worlds the "mothers" inhabit and what they, as a consequence, can offer the daughters. Both Voadicea and Velleda possess power (*Macht*), but Voadicea's is clearly vested in her authority to rule over people as queen, while Velleda's is the power of knowledge (*Wissen*). The daughters' decision to remain with Velleda, rather than return to the world of their mother and the Romans, is framed in terms of the exceptional status of Velleda's offerings:

> ... they would not leave this shore, not even on the hand of the most beloved of mothers, without the consent of their governess. ... Velleda's more than motherly generosity, her *superhuman wisdom, the supernatural knowledge* which her young pupils praised having received from her mouth, her *warnings about the dangers of the world,* thousands of proofs in individual situations of her *loyalty and infallibility,* everything was mentioned ....

> ... sie würden, ohne die Einwilligung ihrer Erzieherin, selbst an der Hand der geliebtesten aller Mütter, nicht diese Küste verlassen. ... Velleda's mehr als mütterliche Güte, ihre *übermenschliche Weisheit, die höheren Kenntnisse,* die ihre jungen Schülerinnen rühmte, durch ihren Mund erhalten zu haben, ihre *Warnungen vor den Gefahren der Welt,* tausende in einzelnen Fällen erhaltene Beweise von ihrer *Treue und Unfehlbarkeit,* alles kam an die Reihe. ... (82–83; emphasis added)

The princesses, "the young pupils," reject the biological mother in favor of the spiritual mentor. The mother, in her redemption attempts, can only offer the daughters a return to a society in which she plays "the *subordinate* role of the wife of the king" (die *unter-geordnete* Rolle der Frau des Königs, 29; emphasis added). Velleda, on the other hand, can offer access to knowledge.

A large number of fairy tales with female protagonists written by German women revolves around this same triad of women. The interaction between the heroine and the mediating wisewoman, with the greatest stress on the young protagonist's intellectual and moral growth, becomes the focus of many later German women's fairy tales, while the biological mother becomes the source of the young protagonist's predicament. The constellation of characters explores the dynamics of female interaction and the sources of women's education. The models female protagonists follow, whether perforce or perchance, almost certainly lead them to experiences and self-actualization unachievable in traditional society.

Amalia Schoppe, in her fairy tale "Das braune Hedchen" (1828), for example, sets up a conflict between the fairy Bambuina, the mother, and the daughter Hedchen. Hedchen's mother asks the fairy godmother to bestow beauty on her other children, but leaves Hedchen's fate to the fairy; Bambuina curses Hedchen, the last daughter, with great ugliness, until Hedchen can discover that physical beauty is only skin deep, while a beautiful spirit will shine forth. Hedchen learns this lesson, literally saves her parents from their other vain and hateful children, and reconciles with her mother in the process. Bambuina has thus shown the mother the folly of her ways and has helped Hedchen, tried by many, if not all, of life's difficulties, on the path to intellectual and moral independence. In Agnes Franz's "Prinzessin Rosalieb," the mother turns to a neighboring fairy "who was reputed to be very wise and insightful," to receive advice about how to raise her wayward daughter. When the mother's efforts fail and Rosalieb is whisked off to the island tower, she is still not completely abandoned by the fairy. The spirits in the tower coach "their pupil" along a path to knowledge; they visit her daily, acquaint her with "all kinds of useful tasks" and bring her "informative books." When Rosalieb finally learns her lessons, she has, thanks to the fairy Amaranth, also learned to shape her own destiny.

Some of the most interesting wisewomen appear in Gisela von Arnim's works: in *Das Leben der Hochgräfin Gritta von Ratten-zuhausbeiuns* the "ancestress of the switch tree" (die Ahnfrau von Rutenbaum), strongly reminiscent of Naubert's *weiße Frau*[22] and Thekla von Thurn;[23] the ghost woman (Geisterfrau) of her epistolary cycle to her nephew Achim von Arnim;[24] and Tante Colette of "Die Rosenwolke." In "Die Rosenwolke" (unpublished, ca 1845)[25] the female triad of biological mother, spiritual mother, and heroine functions to point up the differences between male- and female-conceived fairy tale worlds. The biological mother Sylvia represents the Grimmian fairy tale principles of aggrandizement of material wealth, while the mentoring Aunt Colette leads the heroine Catharine on the path to spiritual wealth.[26] Like the spirits in Rosalieb's tower, Aunt Colette teaches her "inquisitive pupil" (wißbegierige Schülerin) to harness her own reserves and to discipline her native talents. Catharine's primary goal is to achieve a state of knowledge equal to her aunt's, not to aggrandize material goods.

The magical wisewomen, demystified and demonified into loquacious witches and scheming sorceresses through the misogynist redactional practices of various authors, and here I mean in collections like those of the Grimms,[27] serve an important mediating and educating function in most women's tales. They are both mentors and models. The negative figures in women's fairy tales are not the witches and wisewomen, but rather the women who embrace the male world—in *Velleda* the woman who wants to return to civilization; in "Das braune Hedchen" the beauty-seeking, intellectually bankrupt mother; in "Die Rosenwolke" the woman who embraces the Grimmian world.

A diachronic view of German women's fairy tales shows a progression as magic becomes less the ability to affect the physical realm (magic as the ability to influence natural phenomena), and more the mastery of the psychic arena (magic as a way to create a different consciousness). Whereas the wisewomen in Naubert's texts could spin magic cloaks and soar on the wings of an eagle, Gisela von Arnim's magical women sixty years later spin fleecy clouds which enable them to achieve spiritual autonomy and concomitant material independence. Naubert's characters are still very much part of a tradition where magic was a woman's only way to exercise power over her material conditions; Gisela von Arnim's protagonist, with the aid of her mentor, is able to create the conditions for her own education into life and to become financially autonomous—in the 1840s, receiving an education was tantamount to magic.

3. The Rejection of "Redemption" and the Rite of Passage

As Voadicea sets out in the second phase of the story to find her daughters and rescue them from the dreaded sorceress, Velleda,

Naubert shows the folly of a woman's blind belief in "redemption" and the inadequacy of the partriarchal *Erlösungsmärchen* model. When Voadicea finally finds her daughters, she is unable to persuade them to return. The redemption adventure typically crowned in success for men is doomed to failure. Why? Because Naubert's text indicates that the values Voadicea invokes belong to the patriarchal world to which the daughters, under Velleda's guardianship, no longer belong. Like male protagonists of the medieval *Erlösungmärchen*, Voadicea demands open displays of submission, passivity and helplessness. Voadicea appeals to the "rights of a mother" (Rechte einer Mutter) and meets with independence and rejection. The "captives" simply do not want to be saved. The one daughter who firmly believes in a retrograde construct of deliverance wants to leave and embraces the Roman world. She perceives her transformation as a curse, calling out to passing ships "that the daughters [of the queen Voadicea] are being held against their wills by *magical powers* and are waiting for their *redemption*" (durch *Zaubergewalt* werden hier [die] Töchter [der Königin Voadicea] festgehalten und harren auf ihre *Erlösung*, 76; emphasis added). Bunduica's call for a deliverance (*Erlösung*) places her firmly in the medieval narrative as the damsel in distress. But when Bunduica eventually succeeds in leaving the island, her rejection of the women's community leads to death at the hands of the Romans. The other princesses view return to the "civilized" world as a return to captivity from the freedom they have known with Velleda.

Yet the exigencies of the redemption fairy tale plot require that the captives be redeemed. The task to regain them for "civilized society" falls now to the Romans, Julius and Flavius. The sub-plot of the redemption fairy tale, the marriage with the rescuer, is equally subverted. It becomes clear that marriage, or any kind of dependence on men, is not the goal of the female characters. Six princesses prefer ritual death in the last of the earthly elements, fire, to life with the Romans. Naubert makes it clear, however, that mortal women are unfortunately subject to male protection until they transcend the limits imposed on them by patriarchal society.

In "Der Riesentanz," Velleda the younger would prefer to reject her male admirers openly. We are enjoined, however, to understand her predicament: "surely you see that a princess, who is not a sorceress, and whose entire prestige is based on the power of a ruler . . . must take some things into consideration. If Vespasianus were gone, then all the respect the Icanian princess enjoyed from the populus would perhaps not help her further" (ihr seht wohl ein, daß eine Prinzessin, welche keine Zauberin ist, und deren ganzes Ansehn in der Macht eines Fürsten gegründet ist . . . , einige Rücksichten in acht zu nehmen hat. War Vespasianus dahin, so half die Achtung, in welcher die icanische Prinzessin unter ihrem Volke lebte, ihr vielleicht zu nichts weiter . . .). Only when she becomes a sorceress does Velleda become independent of male society.

In Velleda's rite of passage to magical awareness and ultimate independence from men, several themes of Naubert's *Märchen* coalesce. One night, wandering about Salisbury and Marlborough, Velleda suddenly stumbles upon an unknown temple. A mysterious inscription above the entrance invites the "student of wisdom" (Schülerin der Weisheit) to enter, to receive the teachings of the sages. If she enters, the powers of nature will be hers and she will rule over all. When Velleda heeds this call and enters:

> . . . she was a goddess as she exited. Not only more beautiful and wiser than ever before, but also as happy as the children of Heaven. . . . [A]nd now that her vision was sharp and infallible, surveying all regions which had until now lain dark before her *soul thirsty for knowledge,* inasmuch as she combined *superhuman knowledge* with *superhuman powers,* so tell me, what could such a promising lady still desire?

> . . . [s]ie war ganz eine Göttin, als sie wieder hervorging. Nicht allein schöner und weiser als je zuvor, sondern auch glücklich wie die Kinder des Himmels. . . . [U]nd da ihr Blick geschärft und untrüglich, alle Gegenden übersah, welche bisher noch dunkel vor ihrer *wißbegierigen Seele* lagen, da sie mit *übermenschlichem Wissen* auch *übermenschliche Macht* verband, so sprecht, was so einer vielversprechenden Dame noch zu wünschen übrig bleiben konnte? (133–34; emphasis added)

Velleda, "student of wisdom," gains access to the teachings of nature and the sages, and thereby carves the path for later female protagonists in women's tales: her rite of passage is to a higher level of consciousness. The equation of knowledge as power is formulated.

In a final act of independence, Velleda returns from the temple and transforms her male admirers into green boulders in the shape of horned rams. Only when this world becomes too boring does she leave for "lighter regions" (lichtere Gegenden).

Like Naubert and her character Velleda, later German women
writers also rejected the patriarchal paradigm of redemption and
sought instead to facilitate their heroines' access to skills and
knowledge. Patriarchal redemption later became in the social history of Germany and Europe the paradigm of redemption through
marriage. Female protagonists in women's fairy tales do not
marry, at least not for the sake of personal fulfillment. We never
learn if Franz's Rosalieb or von Arnim's Catharine marry; Hedchen's marriage is simply a footnote in Schoppe, an aside; and von
Arnim's Gritta marries into the royal family only in order to gain
sanctuary for her friends. Most frequently women's tales do not
even have a significant male figure in the narrative. Rather than
waiting for their prince to come, most female protagonists redeem
themselves through the accrual of wisdom and experience, mediated by a wisewoman. The real-life nineteenth-century solution to
all of women's woes through matrimony is decidedly lacking. Fairy
tale heroines created by women gain access to a wisdom and
knowledge which enables ultimate independence.

It is telling that all the authors I have discussed mediate the
female's rite of passage not only by a wisewoman, but also by reading. Velleda's legacy at the end of "Der Riesentanz" is a small book
of "foreign sagas" (ausländische[n] Sagen), "with which the sage
woman used to amuse herself—even sages need recreation—in
her free time" (mit welchem sich die Weise in Nebenstunden—
auch Weisen bedürfen der Erholung—zu desennuyieren pflegte).
Reading for the heroines in these tales (Rosalieb's access to her
own life story through a book; Bertha's access to the family archives and "her-story" of the woman in white in Naubert's "Die
weiße Frau"; Hedchen's access to another, kinder world in the
books she reads—I could mention many more) introduces them to
other worlds and echos their authors' belief in the didactic potential of literature. German women authors wrote for an audience
for whom reading was empowerment.

Concluding Remarks

Velleda, Ein Zauberroman, was, by its author's own account,

> one of the worst pieces of the self-avowed scribbler. It was written
> at a time in which my heart was occupied with other things, it
> was the means of a violent breaking away, and still bears traces
> that it was not the final goal. . . .

von den allerschlechtesten der bewußten Vielschreiberin. Sie wurde zu einer Zeit geschrieben, da das Herz anders beschäftigt war, sie war Mittel gewaltsamen Losreißens, und [trägt] noch Spuren, daß sie nicht Entzweck war . . . (to Louise Brachmann, October 22, 1805; Dorsch, 37).

The violent "breaking away" (Losreißen) of which Naubert speaks was her attempt to break away from the patriarchal paradigms in the literature around her. Situated in a time and space when the Romans, the Olympians of imperialistic, hegemonic pursuit, ruled the world, *Velleda, Ein Zauberroman,* becomes in many ways a metaphor for Naubert's own life and her views of her role as writer who lived in a period of Olympian literary hegemony. Tacitus tells us how Velleda, who exercised great influence over the warriors of her nation, dwelt in a tower and refused audiences with her admirers in order to inspire greater awe. Naubert, too, jealously guarded her identity, yet exercised great influence over the writers of her time. She may have perceived a need for anonymity, secluded in her tower in Naumburg, because she spoke of issues taboo to women writers: how women, real and imaginary, could achieve independent stature. Voadicea and Velleda succeed in thwarting masculine power; the princess Velleda is even able to transform her admirers into impotent, lifeless statues. Velleda did not have to be recognized by traditional standards to be powerful—in fact, her anonymity protected her and allowed her to exploit other powers at her disposal.

Benedikte Naubert, whose tales have been dismally ignored in the canonical scholarship, herself anticipated the fate of her work. At the end of "Voadicea und Velleda" the narrator suggests: "once a saga ends up in the mouth of the rabble, the rabble molds and re-molds it until it is abased and becomes like the rabble" (sobald eine Sage in den Mund des Pöbels kommt, so modelt er so lange daran, bis sie herabgewürdigt, und ihm ähnlich wird, 124). The patriarchal rabble of critics and literary historians reduced her work to insignificance, but Naubert re-shaped history to tell the story not of the great men, the Götzs and Herrmanns, but of the women in white, the Velledas, the women of great influence who served as inspiration to later generations of German women writers.

Appendix: Sophie Albrecht's Correspondence with Identified Women

I wish to thank the Hamburg Staats- und Universitätsbibliothek and the Staatsbibliothek Preußischer Kulturbesitz in West Berlin for their kind permissions to publish the following letters.

Letter 1

Halberstadt
d. 21. Ap. 1785

Ein junger Mahler, der mein Freund und Pflegesohn ist, hat mich um ein Empfehlungsschreiben an Sie gebeten.—Herrn Reinhard,[1] meine Theure, kan ich jeder guten feingebildeten Seele empfehlen, den [!] seine Talente,— sein Geist,—sein Herz, verdienen gleiche Hochachtung, und ich bin es Ihnen Bürge, Sie meine Liebe werden mir es selbst danken, Sie mit solch einem talentvollem Künstler, und gutem Menschen bekant gemacht zu haben. Mit wahrer Hochachtung unterzeichne ich mich als
Ihre
ergebene Freundin
Charlotte Elisa Constanzia
von der Recke
gebohrne Gräfin von Medem

Letter 2

Speyer den 3. May 1786

Ich bin nicht ganz ganz wohl, und habe eine Kranke freundin in meinem Hause—aber ich muß doch einige Zeilen an Madame Albrecht schreiben und ihr sagen, daß mir ihr Gram über meinen brief sehr Leid ist daß ich sie bitte sich zu beruhigen, daß ich wünsche meinen Brief nicht geschrieben zu haben wenn er Ihrer Empfindung so nah trat—aber ich konte es

211

nach der erklärung welche mir der Mensch in Gegenwart vieler Personen
machte nicht vermuthen—ich wurde auf der seite getroffen die am meis-
ten würken mußte—
    ich hätte zu viel Mütterliche Liebe für meine Kinder Eltern
    wären nichts als daseyn und sorge für Gesundheit und
    Nahrungs Kunst schuldig—ich gienge zu weit
dieses stük Philosophie, mir in Ihrem nahmen vor mehrern Personen
gepredigt zeigte mir entfernung in der meinerseits nicht mehr zu Ihnen
kommen konte—es war auch nicht möglich jemand für unverschämten
Lügner zu halten—der zum ersten mal mich sah, in ihrem nahmen mit
mir zu sprechen verlangte einen Kaufmann von hier mitbrachte, 2 freunde
antraf Baron V. Hohenfeld[2] mein Mann und 2 Frauenzimer dabey, mir die
seltsame Aufgabe ausrichtete—
    glauben Sie daß es mich schmerzte daß ein solcher Mensch
    sagte er sehe Sie täglich—wisse alles von Ihren grundsäzen
    u. ganz von Ihnen mich trente
gewiß konte ich nach dem Bild, daß bis auf den Augenblik, von Ihnen in
meiner Seele war, mich nicht ohne ursache von Ihrer seitte mich losreis-
sen—gerne Theure Albrecht! glaubte ich was Dalberg und Bethmann mir
sagten—gerne glaube ich Ihnen selbst wieder, und freue mich, daß es betrug war, der den schönen umriß Ihres denkens und Lebens auf einige
Zeit störte beruhigen Sie sich—sagen Sie was Sie von meiner achtung
und Freundschaft wünschen ich schreibe Ihnen bald mehr Leben Sie wohl
v. La Roche
Vergeben Sie ich habe Herrn Legations Rath Bode[3] in Weimar aufgege-
ben mit Ihnen wegen der S 54 sprechen zu laßen wenn es noch nicht ge-
schehen so schiken Sie mir die sume auf meine Kosten zu—es that mir
Leid auf zwey briefe nichts zu hören ich mußte sie geändert glauben.

Letter 3

Hamburg den 4ten May

Ich danke Ihnen liebe Madam Herz für Ihr gütiges Andenken, könt ich
Ihnen doch beweisen wie gern ich Sie ruhig und glüklich sähe. ich fühle
Ihre Lage—und kann Sie nur mit Ihrem Bewußtseyn trösten! Oft ist unsere Ruhe nah, wenn wir noch mit ungewisheit kämpfen. Lyster,[4] wird
Ihnen selbst schreiben damit Sie Ihrer Sache gewis sind—den ich möchte
nicht gern daß Sie sich mit besseren Ausichten täuschten, als Ihnen das
kleine Glück hier versprechen kan—doch Ruhe ist ja viel. Ihr Mann be-
steht darauf in kurzem nach Schleswig zu reisen ob ich ihm gleich alles
sagte was Sie wünschten. Vieleicht ist es besser wenn Sie auch dort mit
ihm sprechen—es muß ja doch Ihre Zukunft entschieden werden—Mil-
gen[?] das gute liebe Kind läst Sie tausendmahl grüßen! ach auch um

dieses liebe Mädchen wünsch ich die Zukunft. Solt es den gar nicht möglich seyn daß Sie sich mit H. Herz wieder vereinten? Gott gebe doch Ihre
Ruhe und Zufriedenheit das wünscht

herzlich Ihre

ergebene Freundin

Sophie Albrecht

Albrecht grüßt Sie aufs beste. Empfehlen Sie mich Pi. Thurn[?] und Ihrer
lieben Betty[?]

Letter 4

Stade den 3ten July 1819

Meine theure Sophie! Wie unendlich mich ihre Zeilen, wie ein Wiederhall
aus schönen Zeiten erfreuten, brauche ich Ihnen nicht zu sagen. Sie sind
dahin diese Zeiten—mir sind ihre fröhlichen Stunden, die zärtlichen
Freunde die sie veranlaßten und theilten, die Kunstgenüße sogar—alles
alles ist mir verschwunden—ich stehe allein—nur dann und wann bang-
licher werdende sorge, um eins meiner kinder; zeigt mir zuweilen daß ich
lebe. Außerdem vegetire ich ohne Wunsch und ohne Hoffnung so fort—Ein
wahres Pflanzenleben. Wollte ich Ihnen meine Begegnisse der letzten 19
Jahre erzählen, daß würde ein wahres Buch werden: so begnüge ich mich
also[5] Ihnen die Hauptpunckte aus jener Zeit anzuführen—bis ich sie
selbst sehe, wo denn ich Ihnen mein ganzes Herz aufschließen werde. Sie
wissen ich ging nohtgedrungen weil mein guter sel. Montenglaut[6] sein
herausgebrachtes Kapital in ein Hamburger Banquerott verloren hatte—
nach Amsterdam, mit der Truppe der Ritter von Steinsberg—dieser
machte einen unritterlichen Banquerott ging durch, und brachte mich um
700 Gulden reinen Verlust. Ich ging nach Cleve von wo aus ich ihren lieben sel. Mann schrieb—aber keine Antwort mehr erhielt. Meine Mutter
starb, sie vermachte meines Bruders 2 Söhne und meinen Kindern 10000
Gulden. Ich solte von etwa 6000 die Zinsen bis zu deren Majorenität zie-
hen. Das liebe kleine Wesen, Montenglauts unglücklicher Nachlaß, den
ich schon wegen der frappanten Aehnlichkeit mit seinem Vater anbetete,
war mir nach 4 wöchentl. Leiden, unter den Händen dreyer Aerzte gestorben in Amsterdam—Seit seinem Tode hörte ich von der Familie aus
Frankreich nichts, als den Tod der Schwiegereltern. Mit den geringen
etwa 300 Th. järl. starken Zinsen von der Verlaßenschaft meiner sel. Mutter, hätte ich nun einsam und still für mich leben können. Ich hätte das
klügere thun und von meiner Kunst leben, jenes Geld aber für die Zeit
zurücklegen legen können, wo die Majorienität meiner Kinder mich reve-
nue los machen wird—so daß ich wie unser göttlicher Freund Christus,
wurde sagen müssen "des Menschen Sohn hat nicht wo er sein Haupt hin-
lege." Nein Liebe das that ich nicht, sondern nachdem ich mehrere Jahre

in Coblenz Mainz und Trier Directrice gewesen, und alles Meinige zuge-
sezt hatte, weil ich jeden Schuldner ehrlich bezahlt, die Schauspieler wie
meine Kinder behandelt hatte und auch sonst betrogen war—so ging ich
nach Strasburg zum Dichter Vogel,[7] in Engagement—Mit ihm war ich in
Str; in Basel und Freiburg bis anno 10—wo ich bis anno 14 am Hoftheater
in Darmstadt mich befand. Diese ganze Zeit über hatte ich meinen
kleinen Fritz bei einem Prediger der ein Erziehungshaus nach Pestalozzi
in Strsb. hat; in pension gethan für 900 Frances järl. Violine, Griechisch,
Zeichnen, franz. Rhetorick [unreadable]—[unreadable] anno 1813 als er
eben nach Heidelberg gehn wollte, um das Camerale zu studieren, er-
stand Teutschl. von seiner Schmach; wir hoften, glaubten, und opferten
viel—und wie ich jezt sehe zwar für eine herrliche "*Idee*", aber in der *realität* vergebens—Auch ich die schon meinen jüngsten Sohn erster Ehe im
russischen Feldzug, und den ältesten durch die Grausamkeit seines ab-
scheulichen Vaters[8] verloren hatte—indem er ihn dahin brachte, daß er
sich als Jüngling erschoß—Ich brachte dem Vaterland und Fritzens Wünschen das Opfer, ihn als Volontair Germaniens [?] zum 7. preussischen
Husaren Regiment zu geben; er machte die 3 Feldzüge 13-14-15 mit, und
sein gutes betragen, und herrliche Kenntniße machten: daß er nach 14
Monaten schon Offizier war. Sein Equipage als Germaniens [?] und port
d'epee Fähndrich, so wie seine Zulage, und frühere Erziehung, haben mir
6400 Gulden gekostet—Ich habe *mir nichts* erspart. Ich habe es beim
König durchgesezt daß seine Lieutnants Equipage von seiner legat
genommen ist—Mein Bruder hat ihn adoptirt, und er führt unseren Nahmen und Wappen. Dieser Bruder der ruhig auf seinem Gute saß, mit
einer englischen pension—als Volontair mit den Denschen [?] Cosaken als
Brigadier; erwirbt sich den Waladimir Orden, und läßt sich sein Gütchen
confisieren vom Könige von Westhfalen, und alle Haabseligkeiten rauben;
nachdem er seine 2. Frau mit 3 Stiefkindern erheiratet hat. Jezt ist er
hier Capitain und ordensritter; hat aber *nichts* mehr, und kan also *nichts*
für mich thun. Dennoch aber plagt ihn, und meinen Sohn so wie er in die
Officiers Uniform stectt, der Hochmuthsteufel, sie geben sich allen Voru-
rtheilen hin, und ich mus die Bühne verlassen—das that ich dann im Mai
1814—Seitdem habe ich mich der Pädagogik in die Armen geworfen, und
habe in Bareuth bei einer Freundin, eine Schwägerin von la Motte Fou-
quet, eine baronin von Schuberth theils als Gesellschafterin, theils als
Gouvernante ihrer Töchter gelebt—Sie ist eine herrliche geistriche Frau,
Jean Paul unser nächster Nachbar, deßen Frau eine meiner besten Freun-
dinnen, und da ich um con amore sein und wirken zu können, von meines
Gleichen *ein Gehalt* oder *präsent nehme*: so ist meine Lage herrlich. Nun
ist aber mein 2ter leider auch geschiedner Mann Müller, vor etwa 20
Monaten in Güstrow gestorben—Er hatte unsern jüngsten Sohn bei sich,
hat ihn trefl erziehen, und die Apotheker Kunst lernen laßen—er ist in
Neuruppin—Seit Müllers Tod habe ich für ihn auch als ehrliche Mutter
sorgen müßen. Er vollendet Michaelis seine Lehrjahre, und braucht nun

Geld, und eine Aussteuer. Ich reiste also im Januar nach Westhfalen, um mit Fritz ein rendesvous zu haben, ihm ein Theil seines Legates zu verschafen, und für den 2t Franz, daßelbe zu bewirken—das Erstere ist mir nur nach langem Aufenthalt und großen Kosten, direct durch den König gelungen—das 2. gar nicht, da Franz noch 4 Jahr bis zur Majorennität hin hat. Dieser möchte dennoch gern Medicin studieren, und wenn dies auch gar nicht ginge: so muß ich ihm doch Michaelis eine Summe schaffen. Meine zinsen werden mir etwas später ausgezahlt, mein Bruder könte vielleicht helfen, ist aber geizig; von ihm ist nichts zu hoffen Ich läugne es nicht, das ruhige Leben, in dem Verhältnis und Kreis, wofür ich geboren bin hat große Reize für mich—es sind mir auch wieder 6 Stellen geboten, u.a. eine in Schlesien, eine in Prag, eine in Eger, u eine in Halle bei einer Schwester meiner Schuberth—Auch habe ich mich mit Erfolg in der Schweiz, um einen Platz in einem Erziehungs Nonnen Kloster vom Orden der Ursalinirin, beworben! / :denn unter uns, ich bin *ohne öffentlichen Uebertritt*—der Misdeutung wegen; / seit langen, langen Jahren catholisch, ich danke Gott und dem Erlöser dafür—und möchte um einen Thron nicht wieder zu der,[9] kaltern herzlosen Grüblerwahn zurück—nach diesem Eingang können Sie meine theure Sophie urtheilen, wie sehr ich meine Mutterpflicht ehre, und meine Kinder Liebe, wenn ich ihnen sage: ich bin bereit ein Engagement wieder anzunehmen—als was, und wofür man will, je unbemerkter je lieber, wenn ich nur so viel verdiene, daß ich selbst kärgl. lebend, noch drei Jahr meinen Franz unter stützen kann. Sollte dies unmöglich sein, wenn ich denn im kommenden Monat irgendwo eine Declamatorium geben könte, und ihm vom Ertrag für den Augenblick schicken. In Bremen, Hamburg und Altona darf es jedoch nicht sein, wegen meines Bruders Nähe, und weil halb Stade immer dort ist. Hier ist man so sehr in Abdera, daß ist die ganze Welt, und das ganze Corps Officier meinen Bruder von aller Gemeinschaft ausschließe, wenn man mein Künstler Thum nur ahnete. Nun gute Sophie geben sie mir guten Raht, oder noch besser verwenden sich für mich an *entfernte* Theater—nur nicht nach Leipzig wegen der Meßen—den ich bin nun zu sehr unter den ersten Zirkeln in meines wahren Nahmens bekant geworden. Auch habe ich ein Bändgen Gedichte heraus gegeben, die Mattison,[10] gütig rezensirt hat—"Herbstblumen Kranz".[11] Manches schrieb ich im Morgenblatt,[12] und arbeite jezt nachdem ich 2 dutzend Hemden für meine Söhne mit blinden Augen durch eine Brille vollendet hatte: an ein Bändgen Erzählungen,[13] daß ich bei Göschen für die Hungernden im Erzgebürge herausgeben will. Alles früher war im Selbstverlag und also mit wenig Vortheil—sagen sie mirs doch, *wie* handelt man mit Buchhändlern, und *wie* macht man sich Geld mit der Schriftstellerei?

Von dem ehrlichen William habe ich seit anno 1805 keine Briefe—ich schrieb ihm unendl. oft, und glaube die reine Seele ist mir ins Vaterland voran gegangen. Nächstens mache ich noch einen Versuch nach England. Kürzl. war hier eine kleine Truppe, und Unzer,[14] Sohn des Professors[15] dabei. Ich durfte mich ihm nicht zu erkennen geben, aber mein Herz schmolz in wehmutigen Erinnerungen!—Altona mit seinen mir so theuren Gräbern *mus* ich wieder sehen! Sie hatte ich überraschen wollen. Schreiben Sie mir doch alles, *wie* und in *welcher Art* Sie leben, auch ob ich ein paar Tage bei Ihnen logiren kan, ist das: so komme ich *bald*. Anfangs Sept. *muß* ich der Kinder Geschäfte wegen wieder in Westhfalen sein, und von dort aus meine künftige Bestimmung antreten, gebe Gott eine lukrative, nur Franzens wegen! Schreiben sie mir *viel, lang*, weitläufig alles, a[lles?] was ihr *Herz*, und ihre Lage betrift. Ich bin besser geworden, daß darf ich sagen, auch ergebner, und christlicher, in Kunsthinsicht bin ich eine *vorzügliche* Rednerin geworden, auch das ist wahr—im Süden gelte ich auch als solche. Im Ganzen aber gemahnt mich die Kunst wie ein längstgeschiedener Freund—dessen Andenken man inig liebt O meine Sophie, liebe Freundin, theures Denkmal aus liebereicher froher Jugend zeit! Ich weine jetzt schon wenn ich daran denke, daß ich Sie sehe; und mit Ihnen nach dem Gottesacker wandeln soll, wo unsrer Jugend süßeste Freuden schlummern. Adieu Ich schreib in der Nacht, und muß enden schreiben Sie bald wieder und lieben fort ihre treue

Henriette v. Monenglaut geb. Cronstain
bei dem HE Hauptmann und Ordensritter v. Cronstain

Die Bürger[16] ist jezt sehr geachtet, was sie verdient—Sie privatisirt in Stuttgardt, und schriftstellert mit Glück. Ist es wahr daß Unzer eine zweite unwürdige Heirath gethan, und unser ehrliche Evers[17] sich erhängt hat? Was macht Deden?—

Ein gewißer Reinhard in Altona hat meine Gedichte von einem hiesigen Baron Spilker bekommen den man hier nicht mag. Wenn sie das Buch kriegen können: so behalten Sie es, ich hatte es Spilker nur geliehen. Machen Sie ja nichts daß dieser etwas von meiner Künstlerschaft erfährt.

Letter 5

Braunschweig den 18t Jan 1832

Theure Freundin! Sie werden durch Herrn von Sidow längst meinen Brief in Händen, und durch den Besuch der Madame Schütz, längst einen Gruß von mir, und einen Trost bekommen haben. Wohl mir meine geliebte Freundin! den Schritten des braven Schauspielers Schütz ist es gelungen, Ihnen von der hiesigen Gesellschaft, eine Kleine Pension, von dritthalb Thaler monatlich zu erwirken. Eine Freundin, von mir außer der Bühne, giebt einen halben Thaler dazu; so daß es drei Thaler machen. Die Differenzen mit dem Gelde, aber macht daß Sie bei der Auszahlung welche Madam Schütz in Hamburg übernimmt; nur 7 Mark aufs Schilling bekommen. In

diesen Tagen schreibe ich nun an Schirmer[18] nach Dresden was gesche-
hen ist,[19] dann werden die doch gewiß ebenso viel thun, und Ihrem
drukendsten Kummer ist abgeholfen. Nach Hanover an Herrn von Holl-
bein schrieb ich gleich, und legte es ihm dringend an das Herz, Ich hoffe
nicht vergebens. Noch eine mir befreundete Mahler familie in Hannover,
(-die Frau ist eine Tochter des sel. Großman,[20] und Schwester der Unzel-
man) dencke ich breit zu schlagen. Genug, es wird schon gehn, vor der
Hand sind Ihnen 7 MK 8 Schil *gewiß*; die erste Zahlung ist, glaube ich am
1t Februar, also in 14 Tagen. Nun mus ich Ihnen doch auch sagen, wer des
hiesigen Schauspieler Schütz, niedliche Frau ist. Es ist die kleine Betty
Herz,[21] der Sie als Kind so freundlich waren sie grüßt Sie ehrerbietig,
und wird Sie diesen Sommer besuchen.

Ich schicke Ihnen hirbei meine Geliebteste Sophie was ich Ihnen
zurecht machen *konte*—mit dem bereitwilligsten Herzen. Den Oberrock
machte ich aus einem Mantel. Sollte er Ihnen zu lang sein: so laßen Sie
über den Samt, einen Saum hineinnähen. Ich sage mit Marie "Stuart"
"Ihr werdet die Gaben meiner Liebe"
"wie arm sie sind, darum gering nicht achten"
Die Schuhe werden Ihnen etwas groß sein, mir waren sie zu klein, aber
warm werden sie sitzen. Das file Schahl knüpfte ich selbst, und trug es
ein paar wochen:—es sitzt schön warm um den Hals. Das Tuch gab mir
eine Freundin für Sie; da es ganz neu ist, können Sie es vertauschen, falls
es Ihnen nicht gefällt. O wie gern meine Theurste, hätte ich Ihnen lauter
neue Ihrer recht würdige Sachen geschickt, aber Gott kennt mein Unvermögen. Also nehmen Sie vorlieb.

Nun auch etwas von mir. *Hier* meine beste *kan* ich nicht bleiben, da
ich wegen der Theurung der entsezlichen, hier nicht *leben kan*. Es ist unmöglich unter 300 Thl jährlich auszukomen. In *diesem* Jahre habe ich
mit Büchern ein paar Prinzeßinnen gebrandschazt auch hatte meine Freundin, etwas geerbt, das flikte mich mit durch. Für das nächste Jahr aber
weiß ich *keinen Rath,*—gar keinen, wenn ich *hier* bliebe. Ich bemühe mich
schon lange um einen Dienst in, oder bei Berlin—vergebens! doch habe
ich seit heute durch einen Brief *etwas* Hoffnung. Sollte es mir nicht gelingen: So thue ich Ihnen folgenden vorschlag. Ich habe von mir selbst jetzt
60 Thl. dazu bezahlen meine Kinder meine Miete mit 40 Thl—macht 100
Thl. Davon kan ich 70 Thl. in monathlich Raten mit sechs/halb Thl, das
andre dann alle Jahr bekommen. Wollen Sie mich nebst meinem Kinde
mit dieser vorläufigen kleinen Beisteuer von 15 MK monath. bei sich
aufnehmen? Wir haben unsre eigenen Betten, die wir mitbrächten—auch
verdiene ich immer etwas nebenbei: so wollte ich zu Ihnen kommen auf
Ostern, falls es mit der Condition nichts wäre. Ich kan jezt *sehr* hübsch
Blumen machen, und könte das lehren, oder auch wohl in einer Fabrick
Arbeit finden. Auf jeden Fall wäre ich doch einmal wieder mit jemandem
eine Zeitlang zusammen, die mich ganz verstünde. Antworten Sie mir
hübsch bald, ob Ihnen die Idee gefällt, ob sie das Päckgen erhalten, und
ob Sie mich noch lieb haben. Gebe Gott daß ich etwas zu Ihrem Trost

beitrug, und Sie zufrieden mit mir sind. Und nun ein herzliches Lebwohl. Ich schrieb Ihnen ja wohl neulich, *daß*, und *warum* ich zu Ostern das M: Blatt aufgebe! Ich spinne jezt fleißig—das, und *recht tiefe Einsamkeit*, sagt mir am besten zu. Noch einmal von ganzem Herzen Adieu, und tausendmal adieu, Gott segne und erhalte Sie! behalten Sie lieb

Ihre treue Montenglaut

Notes

Foreword

1. Elaine Showalter, "Feminist Criticism in the Wilderness," *Critical Inquiry* 8:2 (Winter 1981): 184, 185.

2. Nancy Miller, *Subject to Change: Reading Feminist Writing* (New York: Columbia University Press, 1988), 8.

3. Most recently Denise Riley, *"Am I That Name?" Feminism and the Category of 'Women' in History* (Minneapolis: University of Minnesota Press, 1988).

4. The exceptions are noted in Isobel Grundy, "Samuel Johnson as Patron of Women," *The Age of Johnson: A Scholarly Annual,* ed. Paul J. Korshin, 1 (1987): 59–79.

5. The earliest critical analysis of the terms of this debate in England is to be found in Marilyn Butler, *Jane Austen and the War of Ideas* (Oxford: Oxford University Press, 1975).

6. Syndy McMillen Conger, "The Sorrows of Young Charlotte: Werter's English Sisters 1785–1805," *Goethe Yearbook* 111 (1986): 21–56.

7. Voltaire, *Letters on England,* trans. Leonard Tancock (Harmondsworth: Penguin, 1980), 101.

8. Germaine de Stael, Mme de Genlis and Isabelle de Charrière are the most prominent of these. Stael and Genlis fled or were exiled from France for their association with the government of Louis XVI; while Charrière was a native of Holland, married to a Swiss man, and living permanently in Switzerland. Like the others, however, her affinity for France and her acquaintance with many French people living in exile contributed to Charrière's emotional involvement with events in France.

9. For an overview of French women and French feminism in the eighteenth century, see Léon Abensour, *La Femme et le féminisme avant la Revolution* (Paris: Ernest Leroux, 1923) and Samia Spencer, ed., *French Women and the Age of Enlightenment* (Bloomington: Indiana UP, 1984).

10. English Showalter, Jr. has documented this process for the publication of Mme de Graffigny's *Lettres d'une Péruvienne:* "Les Lettres d'une Péruvienne: Composition, Publication, Suites," *Archives et Bibliothèque de Belgique,* 54 (1983): 14–28.

11. Again Graffigny provides an interesting case in point: "In 1745, just as she was beginning to take her own writing seriously, Mme de Graffigny wrote some poetry; but Mlle Quinault dissuaded her from continuing. According to Mlle Quinault, a 'femme d'esprit' could write prose, but poetry was too ostentatious and marked the author as a bluestocking or 'femme savante.'" Some years later, when Mme de Graffigny thought about versifying her play Cenie, "once again Mlle Quinault vetoed the idea, on the grounds that prose was more decent for a woman." English Showalter, "A Woman of Letters in the French Enlightenment: Madame de Graffigny", *British Journal for Eighteenth-Century Studies,* 1:2 (summer 1978): 99.

12. Claude Labrosse, *Lire au XVIlle siècle: La Nouvelle Héloïse et ses lecteurs* (Lyon: Presses Universitaires de Lyon, 1985), has catalogued 100 of the novel's readers who actually wrote to Rousseau. About one quarter were women.

13. See, for example, his attack on Madame D'Ormoy in the second of the *Rêveries du promeneur solitaire.*

14. There is disagreement over the extent to which women writing after Rousseau slavishly repeated his ideas. For a succinct commentary on this topic, see Nancy K. Miller, "Authorized Versions," *French Review,* 61:3 (February 1988) and "Men's Reading, Women's Writing: Gender and the Rise of the Novel," *Yale French Studies,* 75 (1988): 40–55.

Introduction

1. "Enter, for here too are gods," (Apud gellium). Lessing chose this quote for *Nathan, the Wise.*

2. See Bovenschen and Hoffmann. Hoffmann asserts that only in the last decades of the eighteenth century, did women and men become defined in terms of their difference, rather than as occupying different points in a continuum, or Great Chain of Being

3. An English translation of La Roche's novel has recently appeared: *The History of Lady Sophia Sternheim.* Albany: SUNY, 1991. The page citations here are from the German edition.

4. Luise Gottsched was also a well-known dramatist in her own right, but she was not universally admired. Johanna Schopenhauer, for instance, rejected the offer to learn Greek, citing the "negative" example of Luise Gottsched.

5. The family novel of the late eighteenth century thematized the virtues and precarious social position of bourgeois and aristocratic women. In German literature the family novel is a sub-genre of the sentimental novel.

6. Sally Winkle's valuable study of these two works emphasizes the difference between them as far as their portrait of women is concerned. She views them as transitional works in the transformation of the rationalist ideal into that of gender complementarity. But the influence of La Roche on Goethe is usually considered to have been formal.

7. Although this novel was written very late in, or what some people would consider to be after, the romantic period, much of its content appears to derive from and sometimes directly relay Bettine von Arnim's conversations with Goethe's mother at the turn of the eighteenth century.

8. For a detailed account of the functioning of these salons, see Hertz. For a biography of Rahel Varnhagen, see Arendt.

9. See Goodman "Impact."

10. Maximiliane, Bettine's oldest and most conservative daughter, often did not agree with her mother's political positions and finally introduced the practice of hosting two salons in the same house—one for the "democrats" (Bettine's), the other for the "aristocrats" (Maximiliane's) (See Werner, 196f.)

11. Some, in fact, would trace the origins of this phenomenon back to Goethe's own autobiography *Dichtung und Wahrheit* (1811–32).

12. See, for instance, Weber.

The Beautiful Soul Writes Herself

1. Translation and emphasis mine. The spelling in this letter is quite erratic. In the last sentence of the paragraph it is grammatically not quite clear whether Friederike Unger refers to Goethe as the "love of one's youth" or whether "one's past youth" is in apposition to "lover."

2. Unger's birthdates vary. Depending on the reference work consulted, she was born either in 1741, 1751, or 1754. Since her father died in December 1751, and since after 1745 nothing is known of her mother's situation, whom von Rothenburg married in 1735, the early birthdate seems to be the most likely one.

3. By 1796, Friederike Unger had written numerous translations (Rousseau's *Confessions* and *Rèveries,* plays by Marivaux and Molière), a bestseller novel, *Julchen Grünthal,* a cookbook, stories, calendars for

young people, a comedy and many articles in journals. Although she published anonymously, her authorship was well-known because of her public prominence.

4. See also Ward.

5. Philine is clearly not meant as a model to be emulated by her readers. After all, Wilhelm, the hero, rejects her free ways and her advances.

6. My argument relies heavily on Marianne Hirsch's paradigmatic essay.

7. She was highly educated, married a Berlin publisher with whom, since she remained childless, she cooperated intensely in a variety of literary endeavors and whom, upon his death, she succeeded as manager of the publishing house. See my biographical entry.

8. In her paper on Sophie Mereau, Christa Buerger analyzes a similar dependence on Goethe, and advocates "dependency" studies as a way to understand the complicated mechanisms of literary production in the "Age of Goethe."

9. For a discussion of the impact of *La Nouvelle Heloïse* on Julchen see my paper, "Aus der Not eine Tugend . . . Tugendgebot und Oeffentlichkeit bei Friederike Helene Unger."

10. Curiously, references to Goethe's evil influence appear quite subdued in the third, revised edition of *Julchen Grünthal* which was published in 1798!

11. There are, of course, other "influences" and models: Richardson, Rousseau, Marivaux, and, no doubt, Wobeser's popular *Elisa oder das Weib wie es seyn sollte* (1795) or Caroline von Wolzogen's *Agnes von Lilien* (1795).

12. I am conflating the four categories Beaujean employs, because I know of no work in which they appear in a pure, unadulterated form. In fact, they are complementary properties of one and the same gender definition.

13. I use "beautiful soul" as a generic term here, although I am aware of the subtle differences between Kant's, Schiller's and Goethe's concepts. See Erich Trunz' comments in Goethe, 7:772, and Schiller.

14. See, for instance, La Roche's moral tale "Liebe, Missverstaendnis und Freundschaft," in *Moralische Erzaehlungen* (1784) and Fischer's short stories "Margarethe" and "Justine," in *Kleine Erzaehlungen und romantische Skizzen,* (1816, reprint Hildesheim: Olms, 1988).

15. Caroline Schlegel, 6 Feb. 1800. Quoted in Goedeke, 1875:225.

16. Friederike Unger, letter to August Wilhelm Schlegel, 10 June, 1808. *Krisenjahre der Fruehromantik. Briefe aus dem Schlegel-Kreis.* Ed. Josef Koerner, 2nd ed. (Francke: Bern and Munich), I:553.

17. "Epische, halbepische Dichtung verlangt eine Hauptfigur, die bei vorwaltender Taetigkeit durch den Mann, bei ueberwiegenden Leiden durch die Frau vorgestellt wird."[A] Goethe, apparently unaware of the critical potential of Unger's novel, only found words of praise. In a letter to his publisher Friedrich Unger he wrote: "Der in den ersten Baenden des Journals enthaltene Roman wird gewiss Glueck machen. Er hat das anziehende das solche Produktionen auszeichnen soll, und es kommt mir immer vor als wenn in der neuern Zeit die Romane nur durch Frauenzimmer geschrieben werden sollten." (2 April 1800; reprinted in Biedermann, 171).[B]

[A]"Epic, half-epic literature demands a main character who is introduced with predominant action through the man and with paramount suffering through the woman."

[B]"The novel, contained in the first volumes of the journal, will certainly be a success. It has an attraction about it that should distinguish such productions, and it always seems to me as though in recent times novels should only be written by women."

18. See for example, Mariane's lament in *Wilhelm Meister*: ". . . welch elende Kreatur ein Weib ist, das mit dem Verlangen nicht zugleich Liebe und Ehrfurcht einfloesst" (Goethe 7:34).

19. For Martin Swales, p. 26, "openness" is "the deepest source" of Wilhelm Meister's meaning.

20. See for example Dawson.

21. I am also convinced that commercial reasons play into Unger's ambiguous response to the Goethe reception: on the one hand she knows very well Goethe's "market value" and cannot afford to alienate him; on the other she is waging a long battle against the romantics, in many ways her greatest competitors.

22. Since Unger's authorship of this novel is not completely established—both Unger and the editor Friedrich Buchholz are credited—I do not want to include it in my analysis, although I could not resist using its title for my purposes. See my afterword to *Bekenntnisse einer schönen Seele*.

23. It is also likely that Unger was disappointed by Goethe's generally cool (but not unfavorable) response to her productions. See his letter on *Graefinn Pauline* to Friedrich Unger, 2 April 1800, and his review of *Melanie* in *Jenaische Allgemeine Litteratur-Zeitung* No. 167 (1806), 105, and 109f.

Turns of Emancipation

1. See *Webster's New Universal Unabridged Dictionary,* Second Edition. New York: Dorset & Barber, 1983.

2. *Der große Brockhaus,* Wiesbaden: F. A. Brockhaus, 1953.

3. Gert Mattenklott, "Aufbruch in neue Lebensräume oder Der ungestillte Hunger: Überlegungen zu Briefen der Henriette Herz," *Frankfurter Allgemeine Zeitung* 33 (February 9, 1986, *Beilage*). The following quotations are taken from this article. All translations from the German, here and elsewhere, are mine.

4. The thesis that literature serves as a replacement for actions continues a traditional opposition of art and life. It can often be found in the secondary literature on Rahel Varnhagen, and seems to answer her own complaints about her limitations to act. See, for example, the discussion of Varnhagen even in feminist studies like that of Silvia Bovenschen, *Die imaginierte Weiblichkeit: exemplarische Untersuchungen zu kulturgeschichtlichen und literarischen Präsentationsformen des Weiblichen* (Frankfurt: Suhrkamp, 1979).

5. See Kay Goodman, "Poesis and Praxis in Rahel Varnhagen's Letters," *New German Critique* 27 (1982): 123–139; Goodman refers to Jürgen Habermas' *Strukturwandel der Öffentlichkeit* (Darmstadt: Luchterhand, 1962).

6. Indirectly, Mattenklott himself criticizes his representation of Jewish women writers as women without properties later in his essay, by correcting Wilhelm von Humboldt's similar assertion. In another essay, Mattenklott also touches on the fact that the letter may not be such a "marginal" genre. It is an essay on the letters and epistolary novels of a non-Jewish woman writer, Bettina von Arnim: "Romantische Frauenkultur: Bettina von Arnim zum Beispiel," *Literatur—Frauen—Geschichte: Schreibende Frauen vom Mittelalter bis zur Gegenwart,* eds. Hiltrud Gnüg und Renate Möhrmann (Stuttgart: Metzler, 1985), 123–143.

7. Rahel Varnhagen, *Briefwechsel* I, ed. Friedhelm Kemp (Munich: Winkler, 1979), 248.

8. Compare Alexander von der Marwitz's letter to Rahel Varnhagen, November 12, 1811; *Briefwechsel* I, 125.

9. Letter to David Veit, October 16, 1794. *Briefwechsel zwischen Rahel und David Veit* I, ed. from the papers of Karl August Varnhagens (1861), 240; reprinted as *Rahel-Bibliothek* VII, eds. Konrad Feilchenfeldt, Uwe Schweikert und Rahel E. Steiner (Munich: Matthes & Seitz, 1983).

10. Letter to Alexander von der Marwitz, November 17, 1811; *Briefwechsel* I, 129–130.

11. Hannah Arendt, *Rahel Varnhagen: Lebensgeschichte einer deutschen Jüdin aus der Romantik* (Munich: Piper, 1959), 42.

12. Jean Starobinski, "The Style of Autobiography," *Literary Style: A Symposium,* ed. Seymour Chatman (New York: Oxford UP, 1971), 285–296, esp. 288.

13. Letter to Karl August Varnhagen, February 21, 1809; *Buch des Andenkens* I, ed. Karl August von Varnhagen (1834), 405 [*Rahel-Bibliothek* I].

14. Letter to Friedrich de la Motte Fouqué, July 26, 1809; *Buch des Andenkens* I, 436.

15. See letter to Alexander von der Marwitz, December 8, 1812; *Briefwechsel* I, 217–221, and the following letters.

16. I am grateful to Ursula Isselstein for this reference, who was able to consult Rahel's corrections on the original letters. The copy of the dream narratives has not been censored any further by Rahel or Karl August Varnhagen, however. See " 'daß ich kein Träumender allein hier bin!': Zwei unbekannte Träume Rahel Levins", *MLN* 102 (1987), 648–650, esp. 650. For a history of the publication of Rahel's dream narratives, see Isselstein. Friedrich Kemp gives these narratives the heading "Aus Rahels Tagebuch" [From Rahel's diary] (*Briefwechsel* I, 202).

17. Letter to Alexander von der Marwitz, May 16, 1811; *Briefwechsel* I, 36.

18. See, for example, Goodman, 133; Isselstein, 653 n.12 and Liliane Weissberg, "Writing on the Wall: Letters of Rahel Varnhagen", *New German Critique* 36 (1985): 157–173.

19. Fritz Ernst, "Rahels Traum", *Essais* 2 (Zurich: Artemis, 1946), 211–227.

20. Arendt, 129.

21. Rahel Varnhagen's dreams are quoted from their first publication by Isselstein; the page references follow the quotations in the text.

22. See, for example, the letter to David Veit, December 13 and 17, 1793 and David Veit's letter to Rahel, December 24, 1793; *Briefwechsel zwischen Rahel und David Veit* I (1861), 78 and 85–86.

23. Letter to Alexander von der Marwitz, December 26, 1811; *Briefwechsel* I, 146.

24. Letter to Karl August Varnhagen, December 25, 1811; *Briefwechsel* I, 183.

25. Letter to Alexander von der Marwitz, January 5, 1812; *Briefwechsel* I, 153.

26. Letter to David Veit, June 1, 1795; *Buch des Andenkens* I, 264.

27. Letter to Karl August Varnhagen, February 19, 1809; *Buch des Andenkens* I, 401.

28. Letter to David Veit, February 16, 1805; *Buch des Andenkens* I, 264.

29. Bettina von Arnim, *Goethes Briefwechsel mit einem Kinde. Seinem Denkmal.* Berlin, 1835.

30. Letter to Friedrich de la Motte Fouqué, December 31, 1811; *Buch des Andenkens* I, 585.

The Sign Speaks: Charlotte von Stein's Matinees

1. This despite the fact the *The Spectator* promoted an ideal of womanhood that corresponded neither to that with which we can identify Charlotte von Stein, nor to that portrayed in Goethe's *Iphigenie*. In number 81, for instance, it noted: "Female Virtues are of a Domestick turn. The Family is the proper Province for Private Women to shine in." (cited in Shevelow, 137)

2. For a discussion of some of this literature see Horsley.

3. Actually the 1920s feminist Ida Boy-Ed is one the few scholars to believe there could have been a sexual liaison between Goethe and von Stein. In part, the legacy of the chasteness of their relationship no doubt owes much to the traditional image of von Stein as a pious and humorless proponent of virtue, an image more like the chaste priestess of Diana than the down-to-earth wit who emerges from von Stein's own letters and plays. The somewhat sanctimonious image of her is clearly wrong and now generally admitted to be so. However there is still no evidence as to exactly how intimate the relationship was. Goethe scholars may still not want to consider the possibility that von Stein's later anger toward Goethe was well motivated. However, this is precisely the basis for Boy-Ed's assumption of a sexual relationship between the two. She assumes that such anger was well motivated and that it issued from a profound sense of Goethe's betrayal, not necessarily caused by his relationship with Christiane Vulpius, but (prior to that) by his secretive two-year flight to Italy.

4. Justin was a fifth-century historian, who had excerpted the lost universal history of Pompeius Trogus' *Historiae Philippicae,* written between 14 and 30 AD. The section about Dido is on page 17.

5. Hoff has looked at the meaning of women's self-destruction in three other plays of this period, but in each the woman pines for a love she

cannot have. In this respect *Dido* is quite different. This queen wishes to retain her autonomy and dies for it.

6. Aratus was apparently modeled on the Weimar intellectual Bertuch, Dodus on Hofmeister Knebel, who was frequently refered to in Charlotte von Stein's circle as the "Hofphilosoph". (Stein lvii ff.) Apparently Duke Karl August, who loved his horses passionately, stood model for Jarbus. The faithful Albicerio is reputed to have represented the theologian Herder.

Goethe and Beyond

1. This article is a revised version of parts of Chapter III in my book *Bettine von Arnim and the Politics of Romantic Conversation* (Columbia, SC, Camden House: 1988). All translations are mine. As much as possible, I have retained the grammatical irregularities that are characteristic of some of the writers I quote.

2. "To Achim von Arnim," 13 July 1807, Bettina von Arnim, *Werke und Briefe,* ed. Joachim Müller (Frechen: Bartmann, 1961), V, 149.

3. "To Achim von Arnim," August 1807, Bettina von Arnim, *Werke und Briefe,* V, 151.

4. Even as late as 1830 Goethe writes in his diary (August 7): "Refused Frau von Arnim's importunity." (Frau von Arnims Zudringlichkeit abgewiesen.) Quoted from Gisela Kähler, *Bettine: Eine Auswahl aus den Schriften und Briefen der Bettina von Arnim-Brentano* (Berlin: Verlag der Nation, 1952), 16.

5. Bettine von Arnim denied any support of the existing Goethe cult. See "To K. M. Kertbeny," 16 June 1850, Letter 6; Markgraf, 1861, I, 109–10. But she contributed to it independently (and somewhat belatedly), rather than through group adoration, as was the case in Rahel Varnhagen's salon, for example.

6. Ibid., 111.

7. Hermann Hesse, "Goethe und Bettina," *Gesammelte Werke,* (Frankfurt am Main: Suhrkamp, 1970), XII, 193.

8. "To Achim von Arnim," 7 March 1808, Bettina von Arnim, *Werke und Briefe,* V, 134.

9. Bettina von Arnim, *Werke und Briefe,* ed. Gustav Konrad, *Die Günderode* (Frechen: Bartmann, 1959), I, 331–32.

10. Christa Wolf, "Nun ja! Das nächste Leben geht aber heute an," *Sinn und Form,* 2 (März/April 1980), 414.

11. Waldemar Oehlke, *Bettina von Arnims Briefromane,* ed. Alois Randle, Gustav Roethe and Erich Schmidt. Palaestra: Untersuchungen und Texte aus der deutschen und englischen Philologie, No. 41 (Berlin: Mayer und Müller, 1905).

12. "This coming-to-oneself—what is it?" (Was ist das: Dieses Zusichselber-Kommen des Menschen?) is a quotation from Johannes R. Becher which Christa Wolf uses to introduce her novel *The Quest for Christa T.* and which very accurately expresses Bettine von Arnim's search for self-actualization at this point in her life. Christa Wolf, *The Quest for Christa T.* (New York: Farrar, Straus and Giroux, 1970). That a parallel can be drawn between these two writers is substantiated by Christa Wolf's interest in Bettine von Arnim as an individual and as a writer. See Wolf, "Nun ja!", 392–419 and the edition of von Arnim's second novel to which Wolf wrote the afterword, Bettina von Arnim, *Die Günderode: Briefroman* (Frankfurt: Insel Verlag, 1981). In her biography of Bettine von Arnim, Ingeborg Drewitz also alludes to this subjective interest in the chapter entitled "The I Bettine" (Das Ich Bettine). Ingeborg Drewitz, *Bettine von Arnim: Romantik, Revolution, Utopie* (Düsseldorf: Diederichs, 1969), 150–64.

13. It is interesting to note that this process parallels what Hélène Cixous calls *écriture féminine*. Cixous points to the interconnectedness of the female writing process and the search for self-identity. See Hélène Cixous, "The Laugh of the Medusa," in *New French Feminisms,* ed. Elaine Marks and Isabelle de Courtivron (Amherst: University of Massachusetts Press, 1980), 245. For an analysis of the connection between Cixous' theory and Bettine von Arnim's *Günderode* see Elke Frederiksen and Monika Shafi, "'Sich im Unbekannten suchen gehen': Bettina von Arnims 'Die Günderode' als weibliche Utopie," in Inge Stephan and Carl Pietzcker (eds.), *Frauensprache—Frauenliteratur?: Für und Wider einer Psychoanalyse literarischer Werke* (Tübingen: Max Niemeyer Verlag, 1986), 54–61.

14. In April 1832, after Goethe's death, Bettine von Arnim asked for her letters to Goethe from Kanzler von Müller of Weimar. See Drewitz, 147.

15. See, for example, Hans von Arnim, *Bettina von Arnim* (Berlin: Haude und Spenersche Verlagsbuchhandlung, 1963), 78–81, and Ina Seidel, *Drei Dichter der Romantik: Clemens Brentano, Bettina, Achim von Arnim* (Stuttgart: Deutsche Verlags-Anstalt, 1944), 158, 178–79.

16. Camillus Wendeler, ed., *Briefwechsel des Freiherrn Karl Hartwig Gregor von Meusebach mit Jacob und Wilhelm Grimm* (1880; reprint Wallut bei Wiesbaden: Dr. Martin Sändig oHG, 1974), 406.

17. "To Clemens Brentano," n. d., [End of January 1834], Bettina von Arnim, *Werke und Briefe,* V, 179.

18. Bettina von Arnim, *Werke und Briefe*, II, 127–33. Subsequent references to this edition of *Goethes Correspondence with a Child (Goethes Briefwechsel mit einem Kinde)* are included in the text in parentheses.

19. See Konrad, Bettina von Arnim, *Werke und Briefe*, II, 715.

20. See Konstanze Bäumer's analysis of Bettine von Arnim's relationship to this character in Bäumer's book *"Bettine, Psyche, Mignon": Bettina von Arnim und Goethe* (Verlag Hans-Dieter Heinz: Stuttgart, 1986), 118–44.

21. Ibid.

22. Oehlke, 304–05.

23. Gustav Konrad, ed., Bettina von Arnim, *Werke und Briefe, Die Günderode*, I, 374. Subsequent references to this edition of *Die Günderode* will be included in the text in parentheses.

24. See Gustav Konrad's discussion of a specific case. Konrad, Bettina von Arnim, *Werke und Briefe*, I, 55–57.

25. Gisela Dischner, *Bettine von Arnim: Eine weibliche Sozialbiographie aus dem 19. Jahrhundert* (Berlin: Wagenbach, 1978), 133–35.

26. For an example of how the individual senses and experiences this world, see Caroline's poem "The Wanderer's Descent" (Des Wanderers Niederfahrt), included in a letter to Bettine. *Die Günderode*, I, 360–63.

27. See Christa Wolf, "Der Schatten eines Traumes (Karoline von Günderrode, 1978)" in Christa Wolf, *Fortgesetzter Versuch: Aufsätze Gespräche, Essays* (Leipzig: Reclam, 1979), 321–22 and Gisela Dischner, *Bettina von Arnim*, 142.

28. Wolf, "Nun ja!", 411.

29. For a contemporary feminist discussion of the role of reflection in the search for oneself and in the establishment of female friendship, see Elisabeth Lenk, "Die sich selbst verdoppelnde Frau," *Ästhetik und Kommunikation* 25 (September 1976), 87.

30. Wolf, "Nun ja!", 414. Although Wolf does not cite it, the passage from which she quotes *Die Günderode* is in the aforementioned edition, page 259.

31. See, for example, Caroline's letter to Bettine, in which "this organic meshing" of the two women is articulated in a letter and a poem. *Die Günderode*, I, 241–44.

A Good Woman, and No Heroine

1. The quotations from her letters and, where possible, from the works of others will be cited according to the orthography and punctuation of

Erich Schmidt's 1913 edition. The translations are my own. Caroline Michaelis married J. F. W. Böhmer in 1784, A. W. Schlegel in 1796, and F. W. J. Schelling in 1803 and was known by their names during those marriages; to avoid unnecessary confusion, I refer to her throughout as Caroline Schlegel-Schelling.

2. See Kleßmann for an annotated list of works about her life (296–97). Elke Frederiksen expands the list (91, n.17). She remains even today a ready subject for fictionalized biography, as shown, for example, by Brigitte Struzyk's recent *Caroline unterm Freiheitsbaum* (Darmstadt: Luchterhand, 1988).

3. Her mother was a typical woman of the time; the women she met in her parents' home only proved to her that intelligence in a woman made her the object not of admiration but of scorn (i.e., I, 55).

4. Therese described their relationship well when she referred to Caroline as her "friend . . . enemy" (Freundin . . . Feindin, I, 681). Later, as Therese Huber, she wrote novels; see the article by Jeannine Blackwell in this volume.

5. Her letters to Forster after he had left Mainz, to A. W. Schlegel, and to G. Tatter, a romantic interest, for example, have all disappeared.

6. Although her own letters only alluded to this solution (I, 303), Therese Forster Huber was more direct (I, 696).

7. Therese Forster's fabricated report of a liaison between Caroline and Forster was particularly long-lived; Ingeborg Drewitz even in 1969 identified her as having been divorced from Forster (*Bettine von Arnim*, 311).

8. "Das Lied von der Glocke" (The Song of the Bell), however, survived their mockery. "The poem will have its victory march through the German bourgeoisie like no other, and will be considered for more than one hundred years a part of the canon for German high school students" (Kleßmann, 200).

9. Her treatment of her daughter as an equal was unusual for her time, as was her idea of education (e.g., I, 179).

10. After she left Jena, her relationship with Dorothea Veit and Friedrich Schlegel, who had remained there in her house, was mainly antagonistic. Although F. Schlegel had scandalized society with *Lucinde* and various fragments scorning bourgeois marriage in favor of sexual freedom and love (e.g., *Athenäums-Fragment* 34), he was not able to allow his sister-in-law the freedom of those ideals in her relationship with Schelling.

11. Gisela Dischner, Silvia Bovenschen, Barbara Becker-Cantarino, Katherine Goodman, and Barbara Hahn are among those who have laid the foundation for a theoretical discussion of women's letters around 1800.

12. Quoted in Kleβmann, 129.

13. She was widely recognized as the writer of highly intelligent and lively letters, for example by Wilhelm von Humboldt (I, 701). Friedrich Schlegel knew her through her letters even before he met her in Lucka. In frustration Dorothea Veit wrote from Jena of her reputation: "Like the head of the Gorgon, they are always holding Caroline's intellectual letters up to me" (Wie das Haupt der Gorgo halten sie mir immer [Caroline's] geistreichen Briefe vor, I, 744).

14. See *Lucinde* and *Athenäums-Fragment*, 116.

15. Schlegel had written, "Philosophical morality is subordinate to the political" (II, 584).

16. Later letters, however, show more skepticism toward Napoleon (e.g., II, 422).

17. Dischner has recognized the importance of this perspective (39–40). Hoffmann-Axthelm has recognized it, but does not view it as positively (91).

18. See, for example, Ingeborg Drewitz' *Berliner Salons*.

19. A letter was to him "a free imitation of a good conversation" (eine freye Nachahmung des gutes Gesprächs). Quoted in Bovenschen, 205.

20. A section of F. Schlegel's "Dialogue on Poetry" called "Letter on the Novel" links epistolary writing to art and conversation. The dialogue was originally published in *Athenäum* III, 112–28. For a discussion of "Geselligkeit" or "Romantic sociability," see Dischner, *Bettina von Arnim*, 25–33.

21. In addition to Herrmann and Waldstein, other critics have also discussed the implications of a dialogic structure for women's writing. See for example Dale Bauer.

22. In a chapter on Schlegel-Schelling and "Romantic sociability," Hoffmann-Axthelm places the emphasis on her independence, viewing it as vital for the formation of the Jena circle but detrimental to its continuation. The discussion does not do justice to Schlegel-Schelling's views or her accomplishments.

23. More than most critics, Werner Weiland and Dischner (*Caroline*, e.g., 99) have argued for a new assessment of early German romanticism which values its radicality and revolutionary spirit. The contemporary revisioning of romanticism in the former German Democratic Republic is premised on just such an understanding. See also Lennox and Herminghouse.

24. In 1795 she wrote to F. Schlegel that his brother now "thinks . . . differently about my friends, the Republicans, and is no longer such an

aristocrat" (denkt . . . anders über meine Freunde, die Republikaner, und ist gar nicht mehr Aristokrat, I, 366), a development she attributed to her own example. Weiland's study documents her even more important influence on F. Schlegel and the crucial importance for German romanticism of the time they spent together in Lucka.

25. Her views on art were anticipated and perhaps even influenced by *Werther,* but in her emphasis on autobiography and the dialogic structure, she was clearly going beyond Goethe's epistolary novel.

26. Comments such as the following were not uncommon: "I have almost as little sense for art as Tieck's dear Amalie; yesterday I almost fell asleep while reading" (Fast habe ich so wenig Kunstsinn wie Tieks liebe Amalie, denn ich bin gestern bey der Lektür eingeschlafen, I, 460).

27. She celebrated her first wedding anniversary by writing to her sister "on the anniversary of the day that banished me to an existence between 4 walls, near a heated oven, like a hot house plant that gets to enjoy the sun only through glass" (an der Jahresfeyer des Tages, der mich heut zwischen 4 Wände, bey einem geheizten Ofen, wie eine Mistbeetpflanze, die Sonne und Luft nur durch Glas geniest, verbant, I, 114).

28. I argue in my *The Ardrogyne in Early German Romanticism* that the androgynous wholeness they posited as the paradigm for human perfection was only a male goal, since females in their view were already whole, that is, perfect. The sexual equality they thought they were espousing was thus undermined from the beginning.

29. Shari Benstock's title and the essays she chose for inclusion in her recent collection of essays on women's autobiography problematize this issue, long thought the central motive in women's autobiographical writing.

Marriage by the Book

1. Therese Huber, "Die Frau von vierzig Jahren," *Taschenbuch für Damen auf das Jahr 1800,* 98–184, this quotation from p. 126.

2. The section of the *Landrecht* treating divorce is Part 2, Title 1, Paragraphs 738–750, 823, as well as other paragraphs dealing with property and children's rights. See also the *Reichsanzeiger* Nr. 198 (1798) and Nrs. 44, 46, 187 (1799) for contemporary issues surrounding the new code.

3. For example, *Über Ehescheidung. Für gebildete Leser aus allen Ständen.* Von D. Friedrich Popp, der Reichsstadt Nürnberg Konsulent und der Stadt- und Ehegerichts daselbst Assessor. Amberg und Sulzbach: in der Seidelischen Kunst- und Buchhandlung, 1800.

4. Johnnie Tillmon, "Welfare is a Women's Issue," in Rosalyn Baxandall, et al. *America's Working Women* (New York: Random House, 1976), 355–59.

5. For an overview of the literary works of Therese Huber, see: Wulf Koepke, "Immer noch im Schatten der Männer? Therese Huber als Schriftstellerin," in Detlev Rasmussen, ed. *Der Weltumsegler und seine Freunde* (Tübingen: Narr, 1988) 116–32. See also J. Blackwell, "Therese Huber," in *Dictionary of Literary Biography* 90 (Detroit: Bruccoli, Clark, Layman, 1990) 187–92.

6. An analysis of this novel can be found in Christine Touaillon, *Der deutsche Frauenroman des 18. Jahrhunderts.* (Vienna: Braumüller, 1919) 324–50, and in Helmut Peitsch, "Die Revolution im Familienroman: Aktuelles politisches Thema und konventionelle Romanstruktur in Therese Hubers *Die Familie Seldorf*," *Jahrbuch der deutschen Schillergesellschaft* 28 (1984): 248–69.

7. *Luise. Ein Beitrag zur Geschichte der Konvenienz* (Leipzig: in der Pet. Phil. Wolfischen Buchhandlung, 1796), hereafter *Luise;* "Die Frau von vierzig Jahren," *Taschenbuch für Damen auf das Jahr 1800:* 98–184, hereafter "Vierzig"; "Eine Ehestandsgeschichte," *Taschenbuch für Damen auf das Jahr 1804:* 12–116, hereafter "Ehestand"; "Die ungleiche Heirath," *Erzählungen von Therese Huber. Gesammelt und herausgegeben von V. A. H. In sechs Teilen* (Leipzig: F. A. Brockhaus, 1830–33). Vol. 2 (1830): 205–326; *Die Ehelosen von Therese Huber* (Leipzig: F. A. Brockhaus, 1829).

8. Lydia Schieth discusses the effects of this frame around what she calls "eine Krankengeschichte" in *Die Entwicklung des deutschen Frauenromans im ausgehenden 18. Jahrhundert* (Frankfurt/Main: Peter Lang, 1986), 190–93.

9. Huber presents another version of the perils of the sentimental love match in a subplot of *Hannah, der Herrnhuterin Deborah Findling* (1821) in which the orphan Hannah discovers that she is the first born, but illegitimate daughter of a baron and his wife, who later married. The mother's seduction was accomplished by reading *Siegfried.* To protect their reputations and the family inheritance, the birth is kept secret, and Hannah is given to foster parents. The mother, a sympathetic figure, narrates her own story, but soon dies of guilt and grief after finding her lost child again; thus she cannot survive her own narration of a failed female life as wife and mother, as does Amalie.

10. "Über Weiblichkeit in der Kunst, in der Natur, und in der Gesellschaft," *Erzählungen von L. F. Huber. Zweite Sammlung* (Braunschweig: Friedrich Vieweg, 1802) 412–46.

Escape to America

1. For critical essays on America as a theme in German literature, see Bauschinger. Compare with the actual experience of German

immigrants in Trommler. For an assessment of various mythical projections of "America," see Boerner.

2. A historical overview in Jantz.

3. Henriette Frölich's self-justification for publishing under a pseudonym indicates severe alienation: " . . . since bashfulness and memory of the unjustifiably harsh pronouncement she had often heard mentioned about those educated females who spoke out, made her fear to publicly present her writing attempts or even to identify her name to a publisher [bookseller]." (. . . da Schüchternheit und Erinnerung der unbilligen harten Urtheile, die sie so oft über sich aussprechende weibliche Bildung des Geistes vernahm, sie furchtsam machten, ihre Versuche öffentlich mitzutheilen, oder auch selbst einem Buchhändler ihren Namen zu nennen, Schindel, 141–42.)

4. In the USA, this rare book may be found at the Boston Public Library, a microfilm copy also at Cornell University Library.

5. La Roche worked from an authentic diary, and purposefully shaped an energetic French pioneer woman into a feminine role model of sensibility. In a letter of June 21, 1800 she asked Sophie von Pobeckheim to judge for herself "what my brains and my heart made out of this true story" (was mein Kopf und Herz aus der wahren Geschichte machten). *Ich bin mehr Herz als Kopf*, 451. According to historical sources, the French colonist was a "charming and resolute woman whose energy and friendliness is stressed on all accounts" (Lange, "Visitors", 60).

6. The striking difference between this island experiment in a novel of sensibility and other, more robust island adventures by women in narratives from the early to mid-eighteenth century is apparent; see Blackwell.

7. In the context of his research on early socialist thought in Germany, Gerhard Steiner also rediscovered a pamphlet by Henriette's husband Carl Wilhelm Frölich, *Über den Menschen und seine Verhältnisse* (Berlin: Frankesche Buchhandlung, 1792). This manifesto promotes community living and the abolition of private property. For an intellectual biography of both Frölichs, see Steiner.

8. In Germany, female voting rights were decreed November 30, 1918. Early proposals for women's vote initially surfaced among radical reformers in the 1790s. As a political demand it was proposed in the Reichstag by August Bebel only in 1895. It is interesting to note just how anti-establishment this issue was in Frölich's time. For example, in Goethe's *Wilhelm Meisters Lehrjahre* and also in his *Theatralische Sendung* women and men organize as traveling actors. Forming a "republican" senate, each member has the vote and is entitled to a senate seat. According to Victor Lange, this motif is designed to characterize the eccentricity of the troup to show its distance from conventional middle-class and aristocratic behavior (Lange, "Goethes Amerikabild," 68).

9. Renate Böschenstein-Schäfer traces the influence of such idyllic depictions (which carefully avoid personal and social problems) up to 20th century trivial novels. *Idylle,* 135.

10. Schiller's letter to Goethe, June 30, 1797, in Dagmar von Gersdorff, 125.

Reconstructing Women's Literary Relationships

1. The Weimar list of eight subscribers begins with a court official, Herr Kammerrat von Hendrich, presumably Franz Ludwig Albrecht von Hendrich (1754–1828), Sophie Albrecht's near contemporary. The Lieutenant Luk who follows him is presumably Georg Lebrecht von Luck or Lück (1751–1814). Both the divorced parents of the future actress and mistress of Karl August, Caroline Jägemann (1777–1848) subscribed; Caroline was four years old when the book appeared. The second woman from Weimar—and an important one since she bought three copies of Albrecht's book—is Madam Basch, probably Anna Caroline née Seidler. After the death of her first husband she married C. W. Ettinger, a book publisher in Gotha who published several of Sophie von La Roche's later works. It seems possible that the Consistorial Secretary on the list, Heinrich Friedrich Wilhelm Seidler (1751–1819), is Basch's brother. However that may be, he was an occasional performer in Goethe's amateur theater (Bruford, 122, 129), appearing sometimes with Corona Schröter. His name on Albrecht's subscription list makes it a little more likely that the distinguished Weimar actress is the Demoiselle Schröder on the list; while the deviant spelling does not, for the late eighteenth century, refute this conjecture, nothing else confirms or denies it.

2. Records on Hamburg's Theater am Gänsemarkt show that she made a guest appearance there in 1795, the year when her husband was still busily publishing books with a Leipzig imprint.

3. Since she had a stepmother whose maiden name was Manteuffel, Elise von der Recke may have known Dr. Albrecht's employer at the time.

The Vanished Woman of Great Influence

I would like to express my special thanks to Pilar Garcés for her careful reading and insightful comments on drafts of this paper. I would also like to thank Jeannine Blackwell for initially bringing Naubert to my attention.

1. Dorsch, 35.

2. Beginning in 1805, after her extremely productive years as a novelist, she published her short stories and novellas in journals like the *Journal für deutsche Frauen, Selene,* and *Frauen-Almanach zum Nutzen und Vergnügen* which addressed a predominantly female readership.

3. Yet, while strictly maintaining her anonymity, Naubert did defend her authorship: in 1793 she laid claim in newspaper columns to *Walter von Montbarry, Herrmann von Unna,* and *Thekla von Thurn,* and in 1797 to several more which had been erroneously attributed to the male writers Cramer, Heinse, and Milbiller.

4. For a list of essays and studies dealing with Naubert, see Dorsch 3ff.

5. Dorsch, 232, from *Schillers Briefwechsel mit Körner,* ed. Karl Goedeke (Leipzig, 1874), 1.

6. See Joanna Russ for a general discussion of these issues.

7. It is telling that Schreinert suggests that Naubert's most important influence in England was on Sir Walter Scott, a male writer, although Naubert's effect on Ann Radcliffe has also been noted in other sources.

8. Or even against the scourge of times, illegal reprints of her books. See Schreinert, 107, n.3, for a discussion of the bootlegging of Naubert's work by other publishers (who actually produced books of better quality than her own publisher, Weygand).

9. *Sigurd, der Schlangentödter: Ein Heldenspiel in sechs Abentheuern* appeared in 1808. It was expanded to include second and third parts, *Sigurd's Rache: Ein Heldenspiel in sechs Abenteuern* and *Auslauga: Ein Heldenspiel in drei Abenteuern.* In 1810 the work appeared as a trilogy titled *Der Held des Nordens.*

10. Naubert incorrectly accused Fouqué. In reality it was Karl August de Lamotte, director of the Munich Hof-Theater, who adapted *Ida Münsterin* for the stage.

11. Other "Volksmährchen" collections emulating Musäus' *Volksmährchen der Deutschen* and Naubert's anthology continued to appear in the German-speaking lands, e.g. Friedrich Wilhelm Möller's *Volksmährchen aus Thüringen* (1794, probably Cassel). Grätz considers Möller's work of no literary or folkloristic value, but only "further proof of the great popularity of Musäus and Naubert's oeuvres."

12. See Jennifer Fox for a discussion of the patriarchal "scripts" in Herder's paradigm of folkloristic scholarship.

13. See Anthony for a discussion of Wieland and early studies of folklore and fairy tale theory.

14. See my article "Trivial Pursuit?" for further discussion of the French tradition and its influence on German women's fairy tales.

15. See Ilse Nolting-Hauff for a detailed discussion of the connections between novels and fairy tales of redemption.

16. Ruth Bottigheimer has traced this trajectory for Grimm heroines: those who end up in secluded places are subject to degradation, danger, and ultimate demise until or unless a male redeems them. See chapter 4 of my dissertation.

17. See Jeannine Blackwell 1985.

18. George Sand's fairy tales to her grandchildren were originally published in 1873 and 1876 as *Contes d'une Grand-mère*. They have recently been translated and published in German under the title *Sie sind ja eine Fee, Madame! Märchen aus Schloß Nohant*, ed. Hans T. Siepe (Munich: dtv, 1988).

19. The tower later became in the Grimm tradition the most devastating place a pubescent female could visit. See Bottigheimer 1987, chapter 10.

20. See my afterword to *Gritta* for a discussion of this combination of genres in von Arnim.

21. See Waldstein.

22. See Blackwell 1987 for a discussion of this tale.

23. Naubert's Thekla von Thurn disguised herself as a man in order to be at her lover's side in battle.

24. See my edition of von Arnim's manuscripts and illustrations, (*Märchenbriefe an Achim*) for a further discussion of the *Geisterfrau*.

25. The tale exists only in manuscript form. I am currently working on an edition of fairy tales from the *Kaffeterkreis* that will include this text.

26. See my article "Trivial Pursuit?" for a detailed discussion of this fairy tale, and my dissertation for a discussion of these themes in the Grimms' and women's tales.

27. See, for example, Bottigheimer 1985, 1986, 1987.

Appendix: Sophie Albrecht's Correspondence

The letters 1, 2, 4, 5 are at the Hamburg Staats- und Universitätsbibliothek, Campe 3; Letter 3 is at the Staatsbibliothek Preußischer Kulturbesitz, West Berlin, Nachl. 141 (Slg. Adam), K. 86.

1. Johann Christian Reinhart, 1761–1847, primarily a landscape painter, after 1781 mostly in Rome.

2. Christoph Phillipp Willibald von Hohenfeld, 1743–1822, invited the La Roche family to live in his house in Speyer after Georg von La Roche had lost his position in Koblenz.

3. Johann Joachim Christoph Bode, 1730–1793, translator and writer, wrote the introduction to La Roche's second novel, *Rosaliens Briefe*.

4. Friedrich Lyser, 1783–1839, theater director in Altona after Albrecht.

5. Lined out: bis ich Sie selbst sehe.

6. Baron Pidoux de Montenglaut.

7. Wilhelm Vogel, 1772–1843, actor, director, and playwright.

8. Criminal Director Gonsdruch in Herford (Schindel, 2,15).

9. An earlier *dem* appears changed to *der* but the rest of the syntax was left garbled, as it also is in a few other places where no corrections were made.

10. Friedrich von Matthison, 1761–1831, a celebrated poet of his day.

11. *Herbstblumenkranz. Niedergelegt auf das Grab des ehrwürdigen Greises des lieblichen Dichters Jacobi in Freiburg in Breisgau.* (Darmstadt: Stahl, 1814).

12. Schindel lists some anonymous contributions by Montenglaut.

13. Perhaps *Nordlands Heideblüthen*, listed in Schindel but not found.

14. Carl Unzer; see Hoffman 113–14.

15. Johann Christoph Unzer, 1745–1809, medical doctor and playwright, married the actress Dorothea Ackermann; divorced.

16. Elise Bürger née Hahn, 1769–1833, writer and actress who began her stage career in Altona after divorcing the poet Gottfried August Bürger (1792).

17. Joachim Lorenz Evers, 1758–1807, director of the National Theater in Altona 1801–1802. Montenglaut may have done some translations for him in 1800 (Meusel, 14, 612).

18. Probably the actress Friederike Antonie Sophie Schirmer née Christ 1785–1833, with Albrecht in Seconda's troup.

19. The *Norddeutsche Nachrichten* mention that she was plunged into poverty after the death of a Livonian nobleman.

20. Großmann, famous director who first encouraged Albrecht to become an actress.

21. She is probably mentioned in the postscript to Letter 3 above.

References

Introduction

Arendt, Hannah. *Rahel Varnhagen. The Life of a Jewish Woman.* New York: Harcourt Brace Jovanovich, 1974.

Beaujean, Marion. "Frauen-, Familien-, Abenteuer- und Schauerromane" in Glaser, 216–28.

Becker-Cantarino, Barbara, ed. *Die Frau von der Reformation zur Romantik. Die Situation der Frau vor dem Hintergrund der Literatur- und Sozialgeschichte.* Bonn: Bouvier, 1985.

Becker-Cantarino, Barbara. *Der lange Weg zur Mündigkeit. Frau und Literatur 1500–1800.* Stuttgart: Metzler, 1987.

Bovenschen, Sylvia. *Die imaginierte Weiblichkeit. Exemplarische Untersuchungen zu kulturgeschichtlichen und literarischen Präsentationsformen des Weiblichen.* Frankfurt a.M.: Suhrkamp, 1979.

Engelsing, Rolf. *Der Bürger als Leser. Lesergeschichte in Deutschland 1500–1800.* Stuttgart: Metzler, 1974.

Fink, Gouthier-Louis. "Die Revolution als Herausforderung in Literatur und Publizistik" in Glaser, 110–29.

Frederiksen, Elke. "German Women Writers in the Nineteenth Century: Where are They?" in Cocalis & Goodman, eds. *Beyond the Eternal Feminine: Critical Essays on Women and Literature.* Stuttgarter Arbeiten zur Germanistik. Vol. 98. Stuttgart: H. D. Heinz, 1982, 177–201.

Friedrichsmeyer, Sara. *The Androgyne in German Romanticism.* Bern: Lang, 1983.

Glaser, Horst Albert, ed. *Deutsche Literatur. Eine Sozialgeschichte. Zwischen Revolution und Restauration: Klassik, Romantik 1786–1815.* Vol. 5. Reinbeck bei Hamburg: Rowohlt, 1980.

Goodman, Katherine. *Dis/Closures: Women's Autobiography in Germany, Between 1790 and 1914.* New York: Peter Lang, 1986.

Goodman, Katherine. "The Impact of Rahel Varnhagen on Women in the Nineteenth Century." In *Gestaltet und gestaltend: Frauen in der deutschen Literatur.* Ed. Marianne Burkhard, 125–53. Amsterdam: Rodopi, 1981.

Hertz, Deborah. *Jewish High Society in Old Regime Berlin.* New Haven: Yale, 1988.

Heuser, Magdalene Heuser. "Literatur von Frauen/Frauen in der Literatur. Feministische Ansätze in der Literaturwissenschaft." In *Inspektion der Herrenkultur. Ein Handbuch,* ed. Luise F. Pusch, 117–48. Frankfurt a.M.: Suhrkamp, 1983.

Hoffmann, Volker. "Elisa und Robert oder das Weib und der Mann, wie sie sein sollten. Anmerkungen zur Geschlechtercharakteristik der Goethezeit." In *Klassik und Moderne. Die Weimarer Klassik als historisches Ereignis und Herausforderung im kulturgeschichtlichen Prozeß,* ed. Karl Richter and Jörg Schönert, 80–97. Stuttgart: Metzler, 1983.

Hoffmeister, Gerhart. *Deutsche und europäische Romantik.* Stuttgart: Metzler, 1978.

La Roche, Sophie von. *Die Geschichte des Fräulein von Sternheim.* Leipzig: Reclam, 1938.

Leporin, Dorothea Christiane. *Gründliche Untersuchung der Ursachen, die das Weibliche Geschlecht vom Studiren abhalten.* Berlin: Johann Andreas Rüdiger, 1742; reprint. 1977 Hildesheim, Georg Olms.

Lepper, Gisbert. "Literarische Öffentlichkeit—literarische Zentren" in Glaser, 58–73.

Martino, Alberto and Marlies Stützel-Prüsener. "Publikumsschichten, Lesegesellschaften und Leihbibliotheken" in Glaser, 45–57.

Meise, Helga. *Die Unschuld und die Schrift. Deutsche Frauenromane im 18. Jahrhundert.* Berlin: Guttandin & Hoppe, 1983.

Oeser, Hans Ludwig. *Das Zeitalter Goethes.* Berlin: Deutsche Buchgemeinschaft, 1932.

Schieth, Lydia. *Die Entwicklung des deutschen Frauenromans im ausgehenden 18. Jahrhundert.* Frankfurt a.M.: Peter Lang, 1987.

Schiller, Friedrich. *Werke in drei Bänden.* Munich: Hanser, 1966.

Schmidt, Peter. "Buchmarkt, Verlagswesen und Zeitschriften" in Glaser, 74–92.

Schopenhauer, Johanna. *Jugendleben und Wanderbilder.* Danzig: Danziger Verlagsgesellschaft, 1922.

Schumann, Sabine. "Das 'lesende Frauenzimmer:' Frauenzeitschriften im 18. Jahrhundert" in Becker-Cantarino, *Frau,* 138–69.

Touaillon, Christine. *Der deutsche Frauenroman des 18. Jahrhunderts;* reprint. Bern,: Peter Lang, 1979.

Ueding, Gert. *Klassik und Romantik. Deutsche Literatur im Zeitalter der Französischen Revolution 1789–1815. Hansers Sozialgeschichte der deutschen Literatur vom 16. Jahrhundert bis zur Gegenwart,* ed. Rolf Grimminger. Vol. 5. Munich: Hanser, 1987.

Waldstein, Edith. *Bettine von Arnim and the Politics of Romantic Conversation.* Columbia, S.C.: Camden House, 1988.

Walter, Eva. *Schrieb oft, von Mägde Arbeit müde.* Düsseldorf: Schwann, 1985.

Weber, Peter. "Einleitung: 'Kunstperiode' als literaturhistorischer Begriff." In *Kunstperiode. Studien zur deutschen Literatur des ausgehenden 18. Jahrhunderts.* Ed. Weber, et.al. Berlin: Akademie Verlag, 1982.

Werner, Johannes, ed. *Maxe von Arnim: Tochter Bettinas/Gräfin von Oriola, 1818–1894.* Leipzig: Koehler und Amelang, 1937.

Winkle, Sally A. *Woman as Bourgeois Ideal. A Study of Sophie von La Roche's "Geschichte des Fräuleins von Sternheim" and Goethe's "Werther."* New York: Peter Lang, 1988.

Winkler, Lutz. *Autor-Markt-Publikum. Zur Geschichte der Literaturproduktion in Deutschland.* Berlin: Argument, 1986.

The Beautiful Soul Writes Herself

Beaujean, Marion. "Das Bild des Frauenzimmers im Roman des 18. Jahrhunderts." *Wolfenbuetteler Studien zur Aufklaerung.* Ed. Guenter Schulz, III, 9–28. Wolfenbuettel: Jacobi, 1976.

Biedermann, Flodoard von. *Friedrich Unger im Verkehr mit Goethe und Schiller.* Berlin: Berthold, 1927.

Buerger, Christa. " 'Die mittlere Sphaere'. Sophie Mereau—Schriftstellerin im klassischen Weimar." *Deutsche Literatur von Frauen.* Ed. Gisela Brinker-Gabler, I, 366–74, 544. Munich: Beck, 1988.

Dawson, Ruth. "Frauen und Theater: Vom Stegreifspiel zum buergerlichen Ruehrstueck." *Deutsche Literatur von Frauen.* Ed. Gisela Brinker-Gabler, I, 421–24. Munich: Beck, 1988.

Geiger, Ludwig. *Allgemeine Deutsche Biographie,* 56 vols. Leipzig-Duncker und Humblot, 1875–1912. 39:295.

Gilbert, Sandra, and Susan Gubar. *The Madwoman in the Attic: The Woman Writer and the Nineteenth-Century Literary Imagination.* New Haven and London: Yale University Press, 1980.

Goethe, Johann Wolfgang von. *Werke.* HA 7:772. 10th ed. Munich: Beck, 1981.

Heuser, Magdalene. " 'Spuren trauriger Selbstvergessenheit,' Moeglichkeiten eines weiblichen Bildungsromans um 1800: Friederike Helene Unger". In *Kontroversen, alte und neue. Akten des VI. Internationalen Germanisten-Kongresses* 7. 6:30–42. Goettingen: Niemeyer, 1986.

Hirsch, Marianne. "Spiritual *Bildung:* The Beautiful Soul as Paradigm." *The Voyage In.* Ed. Elizabeth Abel, Marianne Hirsch, and Elizabeth Langland, 23–48. Hanover N.H.: New England University Press, 1983.

May, Kurt. "Wilhelm Meisters Lehrjahre, ein Bildungsroman?" *Deutsche Vierteljahresschrift* 31(1957):1–37.

Miller, Nancy K. "Emphasis Added: Plots and Plausibilities in Women's Fiction." *Feminist Criticism. Essays on Women, Literature, and Theory.* Ed. Elaine Showalter. New York: Pantheon, 1985.

Meads, William. "Goethe's Concept of Entsagung." *Pacific Coast Philology* 8 (1973): 34–41.

Schiller, Friedrich. "Ueber Anmut und Wuerde." *Werke.* Nationalausgabe. Weimar: Bohlau, 1943–, vol. 20.

Swales, Martin. *The German Bildungsroman from Wieland to Hesse.* Princeton: Princeton University Press, 1978.

Ward, Margaret. "Ehe und Entsagung: Fanny Lewald's Early Novels and Goethe's Literary Paternity," *Women in German Yearbook* II (Lanham: University Press of America, 1985): 57–77.

Unger, Friederike Helene. *Julchen Grünthal. Eine Pensionsgeschichte. Mit allergnädigsten Freiheiten.* Berlin: Unger, 1784.

———. *Julchen Grünthal.* Third, expanded edition. Berlin: Unger, 1798.

———. *Gräfinn Pauline.* Berlin: Unger, 1800.

———. *Melanie das Findelkind. Von der Verfasserin der Julchen Grünthal.* Berlin: Unger, 1804.

———. *Albert und Albertine.* Berlin: Unger, 1804 (new ed. Leipzig: Lüderitz 1817, quoted here).

———. *Bekenntnisse einer schönen Seele. Von ihr selbst geschrieben.* Berlin: Unger, 1806.

———. *Die Franzosen in Berlin, oder Serene an Clementinen in den Jahren 1806.7.8. Ein Sittengemälde.* Leipzig, Züllichau and Freystadt: Darnmann 1809.

Zantop, Susanne. "Friederike Helene Unger." *Dictionary of Literary Biography: German Writers in the Age of Goethe.* Eds. J. Hardin and Christoph Schweitzer. New York: Bruccoli Clark Layman, 1990. 94:188–93.

Zantop, Susanne. "Aus der Not eine Tugend . . . Tugendgebot und Oeffentlichkeit bei Friederike Helene Unger." In *Untersuchungen zum Roman von Frauen um 1800.* Eds. Helga Gallas and Magdalene Heuser. Tuebingen: Niemeyer, 1990, 132–147.

Zantop, Susanne. Afterword. *Bekenntnisse einer schönen Seele. Von ihr selbst geschrieben.* Reprint Hildesheim: Olms, 1991.

The Sign Speaks

Angst, Joachim and Fritz Hackert. *Erläuterungen und Dokumente. Johann Wolfgang Goethe "Iphigenie auf Tauris."* Stuttgart: Reclam, 1969.

Borchmeyer, Dieter. *Die Weimarer Klassik.* 2 Vols. Königstein: Athenäum, 1980.

Boy-Ed, Ida. *Das Martyrium der Charlotte von Stein. Versuch einer Rechtfertigung.* Stuttgart und Berlin: Cotta, 1920.

Eckermann, Johann. *Gespräche mit Goethe.* Weimar: Kiepenheuer, 1918.

Fränkel, Jonas, ed. *Goethes Briefe an Charlotte von Stein.* 2 vols. Berlin: Akademie Verlag, 1960.

Goethe, Johann Wolfgang von. *Gedenkausgabe der Werke, Briefe und Gespräche.* Ed. Ernst Beutler. Zürich: Artemis, 1954.

Hof, Walter. *Goethe und Charlotte von Stein.* Frankfurt a. M.: Insel, 1979.

Hoff, Dagmar von. "Die Inszenierung des 'Frauenopfers' in Dramen von Autorinnen um 1800." In *Frauen-Literatur-Politik.* Annegret Pelz, Marianne Schuller, Inge Stephan, Sigrid Weigel, Kerstin Wilhelms eds. 255–62. Hamburg: Argument, 1988.

Horsley, Rita Jo. "A Critical Appraisal of Goethe's *Iphigenie.*" *Beyond the Eternal Feminine. Critical Essays on Women and German Literature.* Susan L. Cocalis and Kay Goodman eds. 47–74. Stuttgart: Akademischer Verlag Hans-Dieter Heinz, 1982.

Justinus, Pompeius Trogus. *Weltgeschichte von den Anfängen bis Augustus im Auszug des Justine.* Zürich: Artemis, 1972.

Shevelow, Kathryn. *Women and Print Culture. The Construction of Femininity in the early Periodical.* London: Routledge, 1989.

von Stein, Charlotte. *Dido. Ein Trauerspiel in fünf Aufzügen.* Leipzig: Brockhaus, 1867.

Susman, Margarethe. *Deutung einer großen Liebe. Goethe und Charlotte von Stein.* Zürich: Artemis, 1957.

A Good Woman, and No Heroine

Bakhtin, M. M. *The Dialogic Imagination: Four Essays.* Ed. Michael Holquist. Trans. Caryl Emerson and Michael Holquist. Austin: University of Texas Press, 1981.

Bauer, Dale. *Feminist Dialogics: A Theory of Failed Community.* Albany: State University of New York Press, 1988.

Becker-Cantarino, Barbara. "Leben als Text: Briefe im 18. Jahrhundert." In *Frauen-Literatur-Geschichte. Schreibende Frauen vom Mittelalter bis zur Gegenwart.* Ed. Hiltrud Gnüg und Renate Möhrmann, 83-103. Stuttgart: Metzler, 1985.

Benjamin, Walter. *Gesammelte Schriften.* Ed. Tillman Rexroth, Vol. 4, 872-74. Frankfurt: Suhrkamp, 1972.

Behrens, Katja. "Afterword." *Frauenbriefe der Romantik.* Ed. Katja Behrens. Frankfurt: Insel, 1981.

Benstock, Shari. "Introduction." *The Private Self. Theory and Practice of Women's Autobiographical Writings.* Ed. Shari Benstock. Chapel Hill: North Carolina UP, 1988.

Bovenschen, Silvia. "Is There a Feminine Aesthetics?" Trans. Beth Weckmueller. *Feminist Aesthetics.* Ed. Gisela Ecker, 23–50. Boston: Beacon, 1985.

Damm, Sigrid. "Introduction." *Lieber Freund, ich komme weit her schon an diesem frühen Morgen. Caroline Schlegel-Schelling in ihren Briefen.* Ed. Sigrid Damm. Darmstadt: Luchterhand, 1980.

Dischner, Gisela. *Caroline und der Jenaer Kreis: Ein Leben zwischen bürgerlichen Vereinzelung und romantischer Geselligkeit.* Berlin: Wagenbach, 1979.

Drewitz, Ingeborg. *Berliner Salons: Gesellschaft und Literatur zwischen Auflärung und Industriezeitalter.* Berlin: Haude und Spenersche Verlagsbuchhandlung, 1965.

―――. *Bettine von Arnim: Romantik. Revolution. Utopie.* Düsseldorf: Diederichs, 1969.

Eichner, Hans. *Friedrich Schlegel*. New York: Twayne, 1970.

Frederiksen, Elke. "Die Frau als Autorin zur Zeit der Romantik: Anfänge einer weiblichen literarischen Tradition." *Gestaltet und gestaltend. Frauen in der deutschen Literatur*. Ed. Marianne Burkhard, 83-108. Amsterdamer Beiträge zur Germanistik 10. Amsterdam: Rodopi, 1980.

Friedrichsmeyer, Sara. *The Androgyne in Early German Romanticism: Friedrich Schlegel, Novalis, and the Metaphysics of Love*. Stanford German Studies. Bern: Lang, 1983.

Gilligan, Carol. *In a Different Voice*. Cambridge, MA: Harvard UP, 1982.

————, ed. *Mapping the Moral Domain*. Cambridge, MA: Harvard UP, 1988.

Goodman, Katherine. *Dis/Closures: Women's Autobiography in Germany Between 1790 and 1914*. New York University Ottendörfer Series. Bern: Lang, 1986.

Hahn, Barbara. " 'Weiber verstehen alles à la lettre': Briefkultur im beginnenden 19. Jahrhundert." *Deutsche Literatur von Frauen. Zweiter Band. 19. und 20. Jahrhundert*. Ed. Gisela Brinker-Gabler, 13–27. Munich: Beck, 1988.

Herminghouse, Patricia. "The Rediscovery of Romanticism: Revision and Reevaluations." *Studies in GDR Culture and Society 2*. Ed. Margy Gerber et. al., 1–17. Washington D.C.: University Press of America, 1982.

Herrmann, Anne. *The Dialogic and Difference: "An/Other Woman" in Virginia Woolf and Christa Wolf*. New York: Columbia UP, 1989.

Hoffmann-Axthelm, Inge. *"Geisterfamilie." Studien zur Geselligkeit der Frühromantik*. Frankfurt: Akademische Verlagsgesellschaft, 1973.

Kleßmann, Eckart. *Caroline: Das Leben der Caroline Michaelis-Böhmer-Schlegel-Schelling 1763–1809*. Munich: Deutscher Taschenbuch Verlag, 1979.

Lennox, Sara. "Christa Wolf and the Women Romantics." *Studies in GDR Culture and Society 2*. Ed. Margy Gerber et al., 31–43. Washington, D.C.: University Press of America, 1982.

Schlegel, August Wilhelm and Friedrich Wilhelm Schlegel, eds. *Athenäum*. Reprint, Stuttgart: Cotta, 1960.

Schlegel, Friedrich. *Dialogue on Poetry and Literary Aphorisms*. Trans. and intro. Ernst Behler and Roman Struc. University Park: Pennsylvania State UP, 1968.

————. *Kritsche Friedrich-Schlegel-Ausgabe.* Ed. Ernst Behler. Paderborn: Schöningh, 1962 to the present.

————. *"Lucinde" and the Fragments.* Trans. and intro. Peter Firchow. Minneapolis: Minnesota UP, 1971.

Schlegel-Schelling, Caroline. *Caroline: Briefe aus der Frühromantik.* Ed. Erich Schmidt. 2 vols. Leipzig: Insel, 1913.

Waldstein, Edith. *Bettine von Arnim and the Politics of Romantic Conversation.* Columbia, S.C.: Camden House, 1988.

Weigel, Sigrid. "Die geopferte Heldin und das Opfer als Heldin: Zum Entwurf weiblicher Helden in der Literatur von Männern und Frauen." *Die verborgene Frau.* Inge Stephan und Sigrid Weigel, 138–52. Berlin: Argument, 1983.

Weiland, Werner. *Der junge Friedrich Schlegel oder die Revolution in der Frühromantik.* Stuttgart: Kohlhammer, 1968.

Wolf, Christa. *The Reader and the Writer: Essays, Sketches, Memories.* Trans. Joan Becker. New York: International Publishers, 1977.

Escape to America

Abray, Jane. "Feminism in the French Revolution." *American Historical Review,* 80 (1975): 43–62.

Bauschinger, Sigrid et al., eds. *Amerika in der deutschen Literatur.* Stuttgart: Reclam, 1975.

Bersier, Gabrielle. "Reise als Umrahmung der Utopie." *Reise und soziale Realität am Ende des 18. Jahrhunderts.* Ed. Wolfgang Griep and Hans-Wolf Jäger. Heidelberg: Winter, 1983, 292–301.

Bestor, Arthur E. *Backwood Utopias. The Sectarian Origins and the Owenite Phase of Communitarian Socialism in America, 1663–1829.* 2d ed. Philadelphia: University of Pennsylvania Press, 1970.

Blackwell, Jeannine. "An Island of Her Own: Heroines of the German Robinsonades from 1720 to 1800." *The German Quarterly,* 58 (1985): 5–26.

Boerner, Peter. "Utopia in der Neuen Welt: Vom europäischen Träumen zum American Dream." *Utopieforschung: Interdisziplinäre Studien zur neuzeitlichen Utopie.* Ed. Wilhelm Voßkamp. 3 vols. Stuttgart: Metzler, 1982. 2: 358–74.

Böschenstein-Schäfer, Renate. *Idylle,* 2d ed. Stuttgart: Metzler, 1977.

Cocalis, Susan L. "Der Vormund will Vormund sein: Zur Problematik der weiblichen Unmündigkeit im 18. Jahrhundert." *Amsterdamer Beiträge zur Neuen Germanistik*, 10 (1980): 33–55.

Frevert, Ute, *Frauen-Geschichte zwischen bürgerlicher Verbesserung und neuer Weiblichkeit*. Frankfurt/Main: Suhrkamp, 1986.

Frölich, Henriette. *Virginia oder die Republik von Kentucky*. Berlin: August Rücker, 1820; reprint, Berlin/DDR: Aufbau, 1968.

Gersdorff, Dagmar von. *Dich zu lieben kann ich nicht verlernen. Das Leben der Sophie Brentano-Mereau*. Frankfurt/Main: Insel, 1984.

Habermas, Jürgen. *Strukturwandel der Offentlichkeit*, 3d ed. Neuwied: Luchterhand, 1968.

Hohendahl, Peter Uwe. "Zum Erzählproblem des utopischen Romans im 18. Jahrhundert." *Gestaltungsgeschichte und Gesellschaftsgeschichte*. Ed. Helmut Kreuzer, 79–114. Stuttgart: Metzler, 1969.

Jantz, Harold. "Amerika im deutschen Dichten und Denken." *Deutsche Philologie im Aufriß*. Ed. Wolfgang Stammler, III, 146–204. Berlin: E. Schmidt, 1962.

Köpke, Wulf. "Die emanzipierte Frau in der Goethezeit und ihre Darstellung in der Literatur." *Die Frau als Heldin und Autorin*. Ed. Wolfgang Paulsen, 96–110. Munich: Francke, 1979.

Lange, Victor. "Goethes Amerikabild. Wirklichkeit und Vision." *Amerika in der deutschen Literatur*. Ed. Sigrid Bauschinger et al, 63–74. Stuttgart: Reclam, 1975.

Lange, Victor. "Visitors to Lake Oneida. An Account of the Background of Sophie La Roche's novel 'Erscheinungen am See Oneida.'" *Symposium* 1 (1948): 48–74.

La Roche, Sophie. *Erscheinungen am See Oneida*. 3 vols. Leipzig: Heinrich Gräff, 1798.

Martens, Wolfgang. "Das lesende Frauenzimmer." *Die Botschaft der Tugend*. Stuttgart: Metzler, 1968, 520–42.

Maurer, Michael, ed. *Ich bin mehr Herz als Kopf. Sophie La Roche: Ein Lebensbild in Briefen*. Munich: Beck, 1983.

Mereau, Sophie. *Das Blüthenalter der Empfindung*. Gotha: Justus Perthes, 1794; reprints, Munich: Dreiländerverlag, 1920; Stuttgart: Akademischer Verlag, 1982.

Pfaelzer, Jean. "The Impact of Political Theory on Narrative Structures." *America as Utopia*. Ed. Kenneth M. Roemer, 117–32. New York: Burt Franklin, 1981.

Schindel, Carl von. *Die deutschen Schriftstellerinnen des 19. Jahrhunderts.* Drei Teile in 1 Band; reprint, Heldesheim: Olms, 1978.

Steiner, Gerhard. *Der Traum vom Menschenglück.* Berlin/DDR: Akademie-Verlag, 1959.

Trommler, Frank, McVeigh, Joseph, eds. *America and the Germans.* 2 vols. Philadelphia: University of Pennsylvania Press, 1985.

Reconstructing Women's Literary Relationships

Alberti, Eduard. *Lexikon der Schleswig-Holstein-Lauenburgischen und Eutinischen Schriftsteller von 1829 bis Mitte 1866.* 2 vols. Kiel: Akademische Buchhandlung, 1867–68.

Albrecht, Johann Friedrich Ernst, [and Sophie Albrecht?]. *Erzählungen aus dem Dunkel der Vorzeit.* Hamburg: n.p., 1801.

Albrecht, [Johann Friedrich Ernst, and Sophie Albrecht?.] *Trümmer der Vergangenheit aus ihren Ruinen ans Licht gebracht.* Hamburg: B. G. Hoffman, 1796.

Albrecht, Sophie. *Anthologie aus den Poesien von Sophie Albrecht.* Ed. Fr[iedrich] Clemens [Gerke]. Altona: B. J. F. Hammerich, 1841.

———, ed. *Aramena; eine syrische Geschichte, ganz für unsre Zeiten umgearbeitet.* [By Anton Ulrich Duke of Braunschweig]. 3 parts. Berlin: Rottmann, 1783–87.

———. *Erfurter Kochbuch für die Bürgerliche Küche.* Erfurt: Hilsenberg, 1839.

———. *Gedichte und prosaische Aufsätze.* Vol. 2. Erfurt: Albrecht und Compagnie, 1785. 2nd Ed. Dresden und Liepzig: Richter, 1791.

———. *Gedichte und prosaische Aufsätze.* Vol. 3. Dresden: Richter, 1791.

———. *Gedichte und Schauspiele.* [Vol. 1] Erfurt: Albrecht und Compagnie, 1781. 2nd Ed. Dresden: Richter, 1791.

———. *Das höfliche Gespenst.* Altona: Bechtold, 1797. Also published under the title *Legenden.* Vol. 1. Altona: Bechtold, 1797. And as: *Ida von Duba, das Mädchen im Walde; eine romantische Geschichte aus den grauenvollen Tagen der Vorwelt.* Altona: Bechtold, [1805?].

———. Letter to [Daniel Schütte]. [April 1816.] B:Albrecht. Deutsches Literaturarchiv, Marbach.

———. *Romantische Dichtungen aus der ältern christlichen Kirche.* Hamburg: Vollmer, [1808].

————. *Thüringisches Kochbuch für die bürgerliche Küche.* Erfurt: Hilsenberg, 1839.

Allgemeine Deutsche Biographie. 56 vols. Leipzig: Duncker u. Humblot, 1875–1912.

Baldinger, Friderika. *Lebensbeschreibung von Friderika Baldinger von ihr selbst verfaßt.* Ed. Sophie von La Roche. Offenbach: Weiß u. Brede, 1791.

Becker, Sophie. *Vor hundert Jahren: Elise von der Reckes Reisen durch Deutschland 1784–86.* Stuttgart: Spemann, 1884.

Biereye, Johannes. *Erfurt in seinen berühmten Persönlichkeiten. Eine Gesamtschau.* Erfurt: Stenger 1937.

Bovenschen, Silvia. *Die imaginierte Weiblichkeit. Exemplarische Untersuchungen zu kulturgeschichtlichen und literarischen Präsentationsformen des Weiblichen.* Frankfurt/Main: Suhrkamp, 1979.

Brinker-Gabler, Gisela, ed. *Deutsche Dichterinnen vom 16. Jahrhundert bis zur Gegenwart. Gedichte und Lebensläufe.* Frankfurt/Main: Fischer, 1978.

————, ed. *Vom Mittelalter bis zum Ende des 18. Jahrhunderts.* Vol. 1 of *Deutsche Literatur von Frauen.* 2 vols. Munich: Beck 1988.

Bruford, W. H. *Culture and Society in Classical Weimar 1775–1806.* 1962. New York: Cambridge University Press, 1975.

Brun, Friederike, and Caroline von Humboldt. *Frauen zur Goethezeit. Ein Briefwechsel.* Ed. Ilse Foerst-Crato. Düsseldorf: n.p., 1975.

Dawson, Ruth. "Frauen und Theater: Vom Stegreifspiel zum bürgerlichen Rührstück." Gisela Brinker-Gabler, *Vom Mittelalter* 421–34.

————. "Women Communicating: Eighteenth-Century German Journals Edited by Women." *Archives et Bibliotéques de Belgique* 54 (1983): 95–111.

Devrient, Eduard. *Geschichte der deutschen Schauspielkunst.* 5 vols. Leipzig: Weber, 1848–74.

Eisenberg, Ludwig. *Großes biographisches Lexikon der deutschen Bühne im XIX Jahrhundert.* Leipzig: List, 1903.

Engelhard, Philippine [née Gatterer]. *Neujahrs-Geschenk für liebe Kinder.* Cassel: in Commission, 1787.

Frels, Wilhelm. *Deutsche Dichterhandschriften von 1400 bis 1900.* Leipzig: Hiersemann, 1934.

Friedrichs, Elisabeth. *Die deutschsprachigen Schriftstellerinnen des 18. und 19. Jahrhunderts. Ein Lexikon.* Repertorien zur Deutschen Literaturgeschichte 9. Stuttgart: Metzler, 1981.

[Froriep, Amalie Henriette Sophie]. *Amalie von Nordheim, oder der Tod zur unrechten Zeit*. 2 vols. Gotha: Ettinger, 1783.

[Geisler, Adam Friedrich.] *Gallerie edler deutscher Frauenzimmer*. Vol. 1 Dessau: Buchhandlung der Gelehrten, 1784.

Goedeke, Karl. *Grundriß der Geschichte der deutschen Literatur aus den Quellen*. 10 vols. Dresden: Ehlermann, 1884–1913.

Haferkorn, Hansjürgen. "Der freie Schriftsteller. Eine literatursoziologische Studie über seine Entstehung und Lage in Deutschland zwischen 1750 und 1800." *Archiv für Geschichte des Buchwesens* 5 (1963): 523–712.

Hahn, Karl-Heinz, ed. *Briefe an Goethe. Gesamtausgabe in Regestform*. Weimar: Böhlau, 1980–.

Hamberger, Georg Christoph, and Johann Georg Meusel. *Das Gelehrte Teutschland oder Lexikon der jetzt lebenden teutschen Schriftsteller*. 23 vols. 1797–1831. Hildesheim: Olms, 1966.

Harris, Edward P. "From Outcast to Ideal: The Image of the Actress in Eighteenth-Century Germany." *German Quarterly* 54 (1981): 177–87.

Hoffman, Paul Th. *Die Entwicklung des Altonaer Stadttheaters. Ein Beitrag zu seiner Geschichte*. Altona: Köbner, 1926.

Hutten, M. Joh. Georg. *Verzeichniß der Abonnenten auf Pomona*. N.p.: n.p. 1783.

Joeres, Ruth-Ellen B. and Mary Jo Maynes, ed. *German Women in the Eighteenth and Nineteenth Centuries. A Social and Literary History*. Bloomington: Indiana University Press, 1986.

Jördens, Karl Heinrich. *Lexikon deutscher Dichter und Prosaisten*. 6 vols. Leipzig: Weidmann, 1806–11.

Kiesel, H. and P. Münch. *Gesellschaft und Literatur im 18. Jahrhundert. Voraussetzungen und Entstehung des literarischen Markts in Deutschland*. Munich: Beck, 1977.

Kindermann, Heinz. *Von der Aufklärung zur Romantik*. 2nd ed. Salzburg: Müller, 1972–1976. Vols. 4–5 of *Theatergeschichte Europas*. 1959–76.

Kosch, Wilhelm. *Deutsches Literatur-Lexikon*. 2nd ed. Vol. 1–4. Bern: Francke, 1947–58.

———. *Deutsches Literatur-Lexikon*. 11 vols. to date. Bern: Francke, 1966-.

———. *Deutsches Theater-Lexikon. Biographisches und bibliographisches Handbuch*. 2 vols. to date. Klagenfurt: Kleinmayr, 1953.

La Roche, Sophie. *Pomona für Teutschlands Töchter.* Speier 1783–1784.

Lübker, Detlev Lorenz, and Hans Schröder. *Lexikon der Schleswig-Holstein-Lauenburgischen und Eutinischen Schriftsteller von 1796 bis 1828.* 2 vols. Altona: Busch, 1829–30.

Mahlmann, Siegfried August. Letter to Sophie Albrecht. n.d. Campe 3:226a. Staats- und Universitätsbibliothek, Hamburg.

Maurer, Michael. "Das Gute und das Schöne: Sophie von La Roche (1730–1807) wiederentdecken?" *Euphorion* 79 (1985): 111–38.

Meusel, Johann Georg. *Lexikon der vom Jahr 1750–1800 verstorbenen teutschen Schriftsteller.* 15 vols. Leipzig: Fleischer, 1802–1816.

Mix, York-Gothart. *Die deutschen Musenalmanache des 18. Jahrhunderts.* Munich: Beck, 1987.

Neumann-Strela, [Karl]. Sophie Albrecht, Lebensbeschreibung. [Copy from *Allgemeine Modezeitung,* Leipzig. 30 March 1885. 13: 81.] Freies Deutsches Hochstift, Frankfurt/Main.

―――. "Sophie Albrecht." *Königlich priviligirte Berlinische Zeitung von Staats- und gelehrten Sachen.* *Vossische Zeitung* (8 December 1907) Sonntagsbeilage, 390–92.

Neue Deutsche Biographie. 15 vols. to date. Berlin: Duncker u. Humbolt, 1953–82.

Pies, Eike. *Prinzipale. Zur Genealogie des deutschsprachigen Berufstheaters vom 17. bis 19. Jahrhundert.* Düsseldorf: Aloys Henn, 1973.

Rassmann, Friedrich. *Pantheon deutscher jetzt lebender Dichter und in die Belletristik eingreifender Schriftsteller.* Helmstedt: Fleckeisensche Buchhandlung, 1823.

Recke, Elisa von der. *Elisens Geistliche Gedichte, nebst einem Oratorium und einer Hymne von C. F. Neander.* Leipzig: Dyck, 1783.

[―――]. *Geistliche Lieder einer vornehmen kurländischen Dame mit Melodien von Hiller.* Leipzig 1780.

―――. *Nachricht von des berüchtigten Cagliostro Aufenthalte in Mitau 1779. Tagebücher* 349–99.

―――. *Tagebücher und Selbstzeugnisse.* Ed. Christine Träger. Munich: Beck, 1984.

Recke, Johann Friedrich von, and Karl Eduard Napiersky. *Allgemeines Schriftsteller- und Gelehrten-Lexikon der Provinzen Livland, Esthland, und Kurland.* 6 vols. 1827–61. Reprint, Berlin: Haude und Spener, 1966.

Reden-Esbeck, Johann, ed. *Deutsches Bühnen-Lexikon*. Eichstätt: Stillkrauth, 1879.

Rotermund, Heinrich Wilhelm. *Das gelehrte Hannover*. Bremen: Schünemann, 1823.

Schiller, Friedrich. *Schillers Werke. Nationalausgabe*. Weimar: Böhlau, 1956–.

Schindel, Carl Wilhelm Otto August von. *Die deutschen Schriftstellerinnen des neunzehnten Jahrhunderts*. 3 vols. Leipzig: Brockhaus, 1823–1825.

Schröder, Hans. *Lexikon der Hamburgischen Schriftsteller bis zur Gegenwart*. 8 vols. Hamburg: Perthes-Besser, 1851–83.

Schulz, Gunter. "Elisa v. d. Recke, die Freundin Friedrich Nicolais." *Wolfenbütteler Studien zur Aufklärung* 3 (1976): 159–73.

The Vanished Woman of Great Influence

Anthony, William W. "The Narration of the Marvelous in the Late Eighteenth-Century German 'Märchen'." Ph.D diss., John Hopkins University, 1982.

Arnim, Gisela von. *Märchenbriefe an Achim*. Ed. Shawn C. Jarvis. Frankfurt: Insel, 1991.

————. "Die Rosenwolke." *Märchen aus dem Kaffeterkreis* [working title]. by Gisela and Armgart von Arnim and Herman Grimm. Ed. Shawn C. Jarvis with Roland Specht Jarvis and Werner Moritz. Marburg: Hitzeroth, in progress.

———— and Bettine. *Das Leben der Hochgräfin Gritta von Rattenzuhausbeiuns*. Ed. Shawn C. Jarvis. Frankfurt: Insel, 1986.

Baader, Renate. *Dames de lettres. Autorinnen des preziösen, hocharistokratischen und "modernen" Salons, 1649-1698: Mlle de Scudéry— Mlle de Montpensier—Mme d'Aulnoy*. Romanistische Abhandlungen, 5. Stuttgart: Metzler, 1986.

Bauer, Rudolf. *Der historische Trivialroman in Deutschland im ausgehenden 18. Jahrhundert*. Plauen: Otto Adam, 1930.

Becker-Cantarino, Barbara. Review of *Die weibliche Muse: Sechs Essays über künstlerisch schaffende Frauen der Goethezeit* by Helene M. Kastinger Riley. Studies in German Literature, Linguistics, and Culture, 8. Columbia, S.C.: Camden House, 1986. *Journal of English and Germanic Philology* 88 (1989): 71–74.

Blackwell, Jeannine. "An Island of Her Own: Heroines of the German Robinsonades from 1720–1800." *German Quarterly* 58 (1985): 5–26.

――――. "Fractured Fairy Tales: German Women Authors and the Grimm Tradition." *Germanic Review* 62 (1987): 162–74.

Bottigheimer, Ruth B., ed. *Fairy Tales and Society: Illusion, Allusion, and Paradigm.* Philadelphia: University of Pennsylvania Press, 1986.

――――. *Grimms' Bad Girls and Bold Boys: The Moral and Social Vision of the Tales.* New Haven and London: Yale UP, 1987.

――――. "Silenced Women in the Grimms' Tales: The 'Fit' Between Fairy Tales and Society in Their Historical Context." Bottigheimer, *Fairy Tales and Society,* 53–74.

――――. "Still, Gretel! Verstummte Frauen in Grimms 'Kinder- und Hausmärchen.'" *Frauensprache—Frauenliteratur? Für und Wider einer Psychoanalyse literarischer Werke.* Ed. Inge Stephan and Carl Pietzcker. Vol. 6 of *Kontroversen, alte und neue. Akten des VII. Internationalen Germanisten-Kongresses Göttingen 1985.* Ed. Albrecht Schöne. 11 vols. Tübingen: Niemeyer, 1986.

Church, Alfred J. and Brodribb, W. J., eds. *The Agricola and Germania of Tacitus.* London: Macmillan and Co., 1875.

Dorsch, Nikolaus, ed. *"Sich rettend aus der kalten Würklichkeit": Die Briefe Benedikte Nauberts. Edition—Kritik—Kommentar.* Marburger Germanistische Studien 6. Frankfurt, Bern, New York: Peter Lang, 1986.

Fox, Jennifer. "The Creator Gods: Romantic Nationalism and the Engenderment of Women in Folklore." *Journal of American Folklore* 100 (1987): 563–78.

Franz, Agnes. "Prinzessin Rosalieb: Ein Mährchen." *Kinderlust: Erzählungen, Sagen und Mährchen* (Besonderer und vermehrter Abdruck aus dem "Buch der Kinder"). Breslau: Ferdinand Hirt, 1841.

Grätz, Manfred. *Das Märchen in der deutschen Aufklärung: Vom Feenmärchen zum Volksmärchen.* Germanistische Abhandlungen 63. Stuttgart: Metzler, 1988.

Greiner, Martin. *Die Entstehung der modernen Unterhaltungsliteratur: Studien zum Trivialroman des 18. Jahrhunderts.* Ed. Therese Poser. Reinbek bei Hamburg: Rowohlt, 1964.

Jarvis, Shawn C. "Literary Legerdemain and the *Märchen* Tradition of Nineteenth-Century German Women Writers." Ph.D. diss. University of Minnesota, 1990.

――――, comp. and ed. *Märchenbriefe an Achim.* By Gisela von Arnim. Frankfurt: Insel, 1991.

———. "Trivial Pursuit? Women Deconstructing the Grimmian Model in the *Kaffeterkreis*." *The Reception of Grimms' Fairy Tales: Essays on Responses, Reactions and Revisions.* Ed. Donald Haase. Detroit: Wayne State UP, 1991.

Naubert, Benedikte. *Velleda, Ein Zauberroman.* Leipzig: Schäfer, 1795.

Nolting-Hauff, Ilse. "Märchen und Märchenroman. Zur Beziehung zwischen einfacher Form und narrativer Großform in der Literatur." *Poetica* 6 (1974): 129–78.

Russ, Joanna. *How to Suppress Women's Writing.* Austin: Texas UP, 1983.

Schoppe, Amalia. "Das braune Hedchen. Ein Feenmährchen." *Kleine Mährchen-Bibliothek, oder gesammelte Mährchen für die liebe Jugend.* Berlin: Matthisson, 1828.

Schreinert, Kurt. *Benedikte Naubert: Ein Beitrag zur Entstehungsgeschichte des historischen Romans in Deutschland.* Germanische Studien 230. Berlin, 1941; reprint Nendeln/Liechtenstein: Kraus Reprint, 1969.

Tacitus, P. Cornelius. *The History of P. Cornelius Tacitus.* Trans. Albert William Quill. Vol. 1. London: John Murray, 1892. Vol. 2. London, New York and Bombay: Hodges, Figgis, and Co, 1896.

Touaillon, Christine. *Der deutsche Frauenroman des 18. Jahrhunderts.* Vienna, Leipzig: Braumüller, 1919; reprint Bern, Frankfurt, Las Vegas: Lang, 1979.

Waldstein, Edith. "Romantic Revolution and Female Collectivity: Bettine and Gisela von Arnim's *Gritta*." *Women in German Yearbook* 3 (1986): 91–100.

Contributors

Jeannine Blackwell, associate professor of German at the University of Kentucky, is co-editor of *Bitter Healing: German Women Writers 1700–1830, An Anthology* published by University of Nebraska Press, 1990. She has written articles on nineteenth century German women's literary culture, female Robinson Crusoe stories, fairy tales, witch trials, and the authors Sophie von La Roche, Therese Huber, and Benedikte Naubert. She is presently working on a book treating women's religious and judicial confessions in the early modern era.

Ute Brandes is associate professor of German at Amherst College. Her publications include *Zitat und Montage in der neueren DDR-Prosa* (1984); *Anna Seghers* (1992) and *Zwischen Gestern und Morgen: DDR-Autorinnen aus amerikanischer Sicht* (1991). She has also written articles on Baroque Women writers, the reception of Goethe's *Werther,* and on Christa Wolf, Ulrich Plenzdorf, and Volker Braun. Her current scholarly interest is a history of literary utopias by German woman writers.

Ruth P. Dawson is associate professor in the Women's Studies Program and Associate Dean of the College of Social Sciences at the University of Hawaii at Manoa. While she is especially interested in women writers in eighteenth-century Germany and is finishing a book on this subject, she has also lived and worked in Hong Kong, Singapore, and the People's Republic of China. Her recent publications on eighteenth-century German women concern their emerging feminist consciousness and their connections with the theater.

Sara Friedrichsmeyer is associate professor of German at the University of Cincinnati, Raymond Walters College, where she teaches in German and Women's Studies. She has published on such nineteenth and twentieth century German writers as Novalis, F. Schlegel, Annette von Droste-Hülshoff, Paula Modersohn-Becker, Käthe Kollwitz, and Christa Wolf. She is author of *The Androgyne in German Romanticism*, Stanford German Series (Bern: Lang, 1983), and coeditor with Barbara Becker-Cantarino of *The Enlightenment and its Legacy* (Bonn: Bouvier, 1990); she is coeditor with Jeanette Clausen of the *Women in German Yearbook: Feminist Studies and German Culture*.

Katherine R. Goodman is associate professor of German at Brown University, Providence, Rhode Island. Her book, *Dis/Closures: Women's Autobiography in Germany 1790–1914*, appeared in 1986. She has also published on Goethe, Rahel Varnhagen, Johanna Schopenhauer, Ellen Key and Gabriele Reuter.

Marianne Hirsch teaches French and Comparative Literature at Dartmouth College. She is the author of *The Mother/Daughter Plot: Narrative, Psychoanalysis, Feminism* and *Beyond the Single Vision: Henry James, Michel Butor, Uwe Johnson*. She has co-edited *The Voyage In: Fictions of Female Development* and, most recently, *Conflicts in Feminism*.

Shawn Jarvis has been conducting extensive archival research on *Märchen* by nineteenth-century German women, especially Gisela von Arnim. In an effort to make texts by Arnim more generally available, she has edited the first complete edition of *Das Leben der Hochgräfin Gritta von Rattenzuhausbeiuns* (Frankfurt: Insel, 1986); a facsimile edition of Arnim's fairy tale illustrations and manuscripts, *Märchenbriefe an Achim* (Frankfurt: Insel, 1990); and a third volume of fairy tales and illustrations from the *Kaffeterkreis* by Gisela, Armgart von Arnim and Herman Grimm (in preparation). She is currently associate professor of German at St. Cloud State University, St. Cloud, Minnesota.

Ruth Perry has published widely on eighteenth-century English literature and culture, and about the influence of gender on the production of art. She is the author of *Women, Letters, and the Novel* (1980) and *The Celebrated Mary Astell* (1986), the editor of George Ballard's 1752 *Memoirs of Several La-*

dies of Great Britain (1985), and co-editor and theorist of a
volume of essays on nurturing creativity, *Mothering the
Mind* (1984). She is the founding Director of the Women's
Studies program at MIT.

Virginia E. Swain is associate professor of French and Co-Chair of
Women's Studies at Dartmouth College. She teaches
courses on women in the eighteenth-century for the French
Department and Women's Studies and has written on Diderot, Rousseau, Charrière and Baudelaire.

Edith Waldstein is associate professor of Humanities and Assistant Dean for Academic Affairs at Wartburg College and the
author of *Bettine von Arnim and the Politics of Romantic
Conversation* (1988). She has written articles on other German Romantics and Christa Wolf. Together with Marianne
Burkhard, she is founding editor of the *Women in German
Yearbook: Feminist Studies and German Culture,* which continues to appear annually.

Liliane Weissberg is associate professor of German and Comparative Literature at the University of Pennsylvania. Her most
recent publications include *Geistersprache: philosophischer
und literarischer Diskurs im späten achtzehnten Jahrhundert* (Königshausen und Neumann, 1990) and *Edgar Allan
Poe* (Metzler, 1991). She is currently completing an edition
of German early Romantic letters for the Deutscher Klas-
siker Verlag.

Susanne Zantop is associate professor of German and Comparative Literature at Dartmouth College and Co-chair of Wom-
en's Studies. Holding degrees both in Political Science and
in Comparative Literature, she has concentrated on the interaction between literary and other discourses. Her publications include books on literature and history (*Zeitbilder:
Geschichte und Literatur bei Heinrich Heine und Mariano
José de Larra,* 1988), literature and painting (*Paintings on
the Move: Heinrich Heine and the Visual Arts,* 1989), and an
anthology of texts by German women writers in translation
(*Bitter Healing: German Women Writers from 1700 to 1830,*
co-edited with Jeannine Blackwell, 1990).

Index

Index